HEAVEN

By the same author

HEAVEN

A Prison Diary Volume 3

JEFFREY ARCHER

St. Martin's Griffin

New York

www.stmartins.com

Library of Congress Cataloging-in-Publication Data

Archer, Jeffrey, 1940–
    Heaven: a prison diary / Jeffrey Archer.
        p. cm.
    "Volume 3."
    ISBN-13: 978-0-312-35479-4
    ISBN-10: 0-312-35479-7
    1. Archer, Jeffrey, 1940—Diaries. 2. Novelists, English—20th century—Diaries. 3. Archer, Jeffrey, 1940—Imprisonment. 4. Prisoners—Great Britain—Diaries. 5. Prisons—Great Britain. I. Title.

PR6051.R285Z467 2005
828'.91403—dc22

                                                                    2005042882

First published in Great Britain by Macmillan
an imprint of Pan Macmillan Ltd

First St. Martin's Griffin Edition: August 2006

10 9 8 7 6 5 4 3 2 1

CONTENTS

HEAVEN

DAY 89   MONDAY 15 OCTOBER 2001

2.30 pm

The signpost announces North Sea Camp, one mile. As we approach the entrance to the prison, the first thing that strikes me is that there are no electric gates, no high walls and no razor wire.

I am released from my sweat box and walk into reception, where I am greeted by an officer. Mr Daff has a jolly smile and a military air. He promises that after Wayland, this will be more like Butlins. 'In fact,' he adds, 'there's a Butlins just up the road in Skegness. The only difference is, they've got a wall around them.'

Here, Mr Daff explains, the walls are replaced by roll-calls – 7.30 am, 11.45 am, 3.30 pm, 8.15 pm and 10.00 pm, when I must present myself to the spur office: a whole new regime to become accustomed to.

While Mr Daff completes the paperwork, I unpack my HMP plastic bags. He barks that I will only be allowed to wear prison garb, so all my T-shirts are taken away and placed in a possessions box marked ARCHER FF8282.

Dean, a prison orderly helps me. Once all my belongings have been checked, he escorts me to my room – please note, room, not cell. At NSC, prisoners have their own key, and there are no bars on the windows. So far so good.

However, I'm back to sharing with another prisoner. My room-mate is David. He doesn't turn the music down when I walk in, and a rolled-up cigarette doesn't leave his mouth. As I make my bed, David tells me that he's a lifer, whose original tariff was fifteen years. So far, he's served twenty-one because he's still considered a risk to the public, despite being in a D-cat prison. His original crime was murder – an attack on a waiter who leered at his wife.

4.00 pm

Dean (reception orderly) informs me that Mr Berlyn, one of the governors, wants to see me. He accompanies me to the governor's Portakabin, where I am once again welcomed with a warm smile. After a preliminary chat, Mr Berlyn says that he plans to place me in the education department. The governor then talks about the problem of NSC's being an open prison, and how they hope to handle the press. He ends by saying his door is always open to any prisoner should I need any help or assistance.

5.00 pm

Dean takes me off to supper in the canteen. The food looks far better than Wayland's, and it is served and eaten in a central hall, rather like at boarding school.

6.00 pm

Write for two hours, and feel exhausted. When I've finished, I walk across to join Doug in the hospital. He seems to have all the up-to-date gossip. He's obviously going to be invaluable as my deep throat. We sit and watch the evening news in comfortable chairs. Dean joins us a few minutes later, despite the fact that he is only hours away from being released. He says that my laundry has already been washed and returned to my room.

8.15 pm

I walk back to the north block and report to the duty officer for roll-call. Mr Hughes wears a peaked cap that resembles Mr Mackay's in *Porridge*, and he enjoys the comparison. He comes across as a fierce sergeant major type (twenty years in the army) but within moments I discover he's a complete softie. The inmates like and admire him; if he says he'll do something, he does it. If he can't, he tells you.

I return to my room and push myself to write for another hour, despite a smoke-filled room and loud music.

10.00 pm

Final roll-call. Fifteen minutes later I'm in bed and fast asleep, oblivious to David's smoke and music.

DAY 90   TUESDAY 16 OCTOBER 2001

5.30 am

Alsatians woke me at Belmarsh, at Wayland it was officers jangling keys as they made their early morning rounds, but as NSC is only 100 yards from the coastline, it's the constant squawk of seagulls that causes you to open your eyes. Later, much later, the muffled grunts of swine are added, as the largest group of residents at NSC are the pigs living on the 900-acre prison farm. I drape a pair of black boxer shorts over the light above my head to make sure David is not woken while I continue my writing routine. He doesn't stir. At seven-thirty I make my way to the shower room at the end of the corridor.

8.00 am

Dean accompanies me to breakfast: porridge from Monday to Friday, and cereal at weekends, he explains. I satisfy myself with a very hard-boiled egg and a couple of slices of burnt toast.

8.30 am

Induction. During the first week at NSC, a prisoner spends his time finding out how the place works, while the officers try to discover as much as possible about the new inmate. My first appointment is with Dr Walling, the prison doctor, who asks the usual questions about drugs, smoking, drinking, illnesses and allergies. After twenty minutes of prodding, breathing in, being weighed, and having my eyes, ears, teeth and heart checked, Dr Walling's only piece of advice is not to overdo it in the gym.

'Try not to forget you are sixty-one,' he reminds me.

As I leave the surgery, Doug, the hospital orderly a friend of Darren (Wayland, marijuana only), beckons me into the private ward. Doug is six foot, and about sixteen stone, with a full head of hair just beginning to grey, and I would guess is in his late forties. The ward has eight beds, one of which is Doug's, as someone has to be resident at night in case a prisoner is suddenly taken ill. But what a job; not only does Doug have a room the size of a penthouse suite, but he also has his own television, and his own bathroom. He tells me that he's in for tax evasion, but doesn't elaborate. Doug closes the door to his kingdom and confirms that medical orderly is the best job in the prison. However, he assures me that the second-best position at NSC is orderly at the sentence management unit (SMU). Doug whispers that the SMU job is coming up in just over four weeks' time when the present incumbent, Matthew, will be released. Mr New, the senior officer – equivalent to Mr Tinkler at Wayland – will make the final decision, but Doug will put in a good word for me. 'Whatever you do,' he adds, 'don't end up working on the farm. Winter's not far off, so if the food doesn't kill you, the farm will.' As I leave, he adds, 'Come and have a drink this evening.' (By that he means tea or coffee.) 'I'm allowed two guests from seven to ten, and you'd be welcome.' I thank him and, silently, my old mentor Darren. *Who you know* is just as important on the inside as it is on the outside.

10.30 am

My second induction meeting is to decide what job I'll do while I'm at NSC. I make my way to the sentence management unit, a building that was formerly the governor's house and is situated just a few yards from the front gate. The pathway leading up to the entrance is lined with tired red flowers. The light blue front door could do with a lick of paint; it looks as if it is regularly kicked open rather than pushed.

The first room I enter has the feel of a conservatory. It has a dozen wooden chairs, and a notice board covered in information leaflets. Four officers, including a Mr Gough, who looks like a prep school master, occupy the first room on the ground floor. As he ticks off my name, Mr Gough announces, in a broad Norfolk accent, that he will be speaking to all the new inductees once everyone has come across from their medical examination. But as Dr Walling is taking fifteen minutes with each new prisoner, we may be sitting around for some time. As I wait impatiently in the conservatory, I become aware how filthy the room is. At Wayland, the floors shone from their daily buffing, and if you stood still for more than a few moments, someone painted you.

Eventually, all seven new inductees turn up. Mr Gough welcomes us, and begins by saying that as most prisoners spend less than three months at NSC, the officers aim to make our time as civilized as possible while they prepare us for returning to the outside world. Mr Gough explains that at NSC anyone can abscond. It's all too easy as there are no walls to keep you in. 'But if you do decide to leave us, please remember to leave your room key on your pillow.' He's not joking.

He then tells us about a young man, who absconded sixteen hours before he was due to be released. He was picked up in

Boston the following morning and transferred to a C-cat, where he spent a further six weeks. Point taken.

Mr Gough takes us through the jobs that are available for all prisoners under the age of sixty, pointing out that over half the inmates work on the farm. The other half can enrol for education, or take on the usual jobs in the kitchen, or painting, gardening or as a cleaner.

Mr Gough ends by telling us that we all have to abide by a 'no drugs policy'. Refusing to sign the three documents stating you are not on drugs and will agree at any time to a voluntary drugs test will rule you out of becoming 'enhanced' in eight weeks' time. Enhancement allows you a further £5 a week to spend in the canteen, along with several other privileges. To a question, Mr Gough replies, 'Wearing your own clothes is not permitted in an open prison as it would make absconding that much easier.' However, I did notice that Doug (tax evasion) was wearing a green T-shirt and brown slacks held up by the most outrageous Walt Disney braces. There's always someone who finds a way round the system.

I happily sign all of Mr Gough's drug forms and am then sent upstairs to be interviewed by another officer. Mr Donnelly not only looks like a farmer, but is also dressed in green overalls and wearing Wellington boots. No wonder the place is so dirty. He appears keen for me to join him on the farm, but I explain (on Doug's advice) that I would like to be considered for Matthew's job as SMU orderly. He makes a note, and frowns.

12 noon

After ten weeks locked up in Wayland and always being handed a plate of food, I can't get used to helping myself. One of the kitchen staff laughs when I pass over my plate and expect to be served. 'A clear sign you've just arrived from a closed prison,' he remarks. 'Welcome to the real world, Jeff.'

After lunch, Dean takes me across to view the more secluded, quieter south block, which is at the far end of the prison and houses the older inmates.* Here, there is a totally different atmosphere.

Dean shows me an empty room, large by normal standards, about twenty by eight feet, with a window that looks out over the bleak North Sea. He explains that the whole spur is in the process of redecoration and is scheduled to reopen on Monday. In-cell electricity (ICE) will be added, and all rooms will eventually have a television. On our way back to the north block, an officer informs me that the principal officer, Mr New, wants to see me immediately. I'm nervous. What have I done wrong? Is he going to send me back to Wayland?

PO New is in his late forties, around five feet eleven, with a shock of thick white hair. He greets me with a warm smile. 'I hear you want to work at SMU?' he says, and before I can reply adds, 'You've got the job. As Matthew is leaving in four weeks' time, you'd better start straight away so there can be a smooth takeover.' I've hardly got the words thank you out before he continues, 'I hear you want to move to the south block, which I'm sure will be possible, and I'm also told you want to be transferred to Spring Hill, which,' he adds, 'will not be quite as easy, because they don't want you and the attendant publicity that goes with you.' My heart sinks. 'However,' he says, again before I can respond, 'if that's what you want, I'll have a word with my opposite number at Spring Hill and see if she can help.'

Once Mr New has completed his discourse, we go downstairs

---

* NSC has two blocks, north and south, with about 110 prisoners resident in each.

to meet Matthew, the current orderly. Matthew is a shy young man, who has a lost, academic air about him. I can't imagine what he's doing in prison. Despite Mr New talking most of the time, Matthew manages to tell me what his responsibilities are, from making tea and coffee for the eleven occupants of the building, through to preparing induction files for every prisoner. He's out on a town leave tomorrow, so I will be thrown in at the deep end.

4.45 pm

Dean grabs my laundry bag and then accompanies me to supper, explaining that orderlies have the privilege of eating on their own thirty minutes ahead of all the other inmates.

'You get first choice of the food,' he adds, 'and as there are about a dozen of us,' (hospital, stores, reception, library, gym, education, chapel and gardens; it's quite a privilege). All this within twenty-four hours isn't going to make me popular.

DAY 91   WEDNESDAY 17 OCTOBER 2001

5.30 am

I wake a few minutes after five and go for a pee in the latrine at the end of the corridor. Have you noticed that when you're disoriented, or fearful, you don't go to the lavatory for some time? There must be a simple medical explanation for this. I didn't 'open my bowels' – to use the doctor's expression – for the first five days at Belmarsh, the first three days at Wayland and so far 'no-go' at NSC.

8.00 am

Dean turns up to take me to breakfast. I may not bother in future, as I don't eat porridge, and it's hardly worth the journey for a couple of slices of burnt toast. Dean warns me that the press are swarming all over the place, and large sums are being offered for a photo of me in prison uniform. Should they get a snap, they will be disappointed to find me strolling around in a T-shirt and jeans. No arrows, no number, no ball and chain.

8.45 am

At reception, I ask Mr Daff if it would be possible to have a clean T-shirt, as my wife is visiting me this afternoon.

'Where do you think you fuckin' are, Archer, fuckin' Harrods?'

9.00 am

As a new prisoner, I continue my induction course. My first meeting this morning is in the gym. We all assemble in a small Portacabin and watch a ten minute black-and-white video on safety at work. The instructor concentrates on lifting, as there are several jobs at NSC that require you to pick up heavy loads, not to mention numerous prisoners who will be pumping weights in the gym. Mr Masters, the senior gym officer, who has been at NSC for nineteen years, then gives us a guided tour of the gym and its facilities. It is not as large or well equipped as Wayland, but it does have three pieces of cardiovascular kit that will allow me to remain fit – a rowing machine, a step machine and a bicycle. The gym itself is just large enough to play basketball, whereas the weights room is about half the size of the one at Wayland. The gym is open every evening except Monday from 5.30 pm to 7.30 pm, so you don't have (grunt, grunt – the pigs are having breakfast) to complete the programme in a given hour. I hope to start this weekend, by which time I should have found my way around (grunt, grunt). Badminton is the most popular sport, and although NSC has a football team, the recent foot-and-mouth problems have played havoc when it comes to being allowed out onto the pitch (grunt, grunt).

9.30 am

Education. We all meet in the chapel. The education officer takes us through the various alternatives on offer. Most of the new inmates sit sulkily in their chairs, staring blankly at her. As I have already been allocated a job as the SMU orderly, I listen in respectful silence, and once she's finished her talk, report back to my new job.

10.30 am

Matthew is away on a town visit today, but I quickly discover that the SMU job has three main responsibilities:

a) Making tea and coffee for the eleven staff who regularly work in the building, plus those who drop in to visit a colleague.

b) Preparing the files for new inductees so that the officers have all their details to hand: sentence, FLED (full licence eligibility date), home address, whether they have a home or job to go to, whether they have any money of their own, whether their family want them back.

c) Preparing prisoners' forms for visits, days out, weekend leave, work out and compassionate or sick leave.

It will also be part of my job to see that every prisoner is sent to the relevant officer, according to his needs. Mr Simpson, the resident probation officer tells me, 'I'll see anyone if I'm free, otherwise ask them to make an appointment,' allowing him to deal with those prisoners who have a genuine problem, and avoid those who stroll in to complain every other day.

11.45 am

I go to lunch with the other orderlies. The officer in charge of the kitchen, Wendy, tells me that NSC was commended for having the best food in the prison service. She says, 'You should try the meat and stop being a VIP [vegetarian in prison].' Wendy is a sort of pocket-sized Margaret Thatcher. Her kitchen is spotless, while her men slave away in their pristine white overalls leaving one in no doubt of their respect for her. I promise to try the meat in two weeks' time when I fill in my next menu voucher. (See overleaf.)

2.00 pm

Now I'm in a D-cat prison, I'm allowed one visit a week. After one-third of my sentence has been completed, other privileges will be added. Heaven knows what the press will make of my first town visit. However, all of this could change rapidly once my appeal has been heard. If your sentence is four years or more, you are only eligible for parole, whereas if it's less than four years, you will automatically be released after serving half your sentence, and if you've been a model prisoner, you can have another two months off while being tagged*

Back to today's visit. Two old friends, David Paterson and Tony Bloom, accompany Mary.

The three of them turn up twenty minutes late, which only emphasizes how dreadful the 250-mile round journey from London must be. Mary and I have thirty minutes on our own, and she tells me that my solicitors have approached Sir Sydney Kentridge QC to take over my appeal if it involves that Mr Justice Potts was prejudiced against me before the trial started. The one witness who could testify, Godfrey Barker, is now proving reluctant to come forward. He fears that his wife, who works at the Home Office, may lose her job. Mary feels he will do what is just. I feel he will vacillate and fall by the wayside. She is the optimist, I am the pessimist. It's usually the other way round.

---

* While tagged, you must remain at home between 7 pm and 7 am.

HM PRISON NORTH SEA CAMP

Week 2 — Lunch Menu

Week 2	Lunch Menu	Choice
SUN.	1. Chicken Portions 2. Roast Pork & Stuffing • 3. Mushroom Pasta 4. Stuffed Pepper •H	1
MON.	1. Sausage Rolls 2. Fish Grills •H 3. Vegetable Rolls • 4. Onion Bhajies •	2
TUES.	1. Braised Sausage H 2. Cheese & Tomato Pizza • 3. Braised Veg Sausage • 4. Pilchard Sandwich •H*	#2
WED.	1. Fish Fingers H* 2. Cheese & Onion Pie • 3. Faggots in Gravy 4. 4-Pack Cheese Sandwich •	2
THURS.	1. Quiche Lorraine H 2. Cheeseburger • 3. Vegetarian Quiche • 4. Veg Cheeseburger •	3
FRI.	1. Shepherd's Pie H 2. Chicken Cutlets • 3. Veg Pie • 4. Onion Bhajies •	4
SAT.	1. Pork Hotpot •H 2. Meat & Potato Pie 3. Veg Hotpot • 4. Veg Pie •	1

Week 2 — Dinner Menu

Week 2	Dinner Menu	Choice
SUN.	1. Fish Fingers •H 2. Beefburger 3. Vegburger • 4. Egg Mayonnaise Sandwich •	3
MON.	1. Pork Curry & Rice 2. Chicken & Sweetcorn Pie H 3. Veg Curry & Rice • 4. Veg Pie •	1
TUES.	1. Beef Lasagne 2. Fish Fillets & Parsley Sauce •H 3. Vegetable Lasagne • 4. Vegetable Pie •	2
WED.	1. Ham & Egg 2. Kidney Casserole •H 3. Stir Fried Rice • 4. Vegetable Pie •	1
THURS.	1. Chicken Meatballs in Tomato Sauce 2. Cottage Pie H 3. Veg Meatballs in Tomato Sauce • 4. Vegetarian Soya Pie •	2
FRI.	1. Liver, Sausage & Onions H 2. Chicken Fricassée & Rice • 3. Potato & Lentil Bake • 4. Veg Fricassée & Rice •	3
SAT.	1. Cornish Pasties 2. Welsh Rarebit 3. Vegetarian Pasty • 4. Vegburger •	3

You are responsible for returning your choices by Monday. Please hand to any staff on duty in the Kitchen. Print your name and number and sign the form. Failure to do so will result in you automatically being given a vegetarian meal. The Kitchen will endeavour to keep all meals as laid down on the menu. If, for any reason, the meal indicated cannot be issued, a replacement meal will be substituted. (H – Healthy Eating Option. * - Suitable for Muslims)

NAME: ARCHER   NUMBER: FF8282   SIGNATURE: Jeffrey Atkes

During the visit, both Governor Berlyn, and PO New stroll around, talking to the families of the prisoners. How different from Wayland. Mr New tells us that NSC has now been dubbed 'the cushiest prison in England' (*Sun*), which he hopes will produce a better class of inmate in future; 'The best food in any prison' (*Daily Star*); I have 'the biggest room in the quietest block' (*Daily Mail*); and, 'he's the only one allowed to wear his own clothes' (*Daily Mirror*). Not one fact correct.

The hour and a half passes all too quickly, but at least I can now have a visitor every week. I can only wonder how many of my friends will be willing to make a seven-hour round trip to spend an hour and a half with me.

5.00 pm

Canteen. At Wayland, you filled in an order form and then your supplies were delivered to your cell. At NSC there is a small shop which you are allowed to visit twice a week between 5.30 pm and 7.30 pm so you can purchase what you need – razor blades, toothpaste, chocolate, water, blackcurrant juice and most important of all, phonecards. I also need a can of shaving foam as I still shave every day.

What a difference a D-cat makes.

6.00 pm

I go across to the kitchen for supper and join two prisoners seated at the far end of the room. I select them because of their age. One turns out to be an accountant, the other a retired insurance broker. They do not talk about their crimes. They tell me that they no longer work in the prison, but travel into Boston every morning by bus, and have to back each afternoon by five.

DAY 91

They work at the local Red Cross shop, and earn £13.50 a week, which is credited to their canteen account. Some prisoners can earn as much as £200 a week, giving them a chance to save a considerable sum by the time they're released. This makes a lot more sense than turfing them out onto the street with the regulation £40 and no job to go to.

7.00 pm

I join Doug at the hospital for a blackcurrant juice, a McVitie's biscuit and the Channel 4 news. In Washington DC, Congress and the Senate were evacuated because of an anthrax scare. There seem to be so many ways of waging a modern war. Are we in the middle of the Third World War without realizing it?

8.15 pm

I return to the north block for roll-call to prove I have not absconded.* Doug assures me that it becomes a lot easier after the first couple of weeks, when the checks fall from six a day to four. My problem is that the final roll-call is at ten, and by then I've usually fallen asleep.

---

* You cannot escape from an open prison, only abscond. There are no walls, just a car barrier at the entrance and a public footpath at the back. Most prisoners who abscond do so in the first two weeks. Nine out of ten are back behind bars within forty-eight hours.

DAY 92   THURSDAY 18 OCTOBER 2001

6.00 am

Because so much is new to me, and so much unknown, I am still finding my way around.

Mr Hughes and Mr Jones, the officers in charge of the north block, try to deal quickly with prisoners' queries and, more important, attempt to get things 'sorted', making them popular with the other inmates. The two blocks resemble Second World War Nissen huts. The north block consists of a 100-yard corridor, with five spurs running off each side. Each corridor has nine rooms – you have your own key, and there are no bars on the windows.

Two prisoners share each room. My room-mate David is a lifer (murder), and has the largest room: not the usual five paces by three, but seven paces by three. I have already requested a transfer to the no-smoking spur on the south block, which tends to house the older, more mature prisoners. Despite the *News of the World* headline, 'Archer demands cell change', the no-smoking rule is every prisoner's right. However, Governor Berlyn is unhappy about my going across to the south block because it's next to a public footpath, which is currently populated by several journalists and photographers.

The corridor opposite mine has recently been designated a

no-smoking zone, and Mr Berlyn suggests I move across to one of the empty rooms on that spur. As the prison is presently low in numbers, I might even be left on my own. Every prisoner I have shared a cell with has either sold his story to the tabloids, or been subjected to front-page exposés – always exaggerated and never accurate.

8.30 am

My working day as SMU orderly is 8.30 am to 12, lunch, then 1 pm to 4.30 pm. I arrive expecting to find Matthew so he can begin the handover, but Mr Gough is the only person on parade. He has his head down, brow furrowed, staring at his computer. He makes the odd muttering sound to himself, before asking politely for a cup of tea.

9.00 am

Still no sign of Matthew. I read through the daily duties book, and discover that among my responsibilities are mopping the kitchen floor, sweeping all common areas, vacuuming the carpets and cleaning the two lavatories as well as the kitchen. Thankfully, the main occupation, and the only thing that will keep me from going insane, is dealing with prisoners' queries. By the time I've read the eight-page folder twice, there is still no sign of Matthew, which is beginning to look like a hanging offence.

If you are late for work, you are 'nicked', rare in a D-cat prison, because being put on report can result in loss of privileges – even being returned to a C-cat – according to the severity of your offence. Being caught taking drugs or absconding is an immediate recategorization offence. These privileges and punishments are in place to make sure everyone abides by the rules.

Mr New, the principal officer, arrives just as Mr Gough enters the room.

'Where's Matthew?' he asks.

I then observe the officers at their best, but the Prison Service at its most ineffective.

'That's why I came looking for you,' says Mr Gough. 'Matthew reported back late last night' – an offence that can have you transferred to a C-cat, because it's assumed that you've absconded – 'and he was put on report.' The atmosphere immediately changes. 'But I took him off.'

'Why?' asks Mr New, as he lights a cigarette.

'His father collapsed yesterday afternoon and was taken into Canterbury Hospital. He's been diagnosed with a brain tumour and the doctors think he may not survive the week.'

'Right,' says Mr New, stubbing out his cigarette, 'sign him up for a compassionate leave order, and let's get him off to Canterbury as quickly as possible.'

Mr New tells me that Matthew's mother died a year ago, having suffered from MS, and his grandmother a few weeks later. This all took place soon after he committed the offence that resulted in him being sent to prison for fifteen months.

Matthew walks in.

Mr New and Mr Gough could not have been more sympathetic. Forms are signed and countersigned with unusual speed, and Matthew is even allowed to use the office phone to arrange for his girlfriend to pick him up. A few minutes later, Governor Berlyn appears and agrees with Mr New that the boy (I think of Matthew as a boy because he's even younger than my son) must be shipped out as quickly as possible. Then the problems start to arise.

Matthew, who only has four weeks left to serve, doesn't know anyone in Canterbury, so he'll have to be locked up overnight in the local jail, despite his girlfriend and her mother staying at a hotel near the hospital. But worse, because Matthew is only allowed twenty-four hours compassionate leave, he will have to travel back from Canterbury and spend the second night at NSC, after which he will be released on Friday morning for weekend leave, when he need not return until Sunday evening. 'Why not just let the boy go and be with his father, and return on Sunday night?' I ask. Both Mr Berlyn and Mr New nod their agreement, but tell me that there is no way round the Home Office regulations.

10.30 am

Matthew's girlfriend arrives at the barrier, and he is driven quickly away. I pray that Matthew's father doesn't die while they are on the motorway. I recall with sadness learning that my mother was dying during my trial. Mr Justice Potts wouldn't allow me to leave the court to be with her, as he didn't accept the doctor's opinion that she only had a few hours to live. I eventually arrived at her bedside an hour or so before she died by which time she was past recognizing me.

11.00 am

Three prisoners who arrived yesterday check in for their induction talk. They pepper me with questions. I feel a bit of a fraud, trying to answer them, having only been around for forty-eight hours and still on induction myself. Mr Gough gives them the talk I heard two days ago. I hand out a booklet emphasizing his comments. A young prisoner whispers in my ear that he can't read. HELP. I tell him to come back and see me if he has any further problems.

12.15 pm

Mr New appears, and runs through my responsibilities. We open a large cupboard crammed full of forms and files, which he feels needs reorganizing. He lights up another cigarette.

2.00 pm

Mr Simpson, the probation officer, asks me to join him in his office on the first floor, as he wants to bring my case file up to date. He asks me if I saw a probation officer after being convicted.

'Yes, but only for a few minutes,' I tell him, 'while I was still at the Old Bailey.'

'Good,' he says, 'because that will show you're domiciled in London, and make it easier for you to be moved to Spring Hill.' He checks his computer and gives me the name of my probation officer. 'Drop her a line,' he advises, 'and tell her you want to be transferred.'

3.30 pm

Mr New joins me in the kitchen for another cigarette break. I learn that he's due to leave NSC in January, when he will be transferred to Norwich Prison as a governor, Grade 5.* He then produces all the necessary forms for my transfer. Although he'll speak to Mrs McKenzie-Howe, his opposite number at Spring Hill, he's not optimistic. Not only are they full, but it's a resettlement prison, and I don't need resettling; I'm not looking for a

---

* There are five grades of governor; the top man or woman is known as the governing governor. I still haven't met one.

job when I'm released, or a home and, as I have no financial problems, I just don't fit any of the usual categories.

5.00 pm

I go off to the canteen for supper, and again sit at a table with two older prisoners. They are both in for fraud; one was a local councillor (three and a half months), and the other an ostrich farmer. The latter promises to tell me all the details when he has more time. It's clear there's going to be no shortage of good stories. Belmarsh – murder and GBH; Wayland – drug barons and armed robbers. NSC is looking a little more sophisticated.

7.00 pm

I join Doug in the hospital. He has allowed me to store a bottle of blackcurrant juice and a couple of bottles of Evian in his fridge, so I'll always have my own supply. As Doug chats away, I learn a little more about his crime. He hates drug dealers, and considers his own incarceration a temporary inconvenience. In fact he plans a cruise to Australia just as soon as he's released. On 'the out' he runs a small transport company. He has a yard and seven lorries, and employs – still employs – twelve people. He spends half an hour a day on the phone keeping abreast of what's going on back at base.

Now to his crime; his export/import business was successful until a major client went bankrupt and renegued on a bill for £170,000, placing him under extreme pressure with his bank. He began to replenish his funds by illegally importing cigarettes from France. He received a two-year sentence for failing to pay customs and excise duty to the tune of £850,000.

DAY 93   FRIDAY 19 OCTOBER 2001

6.00 am

I write for two hours. Boxer shorts draped over the little light that beams down onto my desk ensure that I don't disturb David.

8.15 am

I prepare identity cards for the three new prisoners who arrived yesterday. As each officer comes in, I make them tea or coffee. In between, I continue to organize the filing system for inductees. I will still be one myself for another week.

When Mr New arrives, he leaves his copy of *The Times* in the kitchen, and retrieves it at six before going home.

I am slowly getting into a routine. I now meet new prisoners as they appear, and find out what their problems are before they see an officer. Often they've come to the wrong office, or simply don't have the right form. Many of them want to be interviewed for risk assessment, others need to see the governor, whose office is in the administration block on the other side of the prison. But the real problem is Mr New himself, because many prisoners believe that if their request doesn't have his imprimatur, it won't go any further. This is partly because he takes an interest in every prisoner, but mainly because he won't rush them. He can often take twenty minutes to listen to their problems when all that is needed is for a form to be signed, which results in four other prisoners having to sit in the waiting room until he's finished.

During any one day, about thirty prisoners visit SMU. I have to be careful not to overstep the mark, as inmates need to see me as fighting their corner, while the officers have to feel I'm helping to cut down their workload. I certainly need a greater mental stimulation than making cups of tea. But however much I take on, the pay remains 25p an hour, £8.50 a week.

12 noon

I pick up my lunch – vegetable pie and beans. No pudding. I take my tray back to the SMU and read *The Times*.

2.00 pm

A prisoner marches in and demands to be released on compassionate grounds because his mother is ill. Mr Downs, a shrewd, experienced officer, tells him that he'll send a probation officer round to see his mother, so that they can decide if he should be released. The prisoner slopes off without another word. Mr Downs immediately calls the probation officer in Leicester, just in case the prisoner does have a sick mother.

Bob (lifer) comes to see the psychiatrist, Christine. Bob is preparing for life outside once he's released, possibly next year, but before that can happen, he has to complete ten town visits without incident. Once he's achieved this, he will be allowed out at weekends unescorted. The authorities will then assess if he is ready to be released. Bob has been in prison for twenty-three years, having originally been sentenced to fifteen. But as Christine points out, however strongly she recommends his release, in the end it is always Home Office decision.

Christine joins me in the kitchen and tells me about a lifer who went out on his first town visit after twenty years. He was given £20 so he could get used to shopping in a supermarket. When he arrived at the cash till and was asked how he would like to pay, he ran out leaving the goods behind. He just couldn't cope with having to make a decision.

'We also have to prepare all lifers for survival cooking.' She adds, 'You have to remember that some prisoners have had three cooked meals a day for twenty years, and they've become so institutionalized they can't even boil an egg.'

The next lifer to see Christine is Mike. After twenty-two years in prison (he's forty-nine), Mike is also coming to the end of his sentence. He invites me to supper on Sunday night (chicken curry). He's determined to prove that he can not only take care of himself, but cook for others as well.

5.00 pm

I walk over to the canteen and join Ron the fraudster and Dave the ostrich farmer for cauliflower cheese. Ron declares that the food at NSC is as good as most motorway cafés. This is indeed a compliment to Wendy.

6.00 pm

Mr Hughes (my wing officer) informs me I can move across to room twelve in the no-smoking corridor.

When I locate the room I find it's filthy, and the only

27

furniture is a single unmade bed, a table and a chair. I despair. I am so pathetic at times like this.

In the opposite cell is a prisoner called Alan who is cleaning out his room, and asks if he can help. I enquire what he would charge to transform my room so that it looks like his.

'Four phonecards,' he says (£8).

'Three,' I counter. He agrees. I tell him I will return at eight-fifteen for roll-call and see how he's getting on.

8.15 pm

I check in for roll-call before going off to see my new quarters. Alan has taken on an assistant, and they are slaving away. While Alan scrubs the cupboards, the assistant is working on the walls. I tell them I'll return at ten and clear my debts. The only trouble is that I don't have any phonecards, and won't have before canteen on Wednesday. Doug comes to my rescue and takes over Darren's role of purveyor of essential goods.

Doug appears anxious. He tells me that his fourteen-year-old daughter has suffered an epileptic fit. He's being allowed to go home tomorrow and visit her.

We settle down to watch the evening film, and are joined by the senior security officer, Mr Hocking. He warns me that a *News of the World* journalist is roaming around the grounds but, with a bit of luck, will fall into the Wash. Just before he leaves, he asks Doug if he's on home leave tomorrow.

'Yes, I'm off to see my daughter, back by seven,' Doug confirms.

'Then we'll need someone to be on duty after sister leaves at one. We mustn't forget how many drugs there are in this building. Would you be willing to stand in as temporary hospital orderly, Jeffrey?' he asks.

'Yes, of course,' I reply.

10.00 pm

I return to the north block for roll-call, before checking my room. I don't recognize it. It's spotless. I thank Alan, who takes a seat on the corner of the bed

He tells me that he has a twelve-month sentence for receiving stolen goods. He owns two furniture shops, in Leicester whose turnover last year was a little over £500,000, showing him a profit of around £120,000. He has a wife and two children, and between them they're keeping the business ticking over until he has completed his sentence in four weeks' time. It's his first offence, and he certainly falls into that category of 'never again'.

10.45 pm

I spend my first night at NSC in my own room. No music, no smoke, no hassle.

DAY 94   SATURDAY 20 OCTOBER 2001

6.00 am

Weekends are deadly in a prison. Jules, my pad-mate at Wayland used to say the only time you're not in prison is when you're asleep. So over the weekend, a lot of prisoners just remain in bed. I'm lucky because I have my writing to occupy me.

8.00 am

I spot Matthew, who must have returned from Canterbury last night. His father is still in a coma, and he accompanies me to the office so he can phone the hospital. Although my official working week is Monday to Friday, it's not unusual for an officer to be on duty at SMU on a Saturday morning.

Mr Downs and Mr Gough are already at their desks, and after I've made them both a cup of tea, Matthew takes me through my official duties for any given day or week. If I were to stick to simply what was required, it would take me no more than a couple of hours each day.

Over a cup of tea (Bovril for me), Matthew tells me about his nightmare year.

Matthew is twenty-four, six foot one, slim, dark-haired and

handsome without being aware of it. He's highly intelligent, but also rather gauche, and totally out of place in prison. He read marine anthropology at Manchester University and will complete his PhD once he's released. I ask him if he's a digger or an academic. 'An academic,' he replies, without hesitation.

His first job after leaving university was as a volunteer at a museum in his home town. He was happy there, but soon decided he wanted to return to university. That was when his mother contracted MS and everything began to go badly wrong. After his mother was bedridden, he and his sister took it in turns to help around the house, so that his father could continue to work. All three found the extra workload a tremendous strain. One evening while at work in the museum, Matthew took home some ancient coins to study. I haven't used the word 'stole' because he returned all the coins a few days later. But the incident weighed so heavily on his conscience that he informed his supervisor. Matthew thought that would be the end of the matter. But someone decided to report the incident to the police. Matthew was arrested and charged with breach of trust. He pleaded guilty, and was assured by the police that they would not be pushing for a custodial sentence. His solicitor was also of the same opinion, advising Matthew that he would probably get a suspended sentence or a community service order. The judge gave him fifteen months.*

Matthew is a classic example of someone who should not have been sent to jail; a hundred hours of community service might serve some purpose, but this boy has spent the last three months with murderers, drug addicts and burglars. He won't turn to a life of crime, but how many less intelligent people might? It's a rotten system that allows such a person to end up in prison.

---

* Matthew will end up serving five and a half months.

My former secretary, Angie Peppiatt, stole thousands of pounds from me, and still hasn't been arrested. I feel for Matthew.

12 noon

Lunch today is just as bad as Belmarsh or Wayland. Matthew explains that Wendy is off. I must remember to eat only when Wendy is on duty.

2.00 pm

I report to the hospital and take over Doug's caretaker role, while he visits his daughter. I settle down with a glass of blackcurrant juice and Evian to watch England slaughter Ireland, and win the Grand Slam, the Triple Crown and . . . after all, we are far superior on paper. Unfortunately, rugby is not played on paper but on pitches. Ireland hammer us 20–14, and return to the Emerald Isles with smiles on their faces.

I'm still sulking when a tall, handsome black man strolls in. His name is Clive. I only hope he's not ill, because if he is, I'm the last person he needs. He tells me that he's serving the last third of his sentence, and has just returned from a week's home leave – part of his rehabilitation programme.

Clive and I are the only two prisoners who have the privilege of visiting Doug in the evenings. I quickly discover why Doug enjoys Clive's company. He's bright, incisive and entertaining and, if it were not politically incorrect, I would describe him as sharp as a cartload of monkeys. Let me give you just one example of how he works the system.

During the week Clive works as a line manager for a fruit-packing company in Boston. He leaves the prison after breakfast at eight and doesn't return until seven in the evening. For this, he is paid £200 a week. So during the week, NSC is no more than a bed and breakfast, and the only day he has to spend in prison is Sunday. But Clive has a solution for that as well.

Two Sundays in every month he takes up his allocated town visits, while on the third Sunday he's allowed an overnight stay.

'But what about the fourth or fifth Sunday?' I ask.

'Religious exemption,' he explains.

'But why, when there's a chapel in the grounds?' I demand.

'*Your* chapel is in your grounds,' says Clive, 'because you're C of E. Not me,' he adds. 'I'm a Jehovah's Witness. I must visit my place of worship at least one Sunday in every month, and the nearest one just happens to be in Leicester.'

After a coffee, Clive invites me over to his room on the south block to play backgammon. His room turns out not to be five paces by three, or even seven by three. It's a little over ten paces by ten. In fact it's larger than my bedroom in London or Grantchester.

'How did you manage this?' I ask, as we settle down on opposite sides of the board.

'Well, it used to be a storeroom,' he explains, 'until I rehabilitated it.'

'But it could easily house four prisoners.'

'True,' says Clive, 'but remember I'm also the race relations representative, so they'll only allow black prisoners to share a room with me. There aren't that many black prisoners in D-cats,' he adds with a smile.

I hadn't noticed the sudden drop in the black population after leaving Wayland until Clive mentioned it. But I have seen a few at NSC, so I ask why they aren't allowed to room with him.

'They all start life on the north block, and that's where they stay,' he adds without explanation. He also beat me at backgammon – leaving me three Mars Bars light.

DAY 95   SUNDAY 21 OCTOBER 2001

6.00 am

Sunday is a day of rest, and if there's one thing you don't need in prison it's a day of rest.

8.00 am

SMU is open as Mr Downs is transferring files from his office to the administration block before taking up new responsibilities. Fifteen new prisoners arrived on Friday, giving me an excuse to prepare files and make up their identity cards.

North Sea Camp, whose capacity is 220, rarely has more than 170 inmates at any one time. As inmates have the right to be within fifty miles of their families, being stuck out on the east coast limits the catchment area. Two of the spurs are being refurbished at the moment, which shows the lack of pressure on accommodation.* The turnover at NSC is about fifteen prisoners a week. What I am about to reveal is common to all D-cat prisons, and by no means exclusive to NSC. On average, one prisoner absconds every week (unlawfully at large), the figures have a tendency to rise around Christmas and drop a little

---

* This is only true in D-cats – open prisons.

during the summer, so NSC loses around fifty prisoners a year; this explains the need for five roll-calls a day. Many absconders return within twenty-four hours, having thought better of it; they have twenty-eight days added to their sentence. A few, often foreigners, return to their countries and are never seen again. Quite recently, two Dutchmen absconded and were picked up by a speedboat, as the beach is only 100 yards out of bounds. They were back in Holland before the next roll-call.

Most absconders are quickly recaptured, many only getting as far as Boston, a mere six miles away. They are then transferred to a C-cat with its high walls and razor wire, and will never, under any circumstances, be allowed to return to an open prison, even if at some time in the future they are convicted of a minor offence. A few, very few, get clean away. But they must then spend every day looking over their shoulder.

There are even some cases of wives or girlfriends sending husbands or partners back to prison, and in one case a mother-in-law returning an errant prisoner to the front gate, declaring that she didn't want to see him again until he completed his sentence.

This is all relevant because of something that took place today.

When granted weekend leave, you must report back by seven o'clock on Sunday evening, and if you are even a minute late, you are placed on report. Yesterday, a wife was driving her husband back to the prison, when they became involved in a heated row. The wife stopped the car and dumped her husband on the roadside some thirty miles from the jail. He ran to the nearest phone box to let the prison know what had happened and a taxi was sent out to pick him up. He checked in over an hour late. Thirty pounds was deducted from his canteen account to pay for the taxi, and he's been placed on report.

DAY 95

2.00 pm

I go for a two-mile walk with Clive, who is spending a rare Sunday in prison. We discuss the morning papers. They have me variously working on the farm/in the hospital/cleaning the latrines/eating alone/lording it over everyone. However, nothing beats the *Mail on Sunday*, which produces a blurred photo of me proving that I have refused to wear prison clothes. This despite the fact that I'm wearing prison jeans and a grey prison sweatshirt in the photo.

After our walk, Clive and I play a few games of backgammon. He's in a different class to me, so I decide to take advantage of his superiority and turn each session into a tutorial.

6.00 pm

I write for two hours, and then sign in for roll-call with Mr Hughes.

9.00 pm

Doug, Clive and I watch a magnificent period drama set in Guildford and Cornwall in 1946. Mike (lifer) appears twenty minutes into the film, with a chicken curry in plastic containers – part of his cookery rehabilitation course. Doug serves it up on china plates – a real luxury in itself, even though we have to eat the meal with plastic knives and forks.

I eat the meal very slowly, and enjoy every morsel.

DAY 96   MONDAY 22 OCTOBER 2001

8.30 am

I've been at NSC for a week, and am beginning to feel that I know my way around.

I report to work at SMU. Matthew shows me how to make out an order form for any supplies that are needed for the office, which will then be sent to the stores, who should see that we have it the same day. We discover an outstanding order from 5 October for files and paper, marked urgent, and another for 15 October, marked very urgent. Inefficiency is endemic in parts of the Prison Service. Millions of pounds of taxpayers' money is wasted every year. The departments responsible for this differ from prison to prison, but to give you a small example: some years ago there was a prisoner at HMP Gartree who was a vicious killer and needed to be transferred from one cell to another, a distance of less than a hundred yards. Fifteen officers arrived to move him, an operation that took five minutes. All fifteen officers claimed four hours overtime. How do I know this? A senior officer who previously worked at Gartree told me.

DAY 96

12 noon

Matthew and I have lunch in the canteen with the other orderlies, and are joined by Roger (lifer, murdered his wife), who
berated me about England losing to Ireland on Saturday.

'But you sound Welsh?' I venture.

'I am,' he replies, 'but I don't care who beats the English. It's
one of the few pleasures I get in here.'

1.00 pm

Mr New arrives in the office, having spent the morning in court
on a domestic matter. One has a tendency to forget that prison
officers have problems of their own.

Matthew and I discuss how to improve office efficiency. I'd
like to clear out every drawer and cupboard and start again. He
agrees. We're about to begin, when the door opens and the
governing governor walks in. Mr Lewis greets me with a warm,
jovial smile. He asks Matthew to leave us and wastes no time
with small talk.

'The press,' he tells me, 'are still camped at both ends of the
prison.' And he adds that a prisoner has been caught with an
expensive camera and long lens in his room. Mr Lewis has no
idea which paper smuggled it in, or how much money was
involved. The inmate concerned is already on his way to a C-cat,
and will not be allowed to return to an open prison. Apparently
several prisoners have complained about the press invading
their privacy, and the governor has given his assurance that if a
photograph of them appears in a national newspaper, they have
legal recourse – a rule that doesn't seem to apply to me. We
then discuss my move to Spring Hill before the governor calls
Matthew back in. Mr Lewis grants him a further two days

compassionate leave, which will allow Matthew to spend five days with his father. Mr Lewis appears to have combined compassion and common sense, while remaining inside the Home Office guidelines.

4.00 pm

Mr New arrives back in the office, anxious to know what the governor wanted to see me about. I don't mention the camera as Mr Lewis specifically asked me not to. I tell him that Mr Lewis intends to speak to the governor of Spring Hill, but he's leaving all the paperwork to him.

'It's been dealt with,' Mr New replies. 'I've already sent all the documents to my opposite number.'

4.30 pm

I ask Matthew, on a visit to his room in the south block, if he could redo the 'officers list of needs' presently listed on the back of the kitchen cabinet, so that it's as smart as the one Doug displays in the hospital. I glance up at Matthew's bookshelf: Pliny the Younger and Augustus Caesar. He asks me if I've read Herodotes.

'No,' I confess, 'I'm still circa 1774, currently reading about John Adams and the first Congress. I'll need a little longer sentence if I'm ever to get back to 484 BC.'

5.00 pm

I return to my room. I hate the north block. It's noisy, dirty and smelly (we're opposite the pig farm). I lock myself in and write for a couple of hours.

DAY 96

7.00 pm

I stroll across to Doug (tax avoidance) in the hospital. He allows me the use of his bathroom. Once I've had a bath and put on clean clothes, I feel almost human.

Clive (fraud) joins us after his day job in the fruit factory. He tells me that his fellow workers believe what they read about me in the *Sun* and the *Mirror*. I despair.

8.15 pm

I leave the hospital and return for roll-call before going back to my room to write for a couple hours. The tannoy keeps demanding that Jackson should report for roll-call. He's probably halfway to Boston by now.

10.00 pm

Final roll-call. Mr Hughes waves from the other end of the corridor to show my name has been ticked off. He's already worked out that I will be the last person to abscond. I certainly wouldn't get halfway to Boston before being spotted.

DAY 97 TUESDAY 23 OCTOBER 2001

6.03 am

All the lifers at NSC are coming to the end of their sentence and are being prepared to re-enter the outside world. The very fact that they have progressed from an A-cat, through B, C to D over a period of twenty years, is proof that they want a second chance.

One of the fascinating things about murderers – and we have a dozen or more at NSC – is that you cannot generalize about them. However, I have found that they roughly fall into two categories: those who are first offenders and unlikely to commit another crime, especially after twenty years in jail, and those who are evil and should be locked away in an A-cat for the rest of their lives.

Almost all the lifers at NSC fall into the former category; otherwise they would never have made it to an open prison. Bob, Chris, Mike and Roger are all now middle aged and harmless. This might seem strange to those reading this diary, but I feel none of the fear when I'm with them that I do with some of the young tearaways who only have a few weeks left to serve.

DAY 97

8.30 am

Matthew starts cleaning out the cupboard and drawers, while I concentrate on the new inductees. There are fifteen of them, and it's lunchtime before the last one has all his questions answered.

12 noon

Lunch is memorable only because Wendy says my menu sheet is missing. She suspects it's been stolen and will appear in one of the tabloids tomorrow. She supplies me with a new one, but asks me not to put my name on the top or sign it, just hand the sheet over to her.

2.00 pm

While clearing out the drawers, Matthew comes across a box of biros marked 1987, and a ledger with the initials GR and a crown above it. Two hours later, every shelf has been washed and scrubbed. All the documents we need for inductees are in neat piles, and we have three bin bags full of out-of-date material.

4.45 pm

I join Doug and Matthew for supper: vegetarian sausage and mash.

5.00 pm

Back in my room I write for two hours. Tomorrow I must – I repeat, must – go to the gym.

DAY 98   WEDNESDAY 24 OCTOBER 2001

8.30 am

Today is labour board. All inductees, having completed their other interviews, must now be allocated a job, otherwise they will receive no income. The board consists of two members from management (the farm and other activities) and a senior officer. Before any inductee faces the board I brief them on what to expect, as I went through the process only a week ago. I tell them it helps if they know what they want to do, and one of them, a bright young Asian called Ahmed, tells me he's after my job. Another, Mr Clarke, informs me that he's sixty-seven and wants a part-time cleaning job, perhaps a couple of hours a day. I immediately go upstairs and ask the board if he could be allocated to this office, which would allow me to concentrate on the weekly inductions and the several prisoners who pop in during the day to talk about their problems. They tell me they'll think about it.

12.15 pm

I return to the SMU after lunch to find a drugs officer in the kitchen. His black Labrador Jed is sniffing around. I melt into the background, and listen to a conversation he's having with Mr New. It seems there's going to be another clampdown on drugs. The drugs officer tells Mr New that last year, thirty-six visitors were found with drugs on them, two of them solicitors and one a barrister. I am so surprised by this that I later ask Mr New if he believes it. He nods. Ironically, the headline in today's *Times* is, 'Cannabis to be legalized?' I leave the office at 1.30 pm as I have a visit myself today.

2.00 pm

Alison, my PA, David, my driver, and Chris Beetles are sitting at a little square table in the visitors' room waiting for me. After we've picked up Diet Cokes and chocolate, mostly for me, we seem to chat about everything except prison; from Joseph my butler, who is in hospital, seriously injured after being knocked down by a bus on his way to work, and the 'folly' at the bottom of the garden in Grantchester being flooded, to how the public are responding to the events of 11 September.

Alison and I then go through my personal letters and the list of people who have asked to visit me at NSC. These weekly visits are a wonderful tonic, but they also serve to remind me just how much I miss my friends, holed up in this God-forsaken place.

4.00 pm

I return to the office, to find Mr New and a security officer, Mr Hayes, waiting to see me. The photographers just won't go away. One has even offered Mr Hayes £500 for the charity of his choice if I will agree to pose for a picture. I refuse, aware how much more will go into the journalist's pocket. It's against the law to take a photograph of a serving prisoner, not that that seems to bother any of the vultures currently hovering around. Both officers promise to do their best to keep them at bay. Mr New then tells me that a second camera has been found in an inmate's room, and the prisoner involved was transferred back to a closed prison this morning. I try to concentrate on my work.

7.00 pm

I visit the canteen to discover I have £18.50 in my account: £10 of my own money, and £8.50 added as my weekly wage. My Gillette blades alone cost £4.29, and two phonecards £4.00, so there's not a lot over for extras like toothpaste, soap, bottles of Evian water and perhaps even a bar of chocolate. I mention this only in passing lest any of you should imagine that I am, as the tabloids suggest, living the life of Riley.

7.15 pm

I stroll across to the hospital, and enjoy the fresh country air, even if the surroundings are rather bleak. Doug tells me that my application to Spring Hill is being processed. How does Doug know before Mr New? It turns out that he has a friend (inmate) who works in the administration block at Spring Hill.

I have a long, warm bath. Heaven.

DAY 99   THURSDAY 25 OCTOBER 2001

8.30 am

Mr Simpson (probation) and Mr Gough (induction officer) are
the first to arrive in the office. They supply me with today's list
of appointments. This has two advantages. I can process those
inmates who have booked in, while dealing with the ones that
just drop by on the off chance. Mr Clarke (crime not yet identified), our sixty-seven-year-old cleaner, also turns up on time.
Matthew runs through his duties with him, while I make tea for
the officers.

10.10 am

Mr Hocking (security officer) appears in the kitchen to let me
know that a *Daily Mail* photographer (whose hair is longer than
that of any of the inmates), has entrenched himself on a local
farmer's land. He'll be able to take a picture whenever I return
to the north block. Mr Hocking is going to seek the farmer's
permission to eject him.

10.30 am

Mr Clarke has done a superb job; not only is the office spotless, but tomorrow he plans to get a grip on the waiting room – which presently resembles a 1947 GWR tea room.

12 noon

I have lunch with Malcolm (fraud and librarian orderly). He's quiet, well spoken and intelligent, and even in prison garb has the air of a professional man. What could he have done to end up here?

1.00 pm

Mr New appears, then disappears upstairs to join Mr Simpson, the probation officer. This afternoon they'll conduct interviews with three prisoners to discuss their sentence plans. That usually means that the inmate concerned only has a few months left to serve, so judgments have to be made on whether he is ready to take up work outside the prison, and if he is suitable for tagging.

The main factors in any decision are:

a) Is the prisoner likely to reoffend based on his past record?

b) Has he any record of violence?

c) Is he, or has he been, on drugs?

d) Has he completed all his town visits, and his week's leave, without incident?

Ticks in all those boxes means he can hope for early release, i.e. a two-year sentence becomes one year with an extra two months off for tagging. All three of today's applicants leave SMU with smiles on their faces.

2.20 pm

Mr Hocking returns, accompanied by a police officer. He tells me another camera has been found in an inmate's room. Once again, the prisoner concerned has been shipped off to a C-cat prison. The third in less than a week. No doubt whichever newspaper was responsible will try again. A few weeks of this, and I'll be the only prisoner still in residence.

4.30 pm

Mr Lewis the governing governor calls in to discuss the problem of lurking photographers. He asks me if I wish to return to Wayland.

'You must be joking,' are my exact words.

Mr New later explains that he only asked to protect the Prison Service, so that when a picture eventually appears in the press, I won't be able to suggest that I wasn't given the opportunity to return to closed conditions.

5.00 pm

Supper with Malcolm (fraud), Roger (murdered his wife), Martin (possession of a firearm which went off) and Matthew (breach of trust). All the talk is about an absconder who missed his girlfriend so much that he decided to leave us. He only had another nine weeks to go before his release date.

DAY 100   FRIDAY 26 OCTOBER 2001

A century of days in prison.

8.07 am

Breakfast. As it's Friday, we're offered weekend provisions: a plastic bag containing half a dozen tea bags, four sachets of sugar, some salt and pepper and a couple of pats of butter. Those of you who have read the previous two volumes of these diaries will recall my days in Belmarsh when I was on a chain gang, along with five other prisoners, putting tea bags into a plastic bag. Well, they've finally turned up at North Sea Camp. Prisoners do make useful contributions that can then be taken advantage of in other prisons, thus saving the taxpayer money, and giving inmates an occupation as well as a small weekly wage. For example, the tea towels in the kitchen were made in Dartmoor, the green bath towels in Liverpool, the brown sheets and pillow-cases at Holloway and my blankets at Durham.

Now don't forget the tea bags, because Doug has just told me over his eggs and bacon that a lifer has been shipped out to Lincoln Prison for being caught in possession of drugs. And where were they discovered? In his tea bags. Security staff raided his room this morning and found sixty tea bags containing cannabis, along with £40 in cash, which they consider proof that he was a dealer. But now for the ridiculous, sad, stupid, lunatic (choose your own word) aspect of this story – the prisoner in question was due for parole in eleven weeks' time. He will now spend the next eighteen months in a B-cat, before going on to a C-cat, probably for a couple of years, before being allowed to return to a D-cat in around four years' time. Doug adds that the security staff didn't know what he was up to, until another prisoner grassed on him.

'Why would anyone do that?' I ask.

'Probably to save their own skin,' Doug replies. 'Perhaps he was about to be shipped out for a lesser offence, so he offered them a bigger fish in exchange for a reprieve. It happens all the time.'

8.30 am

When I arrive at SMU, Mr Clarke is already standing by the door. He immediately sets about emptying the bins and mopping the kitchen floor. While we're working, I discover that it's his first offence, and he's serving a fifteen-month sentence for misappropriation of funds and is due to be released in March.

10.00 am

In the morning post there is a registered letter from my solicitors. I read the pages with trembling hands. My leave to appeal against conviction has been turned down. Only my leave to appeal against length of sentence has been granted. I can't describe how depressed I feel.

12 noon

Lunch. Doug nods in the direction of another prisoner who takes a seat at the next table. 'That's Roy,' he says, 'he's a burglar serving his fifteenth sentence. When the judge sentenced him this time to six months, he said, thank you, my Lord, I'll do that standing on my head.'

'Then I'll add a couple of months to help you get back on your feet,' replied the judge.

3.00 pm

I call my barrister, Nick Purnell QC. He feels we should still go for an appeal on conviction because three elements of our defence have been overlooked. How can Ted Francis be innocent if I am guilty? How can Mrs Peppiatt's evidence be relied upon when she confessed in the witness box to being a thief? How can I have perverted the course of justice, when the barrister representing the other side, Mr Shaw, said he had never considered the first diary date to be of any significance?

We also discuss the witness who could help me prove that Potts should never have taken the case. Nick warns me that Godfrey Barker is getting cold feet, and his wife claims she cannot remember the details.

5.30 pm

I see David (murder) in the corridor; he has a big grin on his face. He'll be spending tomorrow with his wife for the first time in two decades. He's very nervous about going out on his own, and tells me the sad story of a prisoner who went on a town visit for the first time in twenty-five years and was so frightened that he climbed up a tree. The fire service had to be called out to rescue him. The police drove him back to prison, and he's never been out since.

6.00 pm

My evenings are now falling into a set pattern. I join Doug at six-thirty and have a bath, before watching the seven o'clock news on Channel 4.

8.15 pm

I report for roll-call, and then return to play a few games of backgammon with Clive.

10.00 pm

Final roll-call.

DAY 101   SATURDAY 27 OCTOBER 2001

8.07 am

There are some prisoners who prefer to remain in jail rather than be released: those who have become institutionalized and have no family, no friends, no money and no chance of a job. And then there is Rico.

Rico arrived at NSC from Lincoln Prison this morning. It's his fourth burglary offence and he's always welcomed back because he enjoys working on the farm. Rico particularly likes the pigs, and by the time he left, he knew them all by name. He even used to sleep with them at night – well, up until final roll-call. He has a single room, because no one is willing to share with him. That's one way of getting a single room.

9.00 am

I check in at SMU, but as there are no officers around I write for two hours.

11.00 am

I try to phone Mary at Grantchester, but because the flash flood has taken the phones out, all I get is a long burr.

DAY 101

12 noon

On the way to lunch, I pass Peter (lifer, arson), who is sweeping leaves from the road. Peter is a six-foot-four, eighteen-stone Hungarian who has served over thirty years for setting fire to a police station, although no one was killed.

I have lunch with Malcolm (fraud) who tells me that his wife has just been released from Holloway having completed a nine-month sentence for money laundering. The £750,000 he made was placed in her account without her knowledge (Malcolm's words) but she was also convicted. Malcolm asked to have her sentence added to his, but the judge declined.

Wives or partners are a crucial factor in a prisoner's survival. It's not too bad if the sentence is short, but even then the partner often suffers as much, if not more, being alone on the outside. In Mary's case, she is now living her life in a glare of publicity she never sought.

4.15 pm

There's a timid knock on the door. I open it to find a prisoner who wants to talk about writing a book (this occurs at least once a week). His name is Saman, and he's a Muslim Kurd. He is currently working on a book entitled *The History of Kurdistan*, and wonders if I'll read a few chapters. (Saman read engineering at a university in Kurdistan.) When he has completed his sentence, Saman wants to settle down in this country, but fears he may be deported.

'Why are you at NSC?' I ask him.

Saman tells me that he was convicted of causing death by dangerous driving, for which he was sentenced to three years. He's due to be released in December.

DAY 102   SUNDAY 28 OCTOBER 2001

6.00 am

Today's is my mother's birthday. She would have been eighty-nine.

8.15 am

After breakfast I read *The Sunday Times* in the library. Rules concerning newspapers differ from prison to prison, often without rhyme or reason. At Wayland the papers were delivered to your cell, but you can't have your own newspaper at NSC.

While I'm reading a long article on anthrax, another prisoner looks over his copy of the *News of the World*, and says, 'I'm glad to find out you're earning fifty quid a week, Jeff.' We both laugh. He knows only too well that orderlies are paid £8.50 a week, and only those prisoners who go out to work can earn more. Funnily enough, this sort of blatant invention or inaccuracy has made my fellow inmates more sympathetic.

10.00 am

Phone Mary in Grantchester and at last get a ringing tone. She's just got back from Munich, which she tells me went well. Not all the Germans are aware that her husband is a convict. Her book, *Clean Electricity from Photovoltaics*, was received by the conference with acclaim. After struggling for some years to complete volume one, she ended up selling 907 copies. Mind you, it is £110 a copy, and by scientific standards, that is a best-seller. I use up an entire phonecard (twenty units) getting myself up to date with all her news.

11.00 am

A message over the tannoy informs inmates that they can report to the drug centre for voluntarily testing. A negative result can help with parole or tagging applications. By the time I arrive, there's already a long queue. I stand behind Alan (fraud) who is being transferred to Spring Hill tomorrow. He says he'll write and let me know how the place compares to NSC and try and find out how my application is progressing.

I reach the head of the queue. Mr Vessey – he of the hatchet face who never smiles – points to a lavatory so I can give him a sample of urine in a little plastic bottle. He then places a filter into the bottle that will show, by five separate black lines, if I am positive or negative, for everything from cannabis to heroin. If two little black lines come up opposite each drug, then you're clear, if only one line appears, you've tested positive and will be up in front of the governor first thing in the morning.

An inmate three ahead of me tests positive for cannabis, and explodes when Mr Vessey says he'll be on report tomorrow. He storms out, mouthing expletives. Mr Vessey smiles. My own test comes up with only double lines, which is greeted with mock applause by those still waiting in the queue.

'And pour your piss down the drain, Archer,' says Mr Vessey.

'If you leave it hanging around, this lot would happily sell it to the *News of the World.*'

12 noon

Lunch. I'm joined by Brian (chapel orderly and organist). He was convicted of conspiracy to defraud an ostrich farming company of seven million pounds. His barrister convinced him that if he pleaded not guilty, a trial could take ten months, and if he were then found guilty he might end up with a six- or seven-year sentence. He advised Brian to plead guilty to a lesser charge, so that he would be sentenced to less than four years. He took the advice, and was sentenced to three years ten months. His two co-defendants decided on a trial and the jury found them not guilty. Brian considers that pleading guilty was the biggest mistake of his life.

2.00 pm

Write for two hours.

6.30 pm

I go to chapel to be joined by five other prisoners. Brian the ostrich man is playing the organ (very professionally). I take Holy Communion in memory of my mother, and can't help reflecting that it's my first sip of wine in three months. The vicar offers each of us a tiny plastic thimble of wine. It's only later that I work out why: some prisoners would attend the service just to drain the chalice.

The vicar, the Rev Johnson, is over seventy. A short, dapper man, he gives us a short, dapper sermon on why he is not quite sure about born-again Christians. We then pray for those Christians who were murdered while taking part in a church service in Pakistan.

Covering the wall behind the altar and part of the ceiling is a painting of the Last Supper. After the service, the vicar tells me that a former prisoner painted it, and each of the disciples was modelled on an inmate. He chuckles, 'Only Christ isn't a convict.'

DAY 103   MONDAY 29 OCTOBER 2001

6.11 am

I wake early and think about home. I have a little pottery model of the Old Vicarage on the table in front of me, along with a photograph of Mary and the boys, and another of a view of Parliament from our apartment in London; quite a contrast to the view from my little room on the north block. The sky is grey and threatening rain. That's the one thing I share with you.

8.15 am

Breakfast with Malcolm (fraud, chief librarian) and Roger (murder, twelve years so far). Malcolm is able to tell me more about the young man called Arnold who absconded last week. I recall him from his induction at SMU, a shy and nervous little creature. He was sharing a room with two of the most unpleasant men I've ever come across. One of them has been moved from prison to prison during the past seven months because of the disruption he causes wherever he goes, and the other is a heroin addict serving out the last months of his sentence. I have never given a moment's thought to absconding.

However, if I had to spend a single night with either of those men, I might have to reconsider my position.

8.30 am

Today I set myself the task of reorganizing the muddled and misleading notice board in the waiting room. Matthew and I spend the first thirty minutes taking down all thirty-seven notices, before deciding which are out of date, redundant or simply on the wrong notice board. Only sixteen survive. We then pin up five new neatly printed headings – drugs, education, leave, tagging and general information, before replacing the sixteen posters neatly in their correct columns. By lunchtime the waiting room is clean, thanks to Mr Clarke, and the notice board easy to understand, thanks to Matthew, although I think I've also earned my 25p an hour.

12 noon

I have to repeat that as far as prison food goes, NSC is outstanding. Wendy and Val (her assistant) set standards that I would not have thought possible in any institution that has only £1.27 per prisoner for three meals a day. Today I'm down for the pizza, but Wendy makes me try a spoonful of her lamb stew, because she doesn't approve of my being a VIP (vegetarian in prison). It's excellent, and perhaps next week I'll risk a couple of meat dishes.

2.30 pm

The turnover at NSC is continual. Last week fifteen inmates departed, one way or another: end of sentence – twelve, moved to another prison – two, absconded – one. So after only two weeks, 20 per cent of the prison population has changed. Give me another month, and I'll be an old lag.

While I'm washing the teacups, Matthew tells me that his father has taken a turn for the worse, and the governor has pushed his compassionate leave forward by a day. He'll be off to Canterbury first thing in the morning, so he can be at his father's bedside for the next ten days. He doesn't complain about having to spend the ten nights in Canterbury Prison (B-cat), which can't be pleasant when your father is dying, and you don't have anyone to share your grief with.

4.30 pm

Another pile of letters awaits me when I return from work, among them missives from Chris de Burgh, Patrick Moore and Alan Coren. Alan's letter makes me laugh so much, rather than share snippets with you, I've decided to print it in full. (See overleaf.) All my life I have been graced with remarkable friends, who have tolerated my ups and downs, and this latest episode doesn't seem to have deterred them one iota.

5.00 pm

Tomorrow I'm going to the gym. I only write this to make sure I do.

6.00 pm

Write for two hours.

Alan Coren

26 October 2001

My dear Jeffrey:

Lots of forgivenesses to be begged. First off, forgive the typing, but not only is my longhand illegible, I should also be writing for some days, because I haven't picked up a pen for anything but cheques since about 1960. More important, try to forgive the fact that I haven't written before, but the truth is that I should so much have preferred to chat to you face to face (albeit chained to a radiator, or whatever the social protocols required) than to engage in the one-sided conversation of letters, so --- as you probably know --- I kept trying to get a visit, and kept being turned down. Most important of all, forgive me for not trying to spring you: I have spent a small fortune on grapnels, ropes, bolt-cutters, fake number-plates, one-way tickets to Sao Paolo, and drinks for large men from the Mile End Road with busted conks and tattooed knuckles, but whenever I managed to put all these elements together, there was always a clear night and a full moon.

Anyway, I gather from your office that it might now be possible to arrange a visit, once I and they have filled in all sorts of bumf, and you have been given enough notice to stick a jeroboam of Krug on ice and slip into a brocade dressing-gown and fez, so I shall set that in train forthwith --- if, of couurse, you agree. You are, by the way, bloody lucky not to be in that office now, these are bad days to be living at the top of a tall building next to MI6 and opposite the H of C --- and I speak as one who knows, having, as you'll spot from the letterhead, recently moved to a house in Regent's Park; where, from my top-floor study window as I type, I can see the Regent's Park Mosque 500 metres to my right, and the American Ambassador's residence 500 metres to my left. I am ground bloody zero right here: every time His Excellency's helicopter trrobs in, we rush down to the cellar. Could by anybody, or anything. Since even I don't know where Freiston is, I rather doubt that Osama bin Laden could find it, and you are further fortunate in the fact that, because every envelope to the clink is doubtless slit open, poked about in and generally vetted to the last square millimetre, if anybody's going to get anthrax, it won't be you.

Life goes on in London as normal: Anne and I have grown used to wearing our gas-masks in bed, though it's still a bit of a bugger waking up in the night and unthinkingly reaching for a bedside drink, so there's more nocturnal tumble-drying going on than there used to be. Giles and Victoria wish to be remembered to you, and want you to know that they're fine, and settling down well with their foster parents in Timbuktu, where they tell me they have made lots of new friends among the other evacuees, although HP sauce is proving dificult to find. Your beloved Conservative Party has elected a new leader, who may be seen every day at the doors of the Commons handing out his business cards to MPs and officials who would otherwise think we was someone who had turned up to flog them personal pension schemes.

Are you writing a book about chokey? *FF 8282* would make a terrific title, and since I am only one of countless hacks who envy you the opportunity to scribble away unencumbered by all the distractions that stop the rest of us from knocking out *Finnegan's Remembrance of War & Punishment*, I would, if I were you, seriously consider not going ahead with your appeal: giving up the chance of another couple of years at the typewriter could cost you millions.

All right --- if we must --- let's be serious for a moment: do you need anything, is there anything I can do, anyone I can see for you, all that? I know that you have truckloads of closer --- and far more influential --- friends than I, but because it's always on the cards that there may just be something you need that no-one else can come up with, I want you to know that I should do my very best to sort it out.

But if nothing else, do drop me the briefest of notes to let me know whether or not you'd like a visit. If you'd rather be left in peace, I should of course, understand. But it would be nice to meet for the odd laugh --- as if there could be any other kind of laugh, these days.

Alma joins me in sending you our very warmest wishes, Jeffrey. Bear up!

Yours ever,

Alan

DAY 103

8.15 pm

I sign in for roll-call. From tomorrow, as I will have completed my two weeks' induction, I need only sign in at 11 am, 4 pm and 8.15 pm. Because I'll be at work, in future, 8.15 pm will be the one time I have to appear in person. Doug says I will feel the difference immediately.

DAY 104 TUESDAY 30 OCTOBER 2001

6.01 am

Write for two hours. I've now completed 250,000 words since being incarcerated. Perhaps Alan Coren is right.

8.15 am

Ten new prisoners arrived yesterday. They will be seeing the doctor straight after breakfast before coming to SMU to be given their induction pack, and then be interviewed by the labour board. One by one they make an appearance. Some are cocky, know it all, seen it all, nothing to learn, while others are nervous and anxious, and full of desperate questions.

And then there's Michael Keane (lifer, fourteen years so far, aged thirty-nine).

Those of you who've been paying attention for the past 250,000 words will recall my twenty days at Belmarsh, where I met William Keane on the tea-bag chain gang. His brother Michael has the same Irish charm, wit and love of literature, but never forget that all seven Keane brothers have been in jail at the same time, costing the taxpayer a million pounds a year. Michael passes on William's best wishes, and adds that he heard today that his sister has just been released from Holloway after serving nine months for a string of credit-card crimes. Michael is hoping for parole in March, and if Irish charm were enough, he'd make it, but unfortunately, the decision has to be ratified by the Home Office, who will only read his files, and never see him face to face. His fame among the Keanes is legendary, because when he was at Belmarsh – a high-security prison – he got as far as the first outer gate while emptying dustbins. The furthest anyone has manage while trying to escape from hell.

10.20 am

A scruffy, unshaven prisoner called Potts checks into SMU to confirm that he has a meeting with his solicitor this afternoon. I check my day sheet to see that his lawyer is booked in for three o'clock. Potts, who has just come off a three-hour shift in the kitchen, smiles.

'See you at three, Jeff.'

11.40 am

All ten inductees have been seen by the labour board, and are fixed up with jobs on the farm, in the kitchen or at the officers' mess. One, Kevin (six years for avoiding paying VAT), has opted for full-time education as he's in his final year of a law degree.

12 noon

Over lunch, Doug asks me if I've put in my takeaway order for the weekend. I realize I'm being set up, but happily play along. He then tells me the story of two previous inmates, Bruce and Roy, who were partners in crime.

Bruce quickly discovered that it was not only easy to abscond from NSC, but equally straightforward to return unobserved. So one night, he walked the six miles to Boston, purchased some fish and chips, stole a bicycle, rode back, hid the bike on the farm and went to bed. Thus began a thriving enterprise known as 'weekend orders'. His room-mate Roy would spend the week taking orders from the other prisoners for supper on Saturday night (the last meal every day is at five o'clock, so you can be a bit peckish by nine). Armed with the orders, Bruce would then cycle into Boston immediately after the eight-fifteen roll-call, visit the local fish and chip shop, McDonalds or KFC – not to mention the pub – and arrive back within the hour so he could drop off his orders and still be seen roaming round the corridors long before the 10 pm roll-call.

This dot-con service ran successfully for several months, in the best traditions of free enterprise. Unfortunately, there's always some dissatisfied customer who will grass, and one night two officers caught Bruce about a mile away from the prison, laden with food and drink. He was transferred to a C-cat the following morning. His room-mate Roy, aware it would only be a matter of days before he was implicated, absconded with all the cash and hasn't been seen since.

2.50 pm

Potts returns to SMU for the meeting with his solicitor. He has shaved, washed his hair and is wearing a clean, well-ironed shirt, and his shoes are shining. I have the unenviable task of telling him that his solicitor rang a few moments ago to cancel the appointment.

This is a message to all solicitors and barristers who deal with the incarcerated: your visit can be the most important event of the week, if not the month, so don't cancel lightly. Potts walks dejectedly back down the path, head bowed.

4.00 pm

Mr Hocking drops into SMU. He tells me that the whole of spur four on the north block (nine rooms) has just been searched, because an officer thought he heard a mobile phone ringing. Possession of a mobile phone is an offence that will ensure you are sent back to a C-cat the same day.

4.30 pm

Write for two hours, feel exhausted, but at least I no longer have to report for the 10 pm roll-call.

7.00 pm

I join Doug and Clive at the hospital. Clive tells me that the officers found nothing during this morning's search. Often 'hearing a mobile phone' is just an excuse to carry one out when they are actually trying to find something else. Doug chips in, 'Truth is, they were looking for another camera which the press have recently smuggled in. They even know the name of the prisoner involved, and as he's due to be released on Friday, they want to be sure he doesn't leave with a role of photos that would embarrass them.'

11.40 pm

Potts is rushed to Boston Hospital, having taken an overdose.

DAY 105   WEDNESDAY 31 OCTOBER 2001

6.23 am

I wake thinking about Potts. He reminds me how awful being incarcerated is, and why inmates forever live in hope. I later discover that Potts will be moved to Sudbury Prison, so that he can be near his wife and family. I know how he feels. I'm still waiting to hear from Spring Hill.

8.30 am

This morning we have a risk-assessment board. Four prisoners who are applying for early release on tag (HCD) are to appear before the deputy governor, Mr Leighton, and the senior probation officer, Mr Simpson. If a candidate has an unblemished record while in jail – never been put on a charge, never been involved with drugs – he is in with a chance. But the prime consideration is whether the prisoner is likely to reoffend. So if the inmate is in for burglary or credit-card fraud, his chances aren't that good.

During the next hour I take each of the four prisoners up to face the board. They leave twenty minutes later, two with smiles on their faces who want to shake me by the hand, and two who barge past me, effing and blinding anyone who crosses their path.

11.11 am

Mr New has received a fax from Spring Hill, requesting three more documents and five more questions answered: a clearance release from the hospital to confirm I'm fit and well and not on any medication; my records from Belmarsh and Wayland to show I have never been put on report; and confirmation from NSC that I have not been put on a charge since I've been here. They also want to know if I intend to appeal against my sentence, and if so, will I be appearing in court. Mr New looks surprised when I say that I won't. There are two reasons for my decision. I never wish to spend another minute of my life in Belmarsh, which is where they transfer you if you are due to appear at the High Court, and I'm damned if I'll put my wife through the ordeal of facing the press outside the court as she arrives and departs.

11.30 am

At the hospital, sister checks over the forms from Spring Hill. Linda ticks all the little boxes and confirms I am remarkably fit – for my age, cheeky lady.

12 noon

Over lunch, Doug warns me that it still might be a couple of months before Spring Hill have a vacancy because it's the most popular prison in Britain, and in any case, they may not enjoy the attendant publicity that I would attract. Bell (a gym orderly) leans across and informs me, 'It's the best nick I've ever been to. I only moved here to be closer to my wife.'

3.52 pm

Mr New reappears clutching my blameless record from Belmarsh and Wayland.

At 4.04 he faxes Spring Hill with the eight pages they requested. He receives confirmation that they arrived at 4.09 pm. I'll keep you informed.

4.15 pm

The senior Listener, Brian (conspiracy to defraud an ostrich company), turns up at SMU. He asks if the backs of prisoners' identity cards can be redesigned, as they currently advertise the Samaritans and Crimestoppers. Brian points out that as no prisoner can dial an 0800 number the space would be better used informing new arrivals about the Listeners' scheme. He has a point.

5.00 pm

Write for two hours.

7.00 pm

Doug tells me that the governing governor, Mr Lewis, dropped into the hospital today as he'd read in the *News of the World* that I keep a secret store of chocolate biscuits in the fridge.

'Quite right,' Doug informed him, 'Jeffrey buys them from

the canteen every Thursday, and leaves a packet here for both of us which we have with my coffee and his Bovril.'

A week ago I told Linda that you could buy a jar of Marmite from the canteen, but not Bovril, which I much prefer. The following day a jar of Bovril appeared.

Prisoners break rules all the time, often without realizing it. Officers have to turn a blind eye; otherwise everyone would be on a charge every day of the week, and the prison service would grind to a halt. Of course there's a difference between Bovril and beer, between having an extra towel and a mobile phone, or a hardback book and a tea bag full of heroin. Most officers accept this and use their common sense.

8.26 pm

Two officers, Mr Spencer and Mr Hayes, join us in the hospital for a coffee break. We learn that eleven new prisoners came in this evening, and only seven will be released tomorrow, so the prison is nearly full. They also add that another prisoner has been placed in the segregation cell overnight and will be up in front of the governor tomorrow. He's likely to be on his way back to Lincoln Prison. It appears that a camera was found in his room, the third one in the past ten days. They also know which newspaper is involved.

DAY 106   THURSDAY 1 NOVEMBER 2001

6.19 am

In prison, you don't think about what can be achieved long term; all thoughts are short term. When is the next canteen so I can buy another phonecard? Can I change my job? Will I be enhanced? Can I move into a single room? At the moment the only thought on my mind is, can I get to Spring Hill? Not when, can. In prison *when* will only happens after *can* has been achieved.

8.30 am

Fifteen new prisoners in today, among them a Major Willis, who is sixty-four. I look forward to finding out what he's been up to.

Willis, Clarke (the cleaner) and myself do not *have* to work because we're all over sixty. But Willis makes it clear he's looking for a job, and the labour board allocate him to works (engineering).

DAY 106

9.30 am

Mr Hocking, the security officer, drops in for a cup of tea. He tells me that Braithwaite, who was found to have a camera in his room, is now on his way back to Lincoln. The newspaper involved was the *Mail on Sunday*. All the relevant papers have been sent to the local police, as an offence of aiding and abetting a prisoner may have been committed.

12.30 pm

I call Alison. Mary has been invited to Margaret and Denis Thatcher's golden wedding anniversary on 13 December. James will be making the long journey to visit me on Saturday.

7.15 pm

Doug tells me that his contact in the administration office at Spring Hill isn't sure if they'll have me. I'll bet that Doug finds out my fate long before any of the officers at NSC.

8.15 pm

A fight breaks out on spur six. It involves a tragic young man, who has been a heroin addict since the age of fourteen. He is due to be released tomorrow morning. Leaving ceremonies are common enough in prison, and an inmate's popularity can be gauged by his fellow prisoners' farewells on the night before he departs. This particular prisoner had a bucket of shit poured over his head, and his release papers burned in front of him. There's a lookout posted at the end of the spur, and the nearest officer is in the unit office at the far end of the corridor, reading a paper, so you can be sure the humiliation will continue until he begins his right rounds.

When I return to the hospital, I tell Doug the name of the prisoner involved. He expresses no surprise, and simply adds, 'That boy won't see the other side of forty.'

10.30 pm

Returning to my room, I pass Alan (selling stolen goods) in the corridor. He asks if he can leave a small wooden rocking horse in my room, as his is a little overcrowded with two inmates. He paid £20 for the toy (a postal order sent by someone on the outside to the wife of the prisoner who made it). It's a gift for his fourteen month old grandson.

As I write this diary, in front of me are several cards from well-wishers, a pottery model of the Old Vicarage, a photo of Mary and the boys and now a rocking horse.

Alan is due to be released in two weeks' time, and when he leaves, no excrement will be poured over his head. The prisoners will line up to shake hands with this thoroughly decent man.

DAY 107   FRIDAY 2 NOVEMBER 2001

6.19 am

Absconding is a D-cat phenomenon. It's almost impossible to escape from an A- or B-cat prison, and extremely difficult to do so even from a C-cat (Wayland, for example). In order for a prisoner to become eligible for D-cat status, he or she must be judged likely to complete their sentence without attempting to abscond. In practice, prisons are so overcrowded that C-cat establishments, which are desperate to empty their cells, often clear out prisoners who quite simply should not be sent to an open prison.

One intake of eleven such prisoners arrived from Lincoln last year and was down to seven before the final roll-call that night. I discovered today that because of the chronic shortage of staff, there are only five officers on duty at night, and two of them are on overtime, so absconding isn't too difficult.

Prisoners abscond for a hundred and one different reasons, but mainly because of outside family pressures: a wife who is having an affair, a partner who takes the children away or a death in the family that doesn't fulfil the criteria for compassionate leave. The true irony is that these prisoners are the ones mostly likely to be apprehended, because the first place they turn up at is the family abode and there waiting for them on the doorstep are a couple of local bobbies who then return them to closed conditions and a longer sentence.

Before I was sent to prison I would have said, 'Quite right, too, it's no more than they deserve.' However, after 106 days of an intense learning curve I now realize that each individual has to be judged on his own merits. I accept that they have to be punished, but it rarely falls neatly into black or white territory.

Then there's a completely different category of absconders – foreigners. They simply wish to get back to their country, aware that the British police have neither the time nor the resources to go looking for them.

For every Ronnie Biggs there are a hundred Ronnie Smalls.

Mr New tells me about two absconders who are part of North Sea Camp folklore. Some years ago Boston held a marathon in aid of a local cancer charity, and the selected route took the competitors across a public footpath running along the east side of the prison. One prisoner slipped out of the gym in his running kit, joined the passing athletes and has never been seen since.

The second story concerns a prisoner who had to make a court appearance on a second charge, while serving a six-year sentence for a previous conviction. When the jury returned to deliver their verdict, his guards were waiting for him downstairs in the cells. The jury delivered a verdict of not guilty on the second charge. The judge pronounced, 'You are free to leave the court.' And that's exactly what he did.

The reason I raise this subject is because Potts, who's had a bad week, absconded yesterday following his suicide attempt. It turns out that the final straw concerned the custody of his children – the subject he was going to raise with his solicitor.

DAY 107

8.15 am

After the frantic rush of events following the arrival of fifteen new prisoners yesterday, today is comparatively quiet. Allen (cannabis, six years) drops in to tell me that his weekend leave forms still haven't been processed, and it's this weekend. The duty officer Mr Hayes deals with it. Thomas (in charge of a gun that discharged) says his town visit form has not been authorized and asks how much longer he will have to wait to find out if he will be allowed out. Mr Hayes deals with it. Merry (embezzlement) arrives with still no word as to when Group 4 will be transporting him to Sudbury so that he can be nearer his family. Mr Hayes deals with it.

Mr Hayes is an unusual officer. He's not frightened of making decisions and standing by them. He also makes his own tea. When I asked him why, he simply replied, 'You're not here to serve me, but to complete your sentence. I don't need to be waited on.'

10.00 am

Mr Hocking and I agree it would be better for the press to take a photograph and then go away, leaving his little band of security officers to get on with their job.

I walk out of the SMU building and deliberately stop to chat to Peter (lifer, arson), who is sweeping leaves from the path. He keeps his back to the cameras. Three minutes later I return to the building and, true to form, the photographers all disappear.

12 noon

Major Willis comes to SMU to hand back his red induction folder. He tells me that he's sixty-four, first offence, GBH, sentence one year, and that he'll be released in March. He was a major in the army, and after retiring, fell in love with a young Nigerian girl (a prostitute), whom he later married. She soon began to bully him, and to spend what little money he had. One day he could take no more, blew his top and stuck a kitchen knife in her. She reported him to the police. He will end up doing ten months (if he gets his tag), six of them at NSC.

He's puzzled as to why I got four years.

2.30 pm

A quiet afternoon. A fleeting visit from Mr Berlyn to check that I'm wearing a prison shirt as the press keep reporting that mine isn't regulation issue. He checks the blue and white HMP label, and leaves, satisfied.

9.00 pm

Fall asleep in front of the TV. Doug says I snore. I'm writing five hours a day, on top of a thirty-four-hour week, and I'm not even going to the gym.

DAY 108   SATURDAY 3 NOVEMBER 2001

I've written several times about the boredom of weekends, but something takes place today that turns the normal torpor into frantic activity.

8.50 am

The photographers have returned. They either missed getting a good shot yesterday, or work for the Sundays who want a 'today pic'. I agree with the deputy governor, Mr Berlyn, to do another walk on, walk off, in order to get rid of them once and for all. He seems grateful.

2.00 pm

I'm expecting a visit from my son James. When I enter the visitors' room I can't see him, but then spot someone waving at me. It turns out to be my son. He's grown a beard. I hate it, and tell him so, which is a bit rough, as he's just travelled 120 miles to see me.

James tells me that my legal team are concentrating their efforts on my appeal. Mr and Mrs Barker have confirmed that they heard the judge discussing me at a dinner party over a year before I was arrested. This could change my appeal.

5.00 pm

Doug and I are having tea in the hospital when Clive strolls in to announce that he's moving to another room.

'Why?' I ask, when he has the largest space in the prison.

'Because they're fitting electrics into all the other rooms.' I can't believe he'd give up his large abode in exchange for a TV. 'If you want to move in, Jeffrey, you'd better come over to the south block now.' We all go off in search of the duty officer, who approves the move. I spend the next two hours, assisted by Alan (selling stolen goods), transferring all my possessions from the north block to the south, while Clive moves into a little single room at the other end of the corridor.

I am now lodged in a room twenty-one by sixteen feet. Most prisoners assume I've paid Clive some vast sum of money to move out and make way for me, whereas the truth is that Clive wanted out. There is only one disadvantage. There always has to be a disadvantage. My new abode is next to the TV room, but as that's turned off at eleven each night, and I rarely leave Doug in the hospital before 10.30 pm, I don't think it will be a real problem.

I now have an interesting job, a better room, edible food and £8.50 a week. What more could a man ask for?

DAY 109   SUNDAY 4 NOVEMBER 2001

6.19 am

Write for two hours before I join Doug at the hospital. We watch David Frost, whose guests include Northern Ireland's Chief Constable of the Police Service Sir Ronnie Flanagan. While discussing the morning papers, Sir Ronnie says that it's an infringement of my privacy that the tabloid press are taking pictures of me while I'm in jail. The pictures are fine, but the articles border on the farcical.

A security officer later points out that two tabloids have by-lines attributed to women, and there hasn't been a female journalist or photographer seen by anyone at NSC during the past three weeks.

12 noon

Over lunch I sit opposite an inmate called Andy, who is a rare phenomenon in any jail as he previously served ten years – as a prison officer. He is now doing a seven-year sentence, having pleaded guilty to smuggling drugs into prison for an inmate. Andy tells me that the only reason he did so was because the inmate in question was threatening to have his daughter beaten up. She was married to an ex-prisoner.

'Did you fall for that one, Jeffrey?' I hear you ask. Yes, I did.

The police presented irrefutable evidence to the jury showing that Andy's daughter had been threatened, and asked the judge to take this into consideration when he passed sentence. Although Andy claims he didn't know what was in the packages, the final one he smuggled in, a box of Cadbury's Quality Street, contained four grams of pure heroin.

Had it been cannabis, he might have been sentenced to a year or eighteen months. If he hadn't confessed, he might have got away with a suspension. He tells me that he knew he would eventually be caught, and once he was called in for questioning, he wanted to get the whole thing off his chest.

Andy was initially sent to HMP Gartree (B-cat), with a new identity and a different offence on his charge sheet. He had to be moved the moment he was recognized by an old lag. From there he went to Swalesdale, where he lasted twenty-four hours. He was then moved on to Elmsley, a sex offenders' prison, where he lived on the same landing as Roy Whiting, who was convicted of the murder of Sarah Payne. Once he'd earned his D-cat, Andy came to NSC, where he'll complete his sentence.

The only other comment he makes, which I've heard repeated again and again and therefore consider worthy of mention, is, 'sex offenders live in far better conditions than any other prisoners.'

DAY 110   MONDAY 5 NOVEMBER 2001

8.28 am

When I was an MP I often heard the sentiment expressed that life should mean life. I am reminded of this because we have a lifers' board meeting at SMU today.

There are nine lifers at NSC and you can be fairly confident that if they've reached a D-cat, they won't consider absconding. In truth, they're all fairly harmless. Two of them go out each day to work in an old people's home, one in a library in Boston and another for the local Oxfam shop.

Linda, their probation officer, joins us for coffee during the morning break. She adds to the research I've pieced together over the past three months. I began my prison life at Belmarsh on a spur with twenty-three murderers. Lifers range from cold-blooded killers like Denis Nielsen, who pleaded guilty to murdering thirteen victims, down to Chris, who killed his wife in a fit of rage after finding her in bed with another man; he's already spent fourteen years regretting his loss of temper. Nielsen began his sentence, and will end it, in the highest security A-category facility. He is currently locked up in a SSU (a special security unit), a sort of prison within a prison. When he moves anywhere within the prison, he is always accompanied by at least two officers and a dog, and he is searched every time he leaves his cell or returns to it. At night, he places all his clothes outside the cell door, and an officer hands them back to him the following morning. Nielsen told PO New on several occasions that it would have been better for everyone if they'd hanged him.

Now that the IRA terrorists are no longer locked up on the mainland, of the 1,800 murderers in custody, there are currently only seven SSU inmates.

Now Chris, who killed his wife, is at the other end of the scale. He's reached D-cat status after eleven years, and works in the kitchens. He therefore has access to several instruments with which he could kill or maim. Only yesterday, I watched him chopping up some meat – rather efficiently. He hopes that the parole board will agree to release him in eighteen months' time. During the past eleven years, he has moved from A-cat to D-cat via seventeen jails, three of them in one weekend when he was driven to Preston, Swalesdale and Whitemoor, only to find each time that they didn't have a cell for him.

All nine lifers at NSC will be interviewed today, so further reports can be sent to the Home Office to help decide if they are ready to return to the outside world. The Home Office will make the final decision; they are traditionally rather conservative and accept about 60 per cent of the board's recommendations. The board convenes at 9 am when Linda, the lifers' probation officer, is joined by the deputy governor, Mr Berlyn, a psychiatrist called Christine and the lifers' prison officer.

The first prisoner in front of the board is Peter, who set fire to a police station. He's so far served thirty-one years, and frankly is now a great helpless hunk of a man who has become so institutionalized that the parole board will probably have to transfer him straight to an old-peoples' home. Peter told me he has to serve at least another eighteen months before the board would be willing to consider his case. I don't think he'll ever be released, other than in a coffin.

The next to come in front of the board is Leon.

The biggest problem lifers face is their prison records. For the first ten years of their sentences, they can see no light at the end of the tunnel, so the threat of another twenty-eight days added to their sentence is hardly a deterrent. After ten years, Linda says there is often a sea change in a lifer's attitude that coincides with their move to a B-cat and then again when they reach a C-cat. This is even more pronounced when they finally arrive at a D-cat and can suddenly believe release is possible.

By the way, it's almost unknown for a lifer to abscond. Not only would they be returned to an A-cat closed prison, but its possible they never would be considered for parole again.

However, most of the lifers being interviewed today have led a farily blameless existence for the past five years, although there are often scars, missing teeth and broken bones to remind them of their first ten years in an A-cat.

During the day, each of them goes meekly in to face the board. No swagger, no swearing, no attitude; that alone could set them back another year.

Leon is followed by Michael, then Chris, Roger, Bob, John, John and John (a coincidence not acceptable in a novel). At the end of the day, Linda comes out exhausted. By the way, they all adore her. She not only knows their life histories to the minutest detail, but also treats them as human beings.

4.00 pm

Only one other incident of note today – the appearance at SMU of a man who killed a woman in a road accident and was sentenced to three years for dangerous driving. He's a mild-mannered chap who asked me for help with his book on Kurdistan. Mr New tells me that he is going to be transferred to another jail. The husband of his victim lives in Boston and, as the inmate is coming up for his first town visit, the victim's husband has objected on the grounds that he might come across him in his daily life.

The inmate joins me after his meeting with Mr New. He's philosophical about the decision. He accepts that the victim's family have every right to ask for him to be moved. He's so clearly racked with guilt, and seems destined to relive this terrible incident for the rest of his life, that I find myself trying to comfort him. In truth, he's a different kind of lifer.

10.00 pm

It must be Guy Fawkes Day, because from my little window I can see fireworks exploding over Boston.

DAY 111   TUESDAY 6 NOVEMBER 2001

5.49 am

The big news in the camp today is that from 1 November, NSC is to become a resettlement prison. (No doubt you will have noticed that it's 6 November.) The change of status could spell survival for NSC, which has been under threat of closure for several years.

Resettlement means quite simply that once a prisoner has reached his FLED (facility licence eligibility date) – in my case July next year – he can take a job outside the prison working for fifty-five hours a week, not including travelling time. The whole atmosphere of the prison will change when inmates are translated into outmates. They will leave the prison every morning between seven and eight, and not return until seven in the evening.

Prisoners will be able to earn £150 to £200 a week, just as Clive does as a line manager for Exotic Foods. It will be interesting to see how quickly NSC implements the new Home Office directive.

8.30 am

Seven new arrivals at NSC today, who complete their induction talk and labour board by 11.21 am. My job as SMU orderly is now running smoothly, although Matthew tells me that an officer said that for the first week I made the worst cup of tea of any orderly in history. But now that I've worked out how to avoid tea leaves ending up in the mug, I need a fresh challenge.

2.30 pm

Mr New warns me that the prison is reaching full capacity, and they might have to put a second bed in my room. Not that they want anyone to share with me, after the *News of the World* covered three pages with the life history of my last unfortunate cell-mate. It's simply a gesture to prove to other inmates that my spacious abode is not a single dwelling.

5.00 pm

I write, or to be more accurate, work on the sixth draft of my latest novel *Sons of Fortune*.

7.00 pm

Doug and I watch Channel 4 news. Fighting breaks out in Stormont during David Trimble's press conference following his reappointment as First Minister. If what I am witnessing on television were to take place at NSC, they would all lose their privileges and be sent back to closed conditions.

Doug has a natural gift of timing, and waits until the end of the news before he drops his bombshell. The monthly prison committee meeting – made up in equal numbers of staff and prisoners – is to have its next get-together on Friday. The governor is chairman, and among the five prison representatives are Doug and Clive; two men who understand power, however limited. Doug tells me that the main item on the agenda will be resettlement, and he intends to apply to work at his haulage company in Cambridgeshire. His application fulfils the recommended criteria, as March is within the fifty-five-mile radius. It is also the job he will return to once he's released, relieving his wife of the pressure of running the company while he's been locked up.

But now for the consequences. His job as hospital orderly – the most sought-after position in the prison – will become available. He makes it clear that if I want the job, he will happily make a recommendation to Linda, who has already hinted that such an appointment would meet with her approval. This would mean my moving into the hospital, and although I'd be working seven days a week, there is an added advantage of a pay rise of £3.20 so, with my personal income of £10, I'd have over £20 a week to spend in the canteen.

But the biggest luxury of all would be sleeping in the hospital, which has an en-suite bathroom, a sixteen-inch TV and a fridge. It's too much to hope for, and might even tempt me to stay at NSC – well, at least until my FLED.

DAY 112 WEDNESDAY 7 NOVEMBER 2001

5.58 am

They call him Mick the Key. He arrived yesterday, and if he hadn't been turned down for a job in the kitchens, I might never have heard his story. Even now I'm not sure how much of it I believe.

Originally sentenced to two years for breaking and entering, Mick is now serving his ninth year. They have only risked moving him to a D-cat for his last twelve weeks. The reason is simple. Mick likes escaping, or assisting others to escape, and he has one particular gift that aids him in this enterprise. He only needs to look at a key once and he can reproduce it. He first commits the shape to memory, then draws the outline on a piece of paper, before transferring that onto a bar of prison soap – the first impression of the key. The next stage is to reproduce the image in plastic, using prison knives or forks. He then covers the newly minted key with thick paint he obtains from the works department. The next day he has a key.

During his years in prison, Mick has been able to open not only his own cell door, but also anyone else's. In fact, while he was at Whitemoor, they closed the prison for twenty-four hours because they had to change the locks on all 500 cells.

Getting out of prison is only half the enjoyment, this

charming Irishman tells me, 'Getting into kitchens, stores or even the governor's office adds to the quality of one's life. In fact,' he concludes, 'my greatest challenge was opening the hospital drugs cabinet in under an hour.' On that occasion, the officers knew who was responsible, but as nothing was missing (Mick says he's never taken a drug in his life), they could only charge him 'on suspicion', and were later unable to make the charge stick.

Some of the prison keys are too large and complicated to reproduce inside, so, undaunted, Mick joined the art class. He drew pictures of the skylines of New York, Dallas and Chicago before sending them home to his brother. It was some weeks before the innocent art teacher caught on. The security staff intercepted a package of keys brought into the prison by his sister. What a useful fellow Mick would have been in Colditz.

Mick tells me that he hopes to get a job in the kitchen, where he intends to be a good boy, as he wants to be released in twelve weeks' time.

'In any case,' he adds, 'it will do my reputation no good to escape from an open prison.'

The labour board turned down Mick's application to work in the kitchen; after all, there are several cupboards, cool rooms and fridges, all of which are locked, and for him, that would be too much of a temptation. He leaves SMU with a grin on his face.

'They've put me on the farm,' he declares. 'They're not worried about me breaking into a pigsty. By the way, Jeff, if you ever need to get into the governor's office and have a look at your files, just let me know.'

10.00 am

An extra bed has appeared in my room, because two of the spurs are temporarily out of service while they're being fitted for TVs. I found out today that prisoners are charged £1 a week for the hire of their TVs, and NSC will make an annual profit of £10,000 on this enterprise. At Wayland, I'm told it was £30,000. Free enterprise at its best. Still, the point of this entry is to let you know that I will soon be sharing my room with another prisoner.

2.40 pm

At Mr New's request, I join him in his office. He's just had a call from his opposite number at Spring Hill, who asked if I was aware that if transferred I would have to share a room.

'Yes,' I reply.

'And can they confirm that the principal reason for seeking a transfer is the inconvenience to your family of having a 250-mile round trip to visit you?'

'Yes,' I reply.

Mr New nods. 'I anticipated your answers. Although a decision has not yet been made, the first vacancy wouldn't be until 28 November.'

Suddenly it's crunch time. Would I rather stay at NSC as the hospital orderly, with my own room, TV, bathroom and fridge? Or move to Spring Hill and be nearer my family and friends? I'll need to discuss the problem with Mary.

5.00 pm

I return to my room to do a couple of hours writing; so far, no other occupant has appeared to claim the second bed.

DAY 112

6.42 pm

My new room-mate arrives, accompanied by two friends. His name is Eamon, and he seems pleasant enough. I leave him to settle in.

When I stroll into the hospital, Clive has a large grin on his face. He spent eleven months in that room without ever having to share it for one night. I couldn't even manage eleven days.

DAY 113   THURSDAY 8 NOVEMBER 2001

8.15 am

Breakfast. Wendy, the officer in charge of the kitchen, needs three new workers from this morning's labour board.

'But only yesterday you told me that you were overstaffed.'

'True,' she replies, hands on hips, 'but that was yesterday, and I had to sack three of the blighters this morning.'

'Why?' I ask hopefully.

'I knew you'd ask,' she replies, 'and only because you're bound to find out sooner or later, I'll tell you. I set three of them plucking chickens yesterday morning, and last night two of the birds went missing. I don't know who stole them, but in my kitchen I dispense summary justice, so all three were sacked.'

9.30 am

Eight new prisoners arrive for induction today, including my room-mate Eamon. It seems that he worked in the kitchen at his last prison, but 'on the out' is a builder by trade. He's due for release in January, and wants to work outside during the winter months to toughen himself up. Sounds logical to me, so I recommend that he opts for the farm.

DAY 113

10.00 am

Eamon gets his preferred job. I also find three new kitchen workers for Wendy, and the labour board is drinking coffee by 10.39 am. I need a new challenge.

12 noon

Lunch. I sit next to the new visits orderly, who tells me that 'on the out' he was a hairdresser in Leicester. He charged £27.50, but while he's in prison, he'll happily cut my hair once a month for a phonecard. Another problem solved.

2.30 pm

A fax has just been received from Spring Hill, requesting my latest sentence plan, which cannot be updated until I've served twenty-eight days at NSC. Sentence plans make up a part of every prisoner's record, and are an important element when it comes to consideration for parole. Sentence planning boards are held almost every afternoon and conducted by Mr New and Mr Simpson. I am due before the board on 20 November. Mr New immediately brings it forward a week to 12 November – next Monday, which would be my twenty-ninth day at NSC, and promises to fax the result through to Spring Hill that afternoon. I'll be interested to see what excuse they'll come up with next.

3.30 pm

Mr Berlyn (deputy governor) drops in to grumble about the prison being full for the first time in years and say that I'm to blame.

'How come?' I ask.

'Because,' he explains, 'the *News of the World* described NSC as the cushiest jail in Britain, so now every prisoner who qualifies for a D-cat wants to be sent here. It's one of the reasons I hope they take you at Spring Hill,' he continues, 'then we can pass that dubious accolade on to them. By the way,' he adds, 'don't get your hopes up about an early move, because someone up above [prison slang for the Home Office] is out to stop you.'

4.00 pm

John (lifer, murder) arrives in SMU, accompanied by a very attractive lady whom he introduces as his partner. This has me puzzled. If John murdered his wife, and has been in prison for the past fourteen years, how can he have a partner?

5.00 pm

I return to my room and write for two hours, relieved that Eamon doesn't make an appearance. I'm not sure if it's because he's with his friends from Derby, or is excessively considerate. This morning he told me he didn't mind my switching the light on at six o'clock.

'I'm in the building trade,' he explained, 'so I'm used to getting up at four-thirty.'

I feel I should add that he doesn't smoke, doesn't swear and is always well mannered. I still haven't found out why he's in prison.

DAY 113

7.15 pm

I find Doug and Clive at the hospital, heads down, poring over the new resettlement directive in preparation for tomorrow's facility meeting. Doug is determined to be the first prisoner out of the blocks, and if that should happen, then I might become the hospital orderly overnight. For the first time I look at the hospital in a different light, thinking about what changes I would make.

DAY 114   FRIDAY 9 NOVEMBER 2001

6.00 am

Before I went to sleep last night, I studied the latest Lords reform bill, as set out in *The Times* and *Telegraph* by Phil Webster and George Jones, those papers' respective political editors.

When I entered the Commons in 1969 at the age of twenty-nine, I think I was the first elected MP not to have been eligible for national service.* I mention this because, having won a by-election in Louth, Lincolnshire, I experienced six months of a 'fag-end' session of which almost every member had served not only in the armed forces, but also in the Second World War, with half a dozen having done so in the First World War. On the back benches generals, admirals and air marshalls – who could add MC, DSO and DFC to the letters MP – were in abundance. At lunch in the members' Dining Room, you might sit next to Sir Fitzroy McLean, who was parachuted into Yugoslavia to assist Tito, or Airey Neave, who escaped from Colditz.

In 1970, when Ted Heath became Prime Minister, Malcolm Rifkind, Kenneth Clarke and Norman Lamont joined me – a new breed of politician who would, in time, replace the amateurs of

---

* A two-year period of compulsory service in one of the branches of the armed forces, which ceased to apply for anyone born after 1940.

the past. I use the word 'amateur' with respect and admiration, for many of these men had no desire to hold high office, considering Parliament an extension of the armed forces that allowed them to continue to serve their country.

When I entered the Lords in 1992, the House consisted of hereditary peers, life peers and working peers (I fell into the latter category). Peter Carrington (who was Foreign Secretary under Margaret Thatcher) is an example of an hereditary peer, the late Yehudi Menuhin of a life peer who rarely attended the House – why should he? And John Wakeham was a working peer and my first leader – a Cabinet minister appointed to the Lords to do a job of work.

A strange way to make up a second chamber, you may feel, and certainly undemocratic but, for all its failings, while I sat on the back benches I came to respect the skills, dedication and service the country received for such a small outlay. On the other side of that undemocratic coin were hereditary peers, and even some life peers, who never attended the House from one year to the next, while others, who contributed almost nothing, attended every day to ensure they received their daily allowance and expenses.

8.00 am

I learn a little more about John's (lifer) love life over breakfast. It seems John met his partner some six years ago when he was ensconced at Hillgrove, a C-cat prison. She had driven a couple of John's friends over to visit him. At that time John would only have been allowed a visit once a fortnight. On learning that a woman he had never seen in his life was sitting in the car park, he suggested she should join them. For the next few months, Jan continued to drive John's friends to his fortnightly visit, but it wasn't long before she was coming on her own. This love affair developed in the most restrictive and unpromising circumstances. Now John is in a D-cat, Jan can visit him once a week. It's their intention to get married, should he be granted his parole in eighteen months' time.

As you can imagine they still have several obstacles to overcome. John is fifty-one, and has served twenty-three years, and Jan is forty-eight, divorced and with three children by her first marriage. At some time between now and next March, Jan has to tell her three children, twenty-four, twenty-two and fifteen, that she has fallen in love with a murderer, and intends to marry him once he's released.

11.00 am

My name is bellowed out over the tannoy, and I am ordered to report to reception. Those stentorian tones could only come from Sergeant Major Daff (Daffodil to the inmates). I have several parcels to sign for, most of them books kindly sent in by the public; I am allowed to take them away only if I promise they'll end up in the library; also, two T-shirts for gym use only (he winks) and a box of Belgian truffles sent by a lady from Manchester. Now the rule on sweets is clear. Prisoners cannot have them, as they may be full of drugs, so they are passed on to the children who attend the gym on Thursdays for special needs classes (explain that one). I suggest that not many seven year olds will fully appreciate Belgian truffles, but perhaps Mrs Daff might like them (they've been married for forty years).

'No,' he replies sharply, 'that could be construed as a bribe.' Mr Daff suggests they're put in the raffle for the Samaritans' Ball in Boston. I agree. I have for many years admired the work of the Samaritans, and in prison they have unquestionably saved countless young lives.

DAY 114

4.00 pm

When I return to my room, I find Eamon preparing to move out and join his friends from Derby in the eight-room dormitory, so I'll be back on my own again. I take advantage of the time he's packing his HMP plastic bag to discover why he's in prison.

It seems that on the Saturday night of last year's Cup Final, Eamon and his friends got drunk at their local pub. A friend appeared and told them he had been beaten up by a rival gang and needed some help 'to teach the bastards a lesson'. Off went Eamon and his drunken mates armed with pool cues and anything else they could lay their hands on. They chased the rival gang back to their cars in the municipal car park next to the Crown Court, and a fierce battle followed – all of which was recorded on CCTV.

Five of them were charged with violent disorder and pleaded not guilty – one of them a member of Derby County football team. Their solicitor plea-bargained for the charge to be downgraded to affray. One look at the CCTV footage and they quickly changed their plea to guilty. They were each given ten months, and if they're granted tagging, will be released after only twelve weeks (five months minus two months tagging). Incidentally, the gang member who enlisted their help was the first to hear the sirens, and escaped moments before the police arrived.

DAY 115   SATURDAY 10 NOVEMBER 2001

6.38 am

There isn't a day that goes by when I don't wish I wasn't here. I miss my freedom, I miss my friends and above all I miss Mary and the boys.

There isn't a day that goes by when I don't curse Mr Justice Potts for what everyone saw as his prejudicial summing up to the jury, and his apparent delight at handing out such a draconian sentence.

There isn't a day that goes by when I don't wonder why the police haven't arrested Angie Peppiatt for embezzlement.

There isn't a day that goes by when I don't question how I can be guilty of perverting the course of justice while Ted Francis is not; either we are both guilty or both innocent.

I have been in jail for 115 days, and my anger and despair finally surface after a visit by a young man called Derek.

Derek knocks quietly on my door, and I take a break from writing to deal with his simple request for an autograph on the back of a picture of the girlfriend who has stood by him. I ask him about his sentence (most prisoners go into great detail, even though they know I'm writing a diary). Derek is spending three months in jail for stealing from his employers after issuing a personal cheque he knew he hadn't the funds to cover. He spent a month in Lincoln Prison, which the old lags tell me is even worse than Belmarsh. He adds that the magistrate's 'short, sharp shock' has enabled him to witness a violent beating in the shower, the injecting of heroin and language that he had no idea any human being resorted to.

'But,' he adds before leaving, 'you've been an example to me. Your good manners, your cheeriness and willingness to listen to anyone else's problems, have surprised everyone here.'

I can't tell him that I have no choice. It's all an act. I am hopelessly unhappy, dejected and broken. I smile when I am at my lowest, I laugh when I see no humour, I help others when I need help myself. I am alone. If I were to show any sign, even for a moment, of what I'm going through, I would have to read the details in some tabloid the following day. Everything I do is only a phone call away from a friendly journalist with an open cheque book. I don't know where I have found the strength to maintain this facade and never break down in anyone's presence.

I will manage it, even if it's only to defeat my enemies who would love to see me crumble. I am helped by the hundreds of letters that pour in every week from ordinary, decent members of the public; I am helped by my friends who remain loyal; I am helped by the love and support of Mary, Will and James.

I have no thoughts of revenge, or even any hope of justice, but God knows I will not give in.

DAY 116 SUNDAY 11 NOVEMBER 2001

8.05 am

I'm five minutes late for breakfast. Mr Hayes, a thoughtful and decent officer, takes me to one side and asks if I could be on time in future because otherwise some prisoners will complain that I'm getting special treatment.

9.00 am

Doug is out on town leave so that he can visit his family in March, and Linda (hospital matron) asks me if I'll act as 'keeper of the pills'. You need three qualifications for this responsibility:

1) non-smoker,

2) never been involved with drugs,

3) be able to read and write.

In a prison of 172 inmates, only seven prisoners fulfil all three criteria.

10.00 am

I write for two hours.

DAY 116

12.10 pm

Lunch. I'm on time.

1.15 pm

The governing governor, Mr Lewis, drops in to see Linda.

'Glad to catch you,' he says to me. 'I've had a letter from "Disgusted, Bexhill on Sea". She wants to know why you have a private swimming pool and are driven home in your Rolls Royce every Friday to spend the weekend with your family. I have disillusioned her on the first two points, and added that you are now working both Saturday and Sunday in the hospital at a rate of 25p an hour.'

2.00 pm

Mary visits me. It's wonderful to see her, although she looks drawn and tired. She brings me up to date on all my legal problems, including details of all the money that disappeared during the period Angie Peppiatt was my secretary. We also discuss whether I should issue a writ against Baroness Nicholson for her accusation that I stole millions from the Kurds, and how it's possible for Ted Francis to be innocent when I was found guilty of the same charge. Once she's completed the file on Mrs Peppiatt, it will be handed over to the police.

We finally discuss the dilemma as to whether I should remain at NSC and take over as hospital orderly. We decide I should still apply for Spring Hill.

6.00 pm

I read the only Sunday papers I can lay my hands on, the *Observer* and the *News of the World.* One too far to the left for me, the other too far to the right.

7.00 pm

Doug returns from a day out with his family, and I hand back my responsibility as 'keeper of the pills'. He's convinced that they're lining me up for the hospital job just as soon as he's granted leave to do outside work, which would take him out of the prison five days a week. I tell him that both Mary and I still feel it would be better if I could transfer to Spring Hill.

10.30 pm

Back to my room. The communal TV next door is showing some vampire film at full volume. Amazed by what the body learns to tolerate, I finally fall asleep.

DAY 117   MONDAY 12 NOVEMBER 2001

8.50 am

As each day passes, I tell myself that the stories will dry up and this diary with it. Well, not today, because Simon has just walked into SMU.

Simon works in the officers' mess, and although I see him every day I have not yet made his acquaintance. He's visiting SMU to check on an application he submitted to visit his mother in Doncaster. He has, I fear, been dealing with an officer ironically known as 'action man'. After six weeks and several 'apps', Simon has still heard nothing. After I've promised to follow this up, I casually ask him why he's in prison.

'I abducted my son,' he replies.

I perk up. I've not come across an abduction before.

Simon pleaded guilty to abducting ('rescuing' in his words) his five-year-old son for forty-seven days. He whisked him off to Cyprus, via France, Germany, Yugoslavia and Turkey. He did so, he explains, because after he'd left his wife, he discovered that his son was being physically abused by both his ex-wife and her new partner, a police detective sergeant. The judge didn't believe his story, and sentenced him to four years, as a warning to other fathers not to take the law into their own hands. Fair enough, and indeed I found myself nodding.

A year later, his wife's new partner (the detective sergeant) was arrested and charged with ABH (actual bodily harm), and received a three-year sentence for, among other things, breaking the little boy's arm. Simon immediately appealed and returned to court to face the same judge. He pleaded not only extenuating circumstances, but added 'I told you so', to which the judge replied, 'It doesn't alter the fact that you broke the law, so you will complete your sentence.'

Ah, I hear you say, but he could have reported the man to the police and the social services. You try reporting a detective sergeant to the police. And Simon has files stacked up in his room filled with dozens of complaints to the social services with replies bordering on the ludicrous, 'We have looked into the matter very carefully and have no reason to believe...' Simon had to sell his home to pay the £70,000 legal bills, and is now incarcerated in NSC, penniless, and with no knowledge of where his only child is. My heart goes out to this man.

Would you have done the same thing for your child? If the answer is yes, then you're a criminal.

11.00 am

A call for me over the tannoy to report to reception. Sergeant Major Daff is on duty. He is happy to release my drug-free radio. It's a Sony three-band, sensible, plain and workmanlike. It will do the job and one only needs to look at the sturdy object to know it's been sent by Mary.

DAY 117

2.30 pm

A quiet afternoon, so Matthew gives me a lecture on Herodotus. He is rather pleased with himself, because he's come across a passage in book four of the *Histories* that could be the first known reference to sniffing cannabis (hemp). I reproduce the translation in full:

> And now for the vapour-bath. On a framework made up of three sticks, meeting at the top, they stretch pieces of woollen cloth, taking care to get the jams as perfect as they can, and inside this little tent, they place a dish with red-hot stones on it. They then take some hemp seed, enter the tent and throw the seed onto the hot stones. It immediately begins to smoke, giving off a vapour unsurpassed by any vapour bath one could find in Greece. The Scythians enjoy the experience so much that they howl with pleasure.

3.40 pm

Mr New and Mr Simpson interview me for my sentence plan. All the boxes are filled in with 'No History' (N/H) for drugs, violence, past offences, drink or mental disorder. In the remaining boxes, the words 'Low Risk' are entered for abscond, reoffend and bullying. The final box has to be filled in by my personnel officer. Mr New is kind enough to commend my efforts at SMU and my relationship with other prisoners.

The document is then signed by both officers and faxed to Spring Hill at 4.07 pm, and is acknowledged as received at 4.09 pm. Watch this space.

DAY 118   TUESDAY 13 NOVEMBER 2001

5.51 am

Write for two hours.

8.30 am

There are no new inductees today and therefore no labour board. Mr New will not be on duty until one o'clock, so Matthew and I have a quiet morning. He gives me a lecture on Alexander the Great.

12 noon

I phone Chris Beetles at his gallery. His annual *Illustrators' Catalogue* has arrived in the morning post. There is the usual selection of goodies: Vickie, Low, Brabazon, Scarfe, Shepard, Giles and Heath Robinson. However, it's a new artist who attracts my attention.

The first edition of *The Wind in the Willows* was illustrated by E. H. Shepard, and after his death for a short time by Heath Robinson. But a new version has recently been published, illustrated with the most delightful watercolours by Michael

Foreman, who is one of Britain's most respected illustrators. Original Shepards are now changing hands for as much as £100,000 and Heath Robinsons can fetch £10,000. So it was a pleasant surprise to find that Mr Foreman's works were around £500. I decide to select one or two for any future grandchildren.

So in anticipation I turn the pages and begin to choose a dozen or so for Mary to consider. I have to smile when I come to page 111: a picture of Toad in jail, being visited by the washer-woman. This is not only a must for a future grandchild, but should surely be this year's Christmas card. (See below.)

4.00 pm

An inmate called Fox asks me if it's true that I have a laptop in my room. I explain politely to him that I write all my manuscripts by hand, and have no idea how to use a computer. He looks surprised. I later learn from my old room-mate Eamon that there's a rumour going round that I have my own laptop and a mobile phone. Envy in prison is every bit as rife as it is 'on the out'.

5.00 pm

I receive a visit from David (fraud, eighteen months). He has received a long and fascinating letter from his former pad-mate Alan, who was transferred to Spring Hill a week ago. Alan confirms that his new abode is far more pleasant than NSC, and advises me to join him as quickly as possible. He doesn't seem to realize that the decision won't rest with me. However, there is one revealing sentence: 'An officer reported that they've been expecting Jeffrey for the past week, has he decided not to come?' David feels that they must have agreed to take me, and are only waiting for my sentence plan, which was faxed to them yesterday.

Incidentally, David (the recipient of the letter) was a schoolmaster in Sleaford before he arrived at NSC via Belmarsh. Three of his former pupils are also residents; well, to be totally accurate, two – one has just absconded.

7.00 pm

Doug and I watch the tanks as they roll into Kabul while Bush and Blair try not to look triumphant.

DAY 118

10.30 pm

I'm back in my room, undressing, when a flash bulb goes off.* I quickly open my door and see an inmate running down the corridor. I chase after him, but he disappears out of the back door and into the night.

I return to my room, and a few moments later, an officer knocks on the door and lets himself in. He tells me that they know who it is, as several prisoners saw the culprit departing. So everyone will know it was by this time tomorrow; yet another inmate who has been bribed by the press. The last three have been caught, lost their D-cat status, been shipped back to a B-cat and had time added to their sentence. I'm told the going rate for a photograph is £500. If they catch him, I'll let you know. If they don't, you'll have seen it in one of the national papers, captioned: 'EXCLUSIVE: Archer undressing in his cell'.

---

* The door to each inmate's room has a large glass panel in it, covered in wire mesh. On the outside is a green curtain to stop casual passers-by peering in. However, during the night, prison officers hold back the curtain to check you're in bed and haven't absconded.

DAY 119   WEDNESDAY 14 NOVEMBER 2001

8.15 am

As I walk over to breakfast from the south block, I pick up snippets of information about last night's incident. It turns out that the photographer was not a prisoner, but Wilkins, a former inmate who was released last Friday. He was recognized by several inmates, all of whom were puzzled as to what he was doing back inside the prison four days after he'd been released.

But here is the tragic aspect of the whole episode. Wilkins was in prison for driving without a licence, and served only twelve weeks of a six-month sentence. The penalty for entering a prison for illegal purposes carries a maximum sentence of ten years, or that's what it proclaims on the board in black and white as you enter NSC. And worse, you spend the entire term locked up in a B-cat, as you would be considered a high-escape risk. The last such charge at NSC was when a father brought in drugs for his son. He ended up with a three-year sentence.

I look forward to discovering which paper considers this behaviour a service to the public. I'm told that when they catch Wilkins, part of the bargaining over sentence will be if he is willing to inform the police who put him up to it.

2.30 pm

There's a call over the intercom for all officers to report to the gatehouse immediately. Matthew and I watch through the kitchen window as a dozen officers arrive at different speeds from every direction. They surround a television crew who, I later learn, are bizarrely trying to film a look-alike Jeffrey Archer holding up one of my books and claiming he's trying to escape. Mr New tells me he warned them that they were on government property and must leave immediately, to which the producer replied, 'You can't treat me like that, I'm with the BBC.' Can the BBC really have sunk to this level?

DAY 120   THURSDAY 15 NOVEMBER 2001

5.21 am

I'm up early because I have to report to the hospital by 7.30 am to take over my new responsibilities as Doug's stand-in, while he goes off on a three-day forklift truck-driving course. How this will help a man of fifty-three who runs his own haulage company with a two million pound turnover is beyond me. He doesn't seem to care about the irrelevance of it all, as long as he gets out of prison for three days.

I write for two hours.

7.30 am

I report to Linda at the hospital, and witness the morning sick parade. A score of prisoners are lined up to collect their medication, or to see if they can get off work for the day. If it's raining or freezing cold, the length of the queue doubles. Most farm workers would rather spend the day in the warm watching TV than picking Brussels sprouts or cleaning out the pigsties. Linda describes them as malingerers, and claims she can spot them at thirty paces. If I worked on the farm I might well join them.

Bill (fraud, farm worker) has had every disease, affliction and germ that's known to man. Today he's got diarrhoea and asks Linda for the day off work. He feels sure he'll be fine by tomorrow.

'Certainly,' says Linda, giving him her warmest smile. Bill smiles back in response. 'But,' she adds, 'I'm going to have to put you in the san [sanatorium] for the day.'

'Why?' asks Bill, looking surprised.

'I'll need to take a sample every thirty minutes,' she explains, 'before I can decide what medication to prescribe.' Bill reluctantly goes into the hospital, lies on one of the beds and looks hopefully in the direction of the television screen. 'Not a chance,' Linda tells him.

Once Linda has sorted out the genuinely ill from the trying-it-on brigade, I'm handed four lists of those she has sanctioned to be off work for the day. I deliver a copy to the south block unit office, the farm office, the north block, the gatehouse amd education before going to breakfast.

8.30 am

It's Matthew's last day at NSC and he's on the paper chase. He takes a double-sided printed form from department to department, the hospital, gym, canteen, stores and reception, to gather signatures authorizing his release tomorrow. He starts with Mr Simpson, the probation officer at SMU, and will end with the principal officer Mr New. He will then have to hand in this sheet of paper at reception tomorrow morning before he can finally be released. It's not unknown for a prisoner's release paper to disappear overnight, which can hold up an inmate's departure for several hours.

I'll miss Matthew, who, at the age of twenty-four, will be

returning to university to complete his PhD. He's taught me a great deal during the past five weeks. I've met over a thousand prisoners since I've been in jail, and he is one of a handful who I believe should never have been sent to prison. I wish him luck in the future; he's a fine young man.

12 noon

I drop into the hospital to see if sister needs me.

'Not at the moment,' says Linda, 'but as we're expecting seventeen new arrivals this afternoon, please come back around four, or when you see the sweat box driving through the front gate.'

'How's Bill?' I enquire.

'He lasted about forty minutes,' she replies dryly, 'but sadly failed to produce a specimen. I sent him back to the farm, but of course told him to return immediately should the problem arise again.'

2.00 pm

On returning to SMU I find a prisoner sitting in the waiting room, visibly shaking. His name is Moore. He tells me that he's been called off work for a meeting with two police officers who are travelling down from Derbyshire to interview him. He's completed seventeen months of a five-year sentence, and is anxious to know why they want to see him.

2.30 pm

The police haven't turned up. I go to check on Moore – to find he's a gibbering wreck.

DAY 120

2.53 pm

The two Derbyshire police officers arrive. They greet me with a smile and don't look at all ferocious. I take them up to an interview room on the first floor and offer them a cup of tea, using the opportunity to tell them that Moore is in a bit of a state. They assure me that it's only a routine enquiry, and he has nothing to be anxious about. I return downstairs and pass on this message; the shaking stops.

3.26 pm

Moore departs with a smile and a wave; I've never seen a more relieved man.

4.00 pm

The seventeen new prisoners arrive in a sweat box via Birmingham and Nottingham. I report to the hospital to check their blood pressure and note their weight and height. It's not easy to carry out my new responsibilities while all seventeen of them talk at once. What jobs are there? How much are you paid? Can I go to the canteen tonight? What time are roll-calls? Which is the best block? Can I make a phone call?

7.00 pm

Doug returns from his day on the fork-lift trucks. He's pleased to be doing the course because if he hopes to retain his HGV licence, he would still have to take it in a year's time. The course is costing him £340 but he'd be willing to pay that just to be allowed out for three days; 'In fact, I'd pay a lot more,' he says.

8.15 pm

After roll-call I take a bath before going over to the south block to say goodbye to Matthew. By the time I check in at the hospital at 7.30 am tomorrow morning he will be a free man. I do not envy him, because he should never have been sent to prison in the first place.

DAY 121   FRIDAY 16 NOVEMBER 2001

10.00 am

All seventeen new inmates are waiting in the conservatory for their introductory talk before they sign the pledge (on drugs). They're all chatting away, with one exception; he's sitting in the corner, head bowed, foot tapping, looking anxious. This could be for any number of reasons, but even though the officers keep a suicide watch during the first forty-eight hours of a prisoner's arrival, I still report my anxieties to Mr New. He tells me to bring the prisoner into his office but make it look routine.

When the man emerges forty minutes later, he is smiling. It turns out that X is a schedule A conviction, which usually means a sexual offence against a minor. However, X was sentenced to six months for lashing out at his son. He'll only serve twelve weeks, and the fact that he's in a D-cat prison shows there is no previous history of violence. However, if word got out that he's schedule A, other inmates would assume he's a paedophile. Mr New has advised the prisoner to say, if asked what he's in for, that he took a swipe at a guy who tried to jump a taxi queue. As he's only serving twelve weeks, it's just believable.

11.30 am

Storr marches into the building, waving a complaint form. Yesterday, after returning from a town visit, he failed a breathalyser test; yes, you can be breathalysed in prison without having driven – in fact walking is quite enough. Storr protested that he never drinks even 'on the out' and the real culprit is a bottle of mouthwash. Storr is sent back to the north block to retrieve the offending bottle, which has about an inch of red liquid left in the bottom. The label lists alcohol as one of several ingredients. After some discussion, Mr New decides Storr will be retested tomorrow morning. If the test proves negative, his explanation will be accepted.* He will then be subjected to regular random tests, and should one of them prove positive, he will be shipped back to his C-cat. Storr accepts this judgment, and leaves looking pleased with himself.

2.30 pm

I ask Mr New if there is any progress on my transfer to Spring Hill. He shakes his head.

4.00 pm

I report back to the hospital and carry out three more urine tests on the inductees we didn't get round to yesterday, measure their blood pressure and record their weight. Among them is a

---

* Mr New banned all mouthwashes from the canteen following a similar incident a year ago. As Storr purchased the bottle at his last prison, Mr New is issuing a new directive, that any new prisoners arriving at NSC with mouthwash will have the bottles confiscated.

prisoner called Blossom, who is returning to NSC for the third time in as many years.

'He's as good as gold,' says Linda. 'A gipsy, who, once convicted, never puts a foot wrong; he's always released as a model prisoner after serving half his sentence. But once he's left us, he's usually back within a year,' she adds.

10.30 pm

Television news footage reveals Kabul as it had been under the rule of the Taliban. Amongst the buildings filmed is Kabul jail, which makes NSC look like the Ritz; twenty men would have occupied my room with only three urine-stained, ragged mattresses between them.

I sleep soundly.

DAY 122   SATURDAY 17 NOVEMBER 2001

Anyone who's incarcerated wants their sentence to pass as quickly as possible. If you're fortunate enough to have an interesting job, as I have at SMU, that certainly helps kill Monday to Friday. That just leaves the other problem – the weekend. Once you've reached your FLED and can work outside the prison, have a town visit every week and a week out every month, I'm told the months fly by, but should I fail to win my appeal against length of sentence, none of this will kick in until July next year – another eight months. So boredom will become my greatest challenge.

I can write, but not for every hour of every day. With luck there's a rugby match to watch on Saturday afternoon, and a visitor to look forward to seeing on Sunday. So, for the record:

Saturday

> *6.00 am* Write this diary for two hours.

> *8.15 am* Breakfast.

> *9.00 am* Read *The Times*, or any other paper available.

> *10.00 am* Work on the sixth rewrite of *Sons of Fortune*.

> *12 noon* Lunch.

> *2.00 pm* Watch New Zealand beat Ireland 40–29 on BBC1.

4.00 pm Watch Wales beat Tonga 51–7 on BBC2.

4.40 pm Watch the highlights of England's record-breaking win of 134–0 against Romania on ITV.

6.00 pm Continue to work on *Sons of Fortune* and run out of paper. My fault.

8.15 pm Sign in for roll-call to prove I haven't absconded, or died of boredom.

8.30 pm Join Doug in the hospital and watch a Danny de Vito/Bette Midler film, followed by the news.

10.30 pm Return to my room, go to bed and, despite the noise of *Match of the Day* coming from the TV room next door, fall asleep.

DAY 123   SUNDAY 18 NOVEMBER 2001

6.11 am

After five weeks at NSC, you must be as familiar with my daily routine as I am so, as from today, I will refer only to highlights or unusual incidents that I think might interest you.

2.00 pm

You will recall that I'm allowed one visit a week, and my visitors today are Alan and Della Pascoe. I first met Alan when he was an England schoolboy, and even the casual observer realized that he was destined to be a star. He had a decade at the highest level, and if that time hadn't clashed with Al Moses – the greatest 400m hurdler in history – Alan would have undoubtedly won two Olympic gold medals, rather than two silvers. We only ran against each other once in our careers; he was seventeen and I was twenty-six. I prefer not to dwell on the result.

Although I had the privilege of watching Della run for her country (Commonwealth gold medalist and world record holder), we didn't meet until she married Alan, and our families have been close ever since. They remain the sort of friends who don't run round the track in the opposite direction when you've been disqualified.

DAY 124   MONDAY 19 NOVEMBER 2001

5.30 am

The noise of three heavy tractors harvesting acres and acres of Brussels sprouts wakes me. If I'm up every day by five-thirty, what time must the farm labourers rise to be on their tractor seats even before I stir?

8.15 am

Matthew, as you will remember, was released last Friday, and has been replaced in the SMU by Carl.

Carl is softly spoken and well mannered. He's the lead singer in the prison's rock band, and has the striking good looks required for someone who aspires to that calling: around five foot eleven, slim, with wavy fair hair. He tells me that he has a fifteen-year-old daughter born when he was twenty (he's not married), so he must be in his mid-thirties.

Carl arrives at eight-twenty, which is a good start, and as I run through our daily duties, he makes notes. Monday is usually quiet: no inductions or labour board, so I'm able to brief him fully on all personnel resident in the building and their responsibilities. He is a quick study, and also has all the women in the building coming into the kitchen on the flimsiest of excuses. In a week he'll have everything mastered and I'll be redundant.

Now of course you will want to know why this cross between Robbie Williams and Richard Branson is in prison. Simple answer, fraud. Carl took advances on property that he didn't own, or even properly represent. A more interesting aspect of Carl's case is that his co-defendant pleaded not guilty, while, on the advice of his barrister, Carl pleaded guilty. But there's still another twist to come. Because Carl had to wait for the outcome of his co-defendant's trial before he could be sentenced, he was released on bail for nine months, and during that time 'did a runner'. He disappeared off to Barcelona, found himself a job and tried to settle down. However, after only a few weeks, he decided he had to come back to England and, in his words, face the music.

Carl was a little surprised not to be arrested when he landed at Heathrow. He spent the weekend with a friend in Nottingham, and then handed himself in to the nearest police station. The policeman at the desk was so astonished that he didn't quite know what to do with him. Carl was charged later that day, and after spending a night in custody, was sentenced the following morning to three years. His co-defendant also received three years. His barrister says he would only have got two years if he hadn't broken bail and disappeared off to Barcelona. Carl is a model prisoner, so he will only serve sixteen months, half his sentence minus two months with a tag.

2.30 pm

Mr New phones Spring Hill to enquire about my transfer, but as there's no reply from Karen's office, he'll try again tomorrow. If I were back in my office, I'd try again at 3 pm, 4 pm and 5 pm, but not in prison. Tomorrow will be just fine. After all, I'm not going anywhere.

5.00 pm

David (murder) arrives with all my clothes neatly laundered. Lifers have their own washing machine and iron. Jeeves of Pont Street would be proud of him. I hand over three Mars Bars, and my debt is paid.

6.00 pm

I need to buy a plug from the canteen (30p) because I keep leaving mine in the washbasin. I've lost four in the last four weeks. When I get to the front of the queue they're sold out. However, Doug tells me he has a drawer full of plugs – of course he does.

DAY 125   TUESDAY 20 NOVEMBER 2001

Many aspects of prison life are unbearable: boredom, confinement, missing family and friends. All of these might fade in time.
But the two things I will never forget after I'm released will be
the noise and the bad language.

When I returned to my room at 10 pm last night, the TV
room next door was packed with screaming hooligans; the
volume, for a the repeat of the world heavyweight title fight
between Lennox Lewis and Hasim Rahman, was so high that
it reminded me of being back at Belmarsh when reggae music
was blaring out from the adjacent cell. I was delighted to learn
that Lennox Lewis had retained his title, but didn't need to hear
every word the commentator said, or the accompanying cheers,
screams and insults from a highly partisan crowd. In the end I
gave up, went next door and asked if the volume could be
turned down a little. I was greeted with a universal chorus of
'Fuck off!'

10.00 am

Sixteen new inductees turn up for labour board, all clutching
their red folders. The message has spread: if you don't return
your folders, you don't get a job, and therefore no wages.

Because the prison is so full at the moment, most of the good jobs – hospital, SMU, library, education, stores, officers' mess – are filled, leaving only kitchen, cleaners and the dreaded farm. Among the new intake is a PhD and an army officer. I fix it so that the PhD, who only has another five weeks to serve, will work in the stores, and the army officer will then take over from him. Only one of the new intake hasn't a clue what he wants to do, so he inevitably ends up on the farm.

11.00 am

I have already described the paper chase to you, so imagine my surprise when among the three prisoners to turn up this morning, clutching his release papers is Potts. Do you remember Potts? Solicitor didn't turn up, took an overdose? Well, he's fully recovered and went back to court for his appeal. However, he was half an hour late and the judge refused to hear his case, despite the fact that it was the Prison Service's fault that he wasn't on time. Here we are two weeks later and he's off tomorrow, even though he wasn't due for release until the middle of next year. As we are unable to have a lengthy conversation at SMU, I agree to visit him tonight and find out what caused this sudden reversal.

3.00 pm

The governor of Spring Hill (Mr Payne) calls to have a private chat with Mr New. He's concerned about the attendant publicity should he agree to my transfer. Mr New does everything he can to allay Mr Payne's anxieties, pointing out that once the tabloids had got their photograph, the press haven't been seen since. But Mr Payne points out that it didn't stop a series of stories appearing from 'insiders' and 'released prisoners' which, although pure fantasy doesn't help. Mr New tells him that I have settled in well, shared a room with another inmate and am a model prisoner. Mr Payne says he'll make a decision fairly quickly. I am not optimistic.

6.30 pm

I have been invited to attend a meeting of the Samaritans (from Boston) and the Listeners (prisoners). They meet about once a month in the hospital to exchange views and ideas. They only need me to sign some books for their Christmas bazaar. One of the ladies asks me if she can bring in some more books for signing from the Red Cross bookshop.

'Of course,' I tell her.

10.30 pm

There's a cowboy film on TV, so the noise is bearable – that is, until the final shoot-out begins.

DAY 126 WEDNESDAY 21 NOVEMBER 2001

6.18 am

The mystery of Potts's early release has been solved. A clerical error resulted in the judge thinking the case should be heard at 10 o'clock, while Potts was able to produce a piece of paper that requested his attendance in court at 10.30 am. The judge subsequently agreed to hear the appeal immediately and, having considered the facts, halved Potts's sentence. The governor called him out of work at the kitchen to pass on the news that he would be released this morning. The first really happy prisoner I've seen in months.

8.15 am

Twelve new inductees due today, and as always, if you look carefully through the list you'll find a story. Today it's Cormack. He was released just over six weeks ago on a tag (HDC) and is back, but only for eleven days.

Strict rules are applied when you are granted an HDC. You are released two months early with a tag placed around your ankle. You supply an address at which you will reside during those two months. You must have a home phone. You will be confined to that abode during certain hours, usually between seven in the evening and seven the following morning. You also agree in writing not to take drugs or drink.

Cormack is an unusual case, because he didn't break any of these rules. But yesterday morning he turned up at the local police station asking to be taken back into custody for the last eleven days because he was no longer welcome at the house he had designated for tagging.

'Wise man,' said Mr Simpson, the probation officer who recommended his early release. 'He kept to the letter of the law, and won't suffer as a consequence. If he'd attempted to spend the last eleven days somewhere else, he would have been arrested and returned to closed conditions.' Wise man indeed.

12 noon

Leon the PhD joins me for lunch. He's the new orderly in stores, which entitles him to eat early. He thanks me for helping him to secure the job. I discover over lunch that his doctorate is in meteorology. He tells me that there are not many job opportunities in his field, so once he's released he'll be looking for a teaching position; not easy when you have a prison record. Leon was sentenced to six months for driving without a licence, so will serve only twelve weeks. He tells me that this is not his biggest problem. He's engaged to a girl who has just left Birmingham University with a first-class honours degree, and like him, wants to be a teacher. So far, so good. But Leon is currently facing racial prejudice in reverse. She is a high-class Brahmin and even before Leon ended up in jail, her parents didn't consider he was good enough for their daughter. He explains that it is necessary to meet the father on three separate occasions before a daughter's hand can be granted in wedlock, and following that, you still have to meet the mother. All these ceremonies are conducted formally. Before he was sentenced, Leon had managed only one meeting with the father; now he is being refused a second or third meeting, and the mother is adamant that she will never allow him to enter the family home. Does his fiancée defy her parents and marry the man she loves, or does she obey her father and break off all contact? Seven of the twelve weeks have already passed, but Leon points out that it's not been easy to stay in touch while you're only allowed one visit a week, and two phonecards.

3.00 pm

Mr Berlyn (deputy governor) drops into SMU to ask me if I've invited any outsiders to come and hear my talk tomorrow night. To be honest, I'd forgotten that I'd agreed to the librarian's request to give a talk on writing a best-seller. I tell Mr Berlyn that I haven't invited anyone from inside – or outside – the prison.

He tells me that after reading about the 'event' in the local paper, members of the public have been calling in all day asking if they can attend.

Can they? I ask innocently. He doesn't bother to reply.

DAY 127   THURSDAY 22 NOVEMBER 2001

5.55 am

The problem of whether I should remain at NSC and become hospital orderly, or transfer to Spring Hill, has come to a head. Doug (VAT fraud and current hospital orderly) has been told by Mr Berlyn that if he applies for a job at Exotic Foods in Boston, who currently employ Clive (local council fraud and backgammon tutor), he would be granted the status of outside worker, which would take him out of the prison six days a week, even allowing him to use his own car to go back and forth to work.

If Doug is offered the job, then I will only do one more week as SMU orderly before passing on my responsibilities to Carl. I would then have to spend a week being trained by Doug in the hospital routines, so that I could take over the following Monday.

10.30 am

Eight new inductees today, and all seem relieved to be in an open prison, until it comes to job allocation. Once again, most prisoners end up on the farm, resulting in a lot of glum faces as they leave the building. Few of them want to spend their day with pigs, sheep and Brussels sprouts, remembering the temperature on the fens at this time of year is often below zero. One of the prisoners, a West Indian called Wesley, used to warmer climes, is so angry that he asks to be sent back to Ashwell, his old C-cat prison. He says he'd be a lot happier locked up all day with a wall to protect him from the wind. Mr Berlyn assures him that if he still feels that way in a month's time, he'll happily send him back.

5.00 pm

Early supper is, as I have explained, one of the orderlies' privileges, so I was surprised to see a table occupied by six inmates I'd never seen before.

John (lifer, senior kitchen orderly) tells me that they're all Muslims, and as Ramadan has just begun, they can only eat between the hours of sunset and sunrise, which means they cannot have breakfast or lunch with the other prisoners. That doesn't explain why they're having dinner on their own, because it's pitch black by five o'clock on a November evening and . . .

'Ah,' says John, 'good point, but you see the large tray stacked with packets of milk and cornflakes? That's tomorrow's breakfast, which they'll take back tonight and have in their rooms around five tomorrow morning. If the other prisoners find out about this, when they still have to come down to the dining room whatever the weather, can you imagine how many complaints there would be?'

'Or conversions to Allah and the Muslim faith,' I suggest.

6.00 pm

I give my talk in the chapel on writing a best-seller. The audience of twenty-six is made up of prisoners and staff. There are five ladies in the front row I do not recognize, seventeen prisoners and four members of staff, including Mr Berlyn, Mr Gough and Ms Hampton, the librarian.

I enjoyed delivering a speech for the first time in three months, and although I've tackled the subject on numerous occasions in the past, it felt quite fresh after such a long layoff, and the questions were among the most searching I remember.

Two pounds was added to my canteen account.

7.00 pm

I call Mary and foolishly leave my phonecard in the slot. When I return three minutes later, it's disappeared. Let's face it, I am in prison.

7.30 pm

I pick up my letters from the unit office, thirty-two today, including one from Winston Churchill enclosing a book called *The Duel*, which covers the eighty-day struggle between his grandfather and Hitler in 1940. Among the other letters, nearly all from members of the public, is one from Jimmy.

You may recall Jimmy if you've read volume two of these diaries (*Purgatory*). He was the good-looking captain of football who had a three-year sentence for selling cannabis. He's been out for a month, and has a job working on a building site. It's long hours and well paid but, he admits, despite all the sport and daily gym visits while he was in prison, he had become soft after eighteen months of incarceration. He's only just beginning to get back into the work ethic. He assures me that he will never sell drugs again, and as he did not take them in the first place, he doesn't intend to start now. I want to believe him. He claims to have sorted out his love life. He's living with the sexy one, and has ditched the intellectual one. As I now have an address and telephone number, I will give him a call over the weekend.

8.15 pm

After roll-call, Doug and I go through our strategy for a smooth changeover of jobs. However, if our plan is to work, he suggests we must make the officers on the labour board think that it's their idea.

DAY 128   FRIDAY 23 NOVEMBER 2001

8.10 am

John (murder, senior kitchen orderly) tells me over breakfast
that two prisoners absconded last night. He reminds me of an
incident a couple of weeks ago when Wendy sacked both of
them from the kitchen for stealing chickens. A few days later
she gave them a reprieve, only to sack them again the following
day for stealing tins of tuna – not to eat but to trade for cannabis.
They were then put on the farm, where it's quite hard to steal
anything; the pigs are too heavy and the Brussels sprouts are
not a trading commodity. However, last night the two prisoners
were caught smoking cannabis in their room and placed on
report. They should have been up in front of the governor this
morning. It's just possible that they might have got away with a
warning, but it's more likely they would have been shipped back
to the dreaded Lincoln Prison – to sample all its Victorian
facilities. They absconded before any decision could be taken.

12.08 pm

I am writing in my room when Carl knocks on the door. The
Red Cross and KPMG have made a joint statement following

Baroness Nicholson's demand for an enquiry into what happened to the money raised for the Kurds. It's the lead item on the midday news, and I am delighted to have my name cleared.

12.20 pm

I call Alison at the office to find that Mary is at the House of Lords attending an energy resources meeting. Alison runs through the radio and television interview requests received by Mary, but she's decided only to issue this brief press statement.

PRESS RELEASE

LORD ARCHER AND THE SIMPLE TRUTH CAMPAIGN

My family and I are delighted, but not surprised, that KPMG's investigation into the Simple Truth campaign, spearheaded by Jeffrey in 1991, has confirmed that no funds were misappropriated by him or anyone else. We have known this from the outset. We are very proud of the work Jeffrey has done for Kurdish relief, the British Red Cross and many other good causes over the years. We hope that Baroness Nicholson, whose allegations have wasted much time and caused much unjustified distress, will accept KPMG's findings.

Mary Archer

1.00 pm

Lady Thatcher has come out saying she's not surprised by the outcome of the enquiry, which has dropped to the second item on the news following the death, at the age of ninety-two, of Dame Mary Whitehouse.

2.00 pm

Several of the officers are kind enough to comment on the outcome of the enquiry, but I've also fallen to second item with them. It seems that the two prisoners who absconded last night, Marley and Tom, were picked up early this morning by the police, only six miles from the prison. They were arrested, charged and transferred to Lincoln Prison. They will each have forty-two days added to their sentence and will never be allowed to apply for a D-cat status again, as they are now categorized as an escape risk.

5.00 pm

Slipped to third item on *Live at Five*, but as I have been exonerated, it's clearly not news. If I had embezzled the £57 million, or any part of it, I would have remained the lead item for a couple of days, and the prison would have been swarming with photographers waiting for my transfer to Lincoln.

Not one photographer in sight.

10.00 pm

A passing mention of the Red Cross statement on the ten o'clock news. I can see I shall have to abscond if I hope to make the headlines again.

10.30 pm

Irony. Eamon, my former room-mate, is now able to move in with his friend Shaun. They have been offered the room vacated by the two men who absconded.

DAY 129   SATURDAY 24 NOVEMBER 2001

4.00 am

A torch is flashed in my eyes, and I wake to see an officer checking if I'm in bed asleep and have not absconded. I'm no longer asleep.

7.17 am

I oversleep and only start writing just after seven.

10.00 am

The broadsheets all report the findings of the KPMG report. Several point out that none of this would have arisen if Baroness Nicholson, a former Tory MP turned Liberal peer, hadn't made her complaint to Sir John Stevens in the first place. I call Mary to discuss our next move, but there's no reply.

2.00 pm

I have a visit today from Doreen and Henry Miller. Doreen is a front-bench spokesman in the Lords having previously been a minister under John Major. She brings me up to date with news of the Upper House, and tells me that the latest Lords reform bill is detested on both sides of the chamber. The Bill ignores John Wakeham's excellent Royal Commission report, and doesn't placate the Labour party because not a large enough percentage of peers will be elected, and doesn't placate the Tory party because it removes all the remaining hereditary peers. 'It cannot,' Doreen assures me, 'reach the statute book in its present form, because it will meet with so much opposition in both Houses.'*

When Doreen and Henry leave, I don't know where the ninety minutes went.

4.00 pm

I call Mary, but the phone just rings and rings.

4.40 pm

Watch England beat South Africa 29–9 and despite the Irish hiccup, begin to believe we might be the best rugby team in the world. If I'm let out in time, I will travel to Australia to see the next world rugby cup.

7.00 pm

I call Mary. Still no reply.

8.15 pm

After checking in for roll-call I join Doug at the hospital to find four officers in the waiting room. One of them, Mr Harding,

---

* The government dropped the bill in March 2004.

is spattered with blood. Mr Hocking, the chief security officer, is taking a photograph of him. It turns out that Mr Hocking, acting on a tip-off, was informed that two inmates had disappeared into Boston to pick up some booze, so he and three other officers were lying in wait for them. However, when they were spotted returning, the first prisoner grabbed Mr Harding's heavy torch and hit him over the head, allowing his mate enough time to escape. The first prisoner was wrestled to the ground and hand-cuffed, and is now locked up in the segregation block. The second has still to reappear, although they know which prisoner it is. Even a cub reporter would realize there's an ongoing story here.

DAY 130   SUNDAY 25 NOVEMBER 2001

8.04 am

Phone Mary in Cambridge; no reply. Try London and only get the answering machine. Report to Linda at the hospital. Doug's away on a town leave (7 am to 7 pm) so I'm temporary keeper of the pills.

11.30 am

During lunch, I discover from one of the gym orderlies that they caught the second inmate who was trying to bring drink back into the prison. He'll be shipped out to Nottingham this afternoon.

Self-abuse is often one of the reasons they move offenders out so quickly. It's not unknown for a prisoner who is kept in lock-up overnight to cut his wrists or even break an arm, and then blame it on the officer who charged him. The prisoner can then claim he was attacked first, which means that he can't be moved until there has been a full enquiry. Mr Hocking took several photographs of both prisoners, which will make that course of action a little more difficult to explain.

DAY 130

12 noon

The morning papers are predicting that I'll soon be moved to Spring Hill so I can be nearer my family. One or two of them even suggest that I should never have been sent to Wayland or NSC in the first place simply on an allegation made by Ms Nicholson.

10.00 pm

After the news, I call Mary again, but there's still no reply.

DAY 131   MONDAY 26 NOVEMBER 2001

8.30 am

One of my duties at SMU is the distribution of bin liners. At eight-thirty every morning, two prisoners, Alf and Rod, check in for work and take away a bin liner each. This morning Alf demands ten. I will allow you a few seconds to fathom out why, because I couldn't.

I make a weekly order for provisions on a Friday, which is delivered on Monday, and always includes ten bin liners, so Alf is about to wipe out my entire stock in one day. I can't believe he's trading them and they are far too big for the small wastepaper baskets in his room, so I give in and ask why the sudden demand. Alf tells me that the director-general of the Prison Service, Martin Narey, is visiting NSC on Wednesday, and the governor wants the place smartened up for his inspection. Fair enough. However, if Mr Narey is half-intelligent, it won't take him long to realize that NSC is a neglected dump and short of money. If they show him the north or south block, he'll wonder if we have any cleaners as he holds his nose and steps gingerly through the rubbish. The visits room is a disgrace and extra-curricular activities almost non-existent. However, if he is only shown the canteen, gym, farm, hospital and SMU, he will leave with a favourable impression.

DAY 131

I'm told the real purpose for Mr Narey's visit is to discuss how this prison will prepare for resettlement status once the new governor takes over in January.

10.30 am

Mr Belford, a south block officer, pops in for a coffee. He tells me that the inmate who photographed me in my room failed to sell the one picture he managed to snap, because the negative came out so poorly.

11.00 am

Today's new inductees from Nottingham include a pupil barrister (ABH), a taxi driver (overcharging) and a farm labourer (theft from his employer). They all end up on the farm because the prison is overcrowded and there are no other jobs available.

6.00 pm

Canteen. I'm £13.50 in credit (I earn £8.50 a week, and can supplement that with £10 of my own money). I purchase two phonecards, three bottles of Evian, a packet of Gillette razor blades, a roll-on deodorant and a toothbrush, which cleans out my account. I'm not in desperate need of all these items, but it's my way of making sure I can't buy any more chocolate as I need to lose the half stone I've put on since arriving at NSC.

7.00 pm

I phone James at work. He tells me that Mary has been on the move for the past few days – Oundle, London and Cambridge, and then back to London this afternoon.*

I join Doug in the hospital. He is anticipating an interview with Exotic Foods on Wednesday or Thursday, and hopes to begin work next Monday, a week earlier than originally planned. He has already spoken to Mr Belford about a room on the south block, in the no-smoking spur, and to Mr Berlyn about his travel arrangements to Boston. However, there is a fly in the ointment, namely Linda, who feels Doug should train his successor for a week before he leaves.

7.10 pm

I call Chris Beetles' gallery and wish Chris luck for the opening of the illustrators' show. Mary is hoping to drop in and see the picture I've selected for this year's Christmas card. I ask him to pass on my love and tell her I'll ring Cambridge tomorrow evening. For the first time in thirty-five years, I haven't spoken to my wife in five days. Don't forget, she can't call me.

---

*I never phone Mary on her mobile because my two-pound phone card is gobbled up in moments.

DAY 132   TUESDAY 27 NOVEMBER 2001

6.11 am

One incident of huge significance took place today. In fact, it's a short story in its own right. However, as I write, I don't yet know, the ending. But to begin halfway through.

Do you recall Leon, the PhD who joined us about a week ago? He wants to marry an Indian girl of high caste, but her father and mother refuse to entertain the idea, and that was *before* he was sent to prison (driving without a licence, six months). Well, he reappeared at SMU at three o'clock this afternoon in what can only be described as an agitated state. Although we'd had ten new inductees and a labour board this morning, it was turning out to be a quiet afternoon. I sat Leon down in the kitchen while Carl made him a cup of tea. He was desperate to discover if he was going to be granted his HDC and be released early on a tag. The officer who deals with HDC was in her office, so I went upstairs to ask if she would see him.

Ten minutes later Leon reappears and says that a decision will be made tomorrow morning as to whether he can be released early.

'Well, that's another problem solved,' says Carl.

'No, it isn't,' says Leon, 'because if they don't grant my tag, it will be a disaster.'

Leon doesn't strike me as the sort of man who would use the world 'disaster' lightly, so I enquire why. He then briefs us on the latest complication in his love life.

His girlfriend's parents have found out that she plans to marry Leon as soon as he's released from prison on 6 December. She's even booked the register office. She told him over the phone last night that her parents have not only forbidden the match, but three men who she has never met have recently been selected as possible husbands and they will be flying in from India at the weekend. She must then select one of them before she and her intended bridegroom fly back to Calcutta to be married on 6 December.

I now fully understand Leon's desperation; I go in search of Mr Downs, a senior officer, who is a shrewd and caring man. I find him in the officers' room going over tomorrow's itinerary for the director-general's visit. I brief Mr Downs and he agrees to see Leon immediately.

After their meeting, Leon tells us that Mr Downs was most sympathetic and will report his worries direct to the governor. He has asked to see Leon again at eight o'clock tomorrow morning, one hour before the board meet to decide if he will be granted a tag. I had assumed that there would be nothing more to tell you until the outcome of that meeting. However...

7.00 pm

I finally catch up with Mary, and forty minutes later have used up both my phonecards.

I go over to the hospital to have a bath, but before doing so tell Doug about Leon. I fail to reach the bathroom because he tells me he can remember a case where special dispensation was granted to allow an inmate to be married in the prison chapel.

'Why don't you ask the vicar about it?' he suggests.

'Because by then it will be too late,' I tell Doug, reminding him of the timetable of the board meeting at nine o'clock tomorrow morning, and the three gentlemen from India arriving in Sheffield over the weekend.

'But the Rev Derek Johnson is over at the chapel right now,' says Doug, 'it's the prison clergy's monthly meeting.'

I leave Doug and walk quickly over to the chapel. The orderly, John (ostrich fraud), tells me that the vicar has just left, but if I run to the gate I might still catch him. At sixty-one I'm past running fast, but I do jog, and hope that as the vicar is even older than I am I'll make it before he's driven off. When I arrive at the gate, his car is at the barrier waiting to be let out. I wave frantically. He parks the car and joins me in the gatehouse, where I tell him the whole story. Derek listens with immense sympathy and says that he can, in certain circumstances, marry the couple in the prison chapel, and he feels confident that the governor would agree, given the circumstances. He also adds that if the young lady needed to be put up overnight, he and Mrs Johnson could supply a room for her. I thank the vicar and return to the north block in search of Leon.

I find him in his room and impart my latest piece of news. He's delighted, and tells me that he's spoken to his fiancée again, and she's already arranged for the wedding to be held in a local register office as long as he's released early. If he isn't, we have at least come up with an alternative solution. Leon is thanking me profusely when I hear my name over the tannoy, 'Archer to report to the south block unit office immediately.'

I leave Leon to jog over to the south block and arrive at the unit office at one minute to nine. I had, for the first time, forgotten to check in for my eight-fifteen roll-call. If I'd arrived at one minute past nine, I would have been put on report and have lost my chance of being 'enhanced' for another eight weeks. Mr Belford, the duty officer, who knows nothing of my nocturnal efforts, bursts out laughing.

'I was so much looking forward to putting you on report, Jeffrey,' he says, 'but I was pretty sure you would come up with a good excuse as to what you were doing at eight-fifteen.'

'I was with the vicar,' I tell him.

DAY 133 WEDNESDAY 28 NOVEMBER 2001

9.50 am

Leon is sitting in the waiting room at SMU ready for his HDC ajudication with Mr Berlyn (deputy governor) and Mr Simpson (resident probation officer).

Leon called his fiancée again last night. The three suitors have arrived from India, and once Sunita has made her choice (and if she doesn't, her parents will decide for her) she will then be flown back to India to meet the man's parents. The couple will then return to England to prepare for a wedding on 6 December, the day before Leon will be released.

Sunita's plan is to take only hand luggage on the flight, so that when she returns, she will walk straight through customs while her parents wait to pick up their luggage from the baggage hall. Leon's brother will be waiting in the arrivals hall and drive her straight to Birmingham, where she and Leon will be married later that day.

If the board grants Leon his tagging, he will leave NSC at eight o'clock on the Saturday, and drive straight to Birming-ham, and they will be man and wife before the family can work out where she's disappeared. Everything is riding on the result of Leon's interview with the board in a few minutes' time. Mr

Berlyn calls for Leon at ten-eleven and I escort him up to the interview room.

Carl and I run around the kitchen pretending to be busy. SMU is on full alert because Martin Narey, the director-general, arrived a few minutes ago.

10.32 am

Leon appears, almost in tears. The board have turned down his application. I fear he may abscond tonight and take the law into his own hands.

11.30 am

The Rev Derek Johnson drops in to tell us that he's met with the governor, who does not have the authority to sanction a wedding in the chapel. A prisoner must have at least nine months to serve before he can apply for such a privilege. He adds that no one has ever come across such an unusual set of circumstances.

Leon now can't do anything until seven o'clock this evening when he's arranged to phone his fiancée on her mobile. Before he leaves us, he adds two more pieces of information. First, his father, an extremely wealthy man, has offered a dowry of £500,000 to Sunita's family. Leon's mother is a Brahmini, but because his father is Irish, their son is unacceptable. One can only wonder how much the three suitors from India are offering as a dowry for this girl they have yet to meet. Second, Sunita's sister was subjected to the same drama two years ago, and is now going through a messy divorce. Carl and I agree to meet in Leon's room at 7.30 pm and plan his next move.

11.45 am

I leave for lunch a few minutes before the director-general is due to arrive at SMU. By the time I've finished my cauliflower cheese and gone back to the south block to make a couple of phone calls, Mr Narey has moved on to visit the lifers' quarters. I return to work at one o'clock.

5.00 pm

I drop in to see Doug, who confirms that Exotic Foods have agreed to interview him on Friday morning, and he is hoping to begin work with them on Monday week, so I could become hospital orderly in two weeks' time.

7.30 pm

Leon opens the door of his room to greet us with a warm smile. Sunita has escaped from Sheffield and has driven down to Portsmouth to stay with his brother and sister-in-law. She has purchased a new phone, as she is worried that her parents will hire a detective to trace her through the mobile Leon bought for her.

Leon removes a thick bundle of letters from his shelf.

'She writes twice a day,' he says.

I am delighted by the news, but suggest to Carl after we've left that it won't take a particularly bright private detective to work out Sunita might be staying with Leon's brother.

I have a feeling this saga is not yet over.

DAY 134   THURSDAY 29 NOVEMBER 2001

I have mentioned the worthwhile role played by the Samaritans who train selected prisoners as Listeners. At NSC they have taken this trust one stage further and set aside a room where a pre-programmed mobile phone has been provided for inmates who need to call the Samaritans.

This service has become very popular, as more and more prisoners claim to be in need of succour from the Samaritans; so much so that Mr New recently became suspicious. After one particularly long call, which was interspersed with laughter, he confiscated the phone and quickly discovered what the inmates had been up to. They had been removing the Sim card from inside the phone and replacing it with one of their own that had been smuggled in.

As of today, there will no longer be a dedicated room for the Samaritans, or a mobile phone.

11.00 am

This will be my last labour board if I am to join Doug in the hospital next week. I therefore suggest to Carl that he should take charge as if I wasn't there. During the rest of the morning, whenever a prisoner calls in with some problem, Carl handles it.

My only worry is that as Carl has another fifteen months to serve before he'll be eligible for a tag, he may become bored long before his sentence is up.

2.30 pm

Mr New calls Spring Hill to ask Mr Payne why my transfer is taking so long. He's told that Spring Hill is about to face a public enquiry as a consequence of something that happened before he became governor. Mr Payne fears that the press will be swarming all over the place and although he is quite willing to have me, he can't let me know his decision for at least another couple of weeks. I press Mr New for the details of what could possibly cause so much public interest but he refuses to discuss it. I wonder if it's simply a ploy to keep me from being trans-ferred.*

7.00 pm

I visit Leon in the north block. He has just come off the phone to his fiancée, still safely ensconced in Portsmouth with Leon's brother. Sunita's three Indian suitors have returned home accompanied by her mother, leaving her father in Bradford. Sunita has rung her father who has agreed to meet Leon. But he still doesn't know that Leon is in jail and won't be released for another three weeks.

---

* No suggestion of a scandal at Spring Hill appeared in the national press during the next twelve months.

DAY 135   FRIDAY 30 NOVEMBER 2001

9.30 am

The best laid plans of mice and convicts.

I am making tea for Mr Simpson at SMU when the duty officer asks me to report to the hospital for a suicide watch. Doug has gone to Boston for his Exotic Foods interview, so they are short of an orderly.

Suicide watch is quite common in prison, and this is the second I've covered in three weeks. Linda and Gail have to judge whether the prisoner is genuinely considering taking his own life, or simply looking for tea and sympathy and a chance to sit and watch television.

I turn up at the hospital a few minutes later to find my charge is a man of about forty-five, squat, thick set, covered in tattoos, with several teeth missing. David is serving a six-year sentence for GBH. What puzzles me is that he is due to be released on 14 January, so he only has a few more weeks of his sentence to complete. All I'm expected to do is to keep an eye on him while Gail gets on with her other duties, which today include taking care of a prisoner who was injured after being thrown through a window at his previous jail.

David's first request is for a glass of water, which is no problem. He then disappears into the lavatory, and doesn't reappear again for some time, when he requests another glass of water. No sooner has he gulped that down than the vicar arrives. He sits down next to David and asks if he can help. I ask David if he wants me to leave.

'No,' he says, but he would like another glass of water.

He then tells the vicar about the demons that visit him during the night, insisting that he must commit more crimes, and as he wants to go straight, he doesn't know what to do.

'Are you a practising member of any faith?' asks the Reverend.

'Yeah,' replies David, 'I believe in God and life after death, but I've never been sure which religion would be best for me.'

A long and thoughtful discussion follows after which David decides he's Church of England. The only thing of interest that comes out of the talk is that David wants to return to Nottingham jail, because he feels safer from the demons there, and more importantly they have a full-time psychiatrist who understands his problem. This also puzzles me. We have our own psychiatrist, Val, who is on duty at SMU this morning. Why would anyone want to leave NSC to return to a hell-hole like Nottingham?

Once the vicar has left, David disappears back into the lavatory and after another long period of time, returns and requests another glass of water.

Gail pops her head round the door to inform David that the governor has decided he can return to Nottingham, so he should go back to his room and pack his belongings. David looks happy for the first time. He drains the glass of water and gets up to leave. Are you also puzzled?

12 noon

Over lunch Dave (lifer), who after eighteen years has seen it all, tells me what David was really up to. Last night David was rumoured to be high on heroin, and feared having to take an MDT today. Had he failed that test, he would have had twenty-eight days added to his sentence and then been sent back to Nottingham. So we were treated to his little performance with the demons. Drinking gallons of water can flush heroin out of the system in twenty-four hours, and although David's still off to Nottingham, he avoided the added twenty-eight days. I'm so dim. I should have spotted it.

12.30 pm

Mr Lewis (the governing governor) has received a letter from the Shadow Home Secretary, Sir Brian Mawhinney, requesting to visit me.

1.15 pm

Disaster. Doug returns from his interview with Exotic Foods and tells me that they don't need him to start work until the middle of January. As he will be eligible for resettlement in February, and able to return to work with his own company, why should he bother? So he's decided to stay on as hospital orderly for the next couple of months.

My only hope now is the governor of Spring Hill.

DAY 136   SATURDAY 1 DECEMBER 2001

4.19 am

I lie awake for hours, plotting. Although I'm currently revising the sixth draft of *Sons of Fortune*, I've come up with a new idea for the ending, which will require some medical research. I will have to seek advice from Dr Walling.

10.40 am

It's just been officially announced that Mr Lewis will retire as governing governor on 1 January. I go over to the unit office and pick up a labour board change of job application form. If I'm not going to be hospital orderly I've decided to apply for his job. (See opposite).

12 noon

Doug tells me that he's going to try another ploy to get outside work. He has a friend in March who runs a small haulage company (three lorries), who will offer him a job as a driver. The only problem is that he doesn't work out of Boston, which is one of the current specifications for anyone who wishes to take up outside

CHANGE OF LABOUR REQUEST

NB. Eight weeks should elapse before submitting a request.

NO: FF 8282	NAME: . ARCHER	EDR: Up to you
PRESENT PARTY: Orderly SMU	REQUESTED PARTY: Govenor of N.S.C	
HOW LONG ON PRESENT PARTY: Eight weeks Enhanced (just)		
REASON FOR REQUEST: I hear that the Govenor of Leicester is unable to join due to stress, provable caused by the thought of taking care of me. I feel after eight weeks I am more than ready to take over from Mr Lewis.		
Signed:		

Fill in above and give it to Senior Officer i/c unit.

The RT Hon The Lord Archer of Weston-Super-Mare

1. PRESENT PARTY OFFICER'S COMMENTS: (Please return to SO i/c _____ unit)

Archer has all the necessary skills, oratory, written & organisational. He does however lack the freedom to represent NSOU on a national level, which could hamper our fight to stay open. On the other hand his contacts more than balance this weakness. I therefore support this application.

Date: 1-12-01   Signed: .... Tildesley..........

2. REQUESTED PARTY OFFICER'S COMMENTS: (Please return to SO i/c _____ unit)

Jeffrey has proved to be a first class orderly, although Mr Reeves has no opinion of him as a tea maker. He is good both the officers and the other prisoners, showing remarkable skills of communication and presence which may disqualify him from the Job of Governor. However he is willing to do the Job for £8.40p per week

Date: Signed: .... CNEW Head of Res

3. LABOUR BOARD DECISION:

No order, overqualified.

Date: 1/12/2001   Signed: ....
(Head of Inmate Activities)

LPF030

employment. However, Doug's wife Wendy will meet the potential employer today and get him to send a fax offering Doug a job of driving loads from Boston back to March. We will have to wait and see if Mr Berlyn will sanction this. I refuse to get excited.

2.00 pm

I walk down to the football field and watch NSC play Witherton. We lose 5–0 so there's not a lot more to report, other than it was very cold standing on the touch line; the wind was blowing in off the next landmass to the east, which happens to be Russia.

7.00 pm

I sit in my room reading *This Week*, an excellent journal if you want an overall view of the week's events. It gives me a chance to bring myself up to date with the situation in Afghanistan, America and even NSC.

Under the heading, 'A Bad Week', it seems that a Jeffrey Archer look-alike is complaining about being regularly stopped by the police to make sure I haven't escaped. 'It's most unfair,' he protests, 'it's ruined my life.' The paper felt his protests would have been more convincing if he hadn't travelled down to NSC accompanied by a tabloid to have his photograph taken outside the prison.

9.00 pm

I visit Leon in his room on the north block. His fiancée has told her father that he is in Norway on business, and won't be returning to England until 21 December, the day he's released from prison.

DAY 137   SUNDAY 2 DECEMBER 2001

10.30 am

Leon's fiancée is visiting him today, and they'll use the ninety minutes to plan their wedding.

11.30 am

I join Doug at the hospital to read the morning papers. The *People* devote half a page to telling their readers that I am distraught because a prisoner has stolen my diary and I'll have to start again. I wouldn't be distraught. After 137 days and over 300,000 words, I'd be suicidal.

3.00 pm

Doug has just come off the phone with his wife and tells me that his friend is going to place an advertisement in the *Boston Target* this Wednesday, stating that he needs a driver to transport goods from Boston to March. Doug will apply for the job, and a fax will then be sent to Mr Berlyn the same day offering Doug an interview. If Mr Berlyn agrees, Doug will be offered the position the following day.

DAY 138   MONDAY 3 DECEMBER 2001

9.40 am

Mr New comes in cursing. It seems the prison is overcrowded and there are applicants from Nottingham, Lincoln, Wayland, Birmingham and Leicester who will have to be turned away because every bed is occupied. Apparently it's all my fault.

This would not be a problem for Spring Hill, because they always have a long waiting list, and can be very selective. At NSC it now means that if any inmate even *bends* the rules, he'll be sent back to the prison he came from, as three inmates discovered to their cost last week. This was not the case when there were dozens of empty beds.

10.50 am

I see Leon walking back from the gatehouse to the stores where he works, and leave the office to have a word with him. Yesterday's visit went well. 'But I have a feeling,' he adds, 'there's something she isn't telling me.'

I press him as to what this might be, but he says he doesn't know, or has he become wary about how much of his story will appear in this diary? He then asks me to change all the names. I agree and have done so.

2.15 pm

Doug gives me some good news. Mrs Tempest (principal officer in charge of resettlement) has assured him that if he gets an interview with another haulage company, she will accompany him, assuming they fulfil all the usual police and prison criteria. If they then offer him a job, she will recommend he starts immediately, and by that she means next Monday.

It's becoming clear to me that there are several officers (not all) who are determined that NSC will be given resettlement status, and not just remain a D-cat open prison. Should the Home Office agree to this, then several of the inmates will be allowed out during the day on CSV work and eventually progress to full-time jobs. It's clear that Doug is a test case, because he's an obvious candidate for outside work, and if they can get him started, the floodgates might well open and this prison's future would no longer be in doubt. So suddenly my fortunes could be reversed. Once again I envy the reader who can simply turn the pages to discover what happens next in my life.

4.00 pm

Mr Simpson (senior probation officer) has completed his inter-views with the three inmates who are on sentence planning. He comes down to the kitchen for a glass of water.

Over the past six weeks, I've come to know Graham Simpson quite well, despite the fact that he's fairly reserved. I suppose it goes with the territory. He is a consummate professional, and wouldn't dream of discussing another prisoner, however good or bad their record. But he will answer general questions on the penal system, and after thirty years in the profession he has views that are worth listening to. I suspect that the majority of people reading this diary would, in the case of lifers, lock them up and throw away the key, and in some cases, hang them. However . . .

All murderers are sentenced to ninety-nine years, but the judge will then set a tariff that can range from eight years to life. At NSC we have an inmate who is serving his thirty-second year in jail. There are over 1,800 prisoners in the UK doing life sentences, of whom only a tiny percentage ever reach a D-cat open prison. There are twenty-two lifers currently at NSC. After being sentenced, they begin their life in an A-cat and progress through to B and C, and finally arrive at a D-cat with the expectation of release. At NSC, of the twenty-two resident lifers, these tariffs are set from twelve years to Her Majesty's pleasure, and Mr Simpson confirms that although some will become eligible for release, they will never make it. The Home Office simply won't take the risk.

Mr Simpson explains that it's his responsibility to assess which of these prisoners should be considered for release, but he will always err on the side of caution because, however many successes you have 'on the out', it only takes one failure to hit the front pages.

Mr Simpson admits to one such failure – a man with no previous convictions, who had, until murdering his unfaithful wife, led a perfectly normal existence. He was sentenced to life imprisonment, with a tariff of twelve years. Once in prison, his model behaviour saw him progress quickly (by lifers' standards) from A, to B, to C, to NSC in under eight years. While at NSC his record remained unblemished, until he fell in love with a member of staff who had to resign her position, and look for another job. After twelve years he was released, and they were married shortly afterwards. The man found a good job, and settled down into the community. Three years later, on the anniversary of his first wife's murder, he killed his new spouse and then took his own life.

Mr Simpson sighs. 'There was nothing to suggest this would occur, and if he'd not been released, no lifer ever would be. The majority will never be a danger to the public as most murders are one-off crimes and first-time offences; 90 per cent of those released never commit another crime.'

It is possible for a lifer to be released after eight years, but the vast majority serve over twenty, and some never leave prison – other than in a coffin.

DAY 139   TUESDAY 4 DECEMBER 2001

8.57 am

Mr Clarke has been sacked and put on outside duties, while Carl has been sent back to the south block, and all because of a dishonest prison officer. I'll explain.

Mr Clarke is the cleaner at SMU and because he's sixty-seven years old, he only works mornings. It keeps him out of the cold, and gives him something to do rather than sit around in his room all day. You will all know from past reports that he carried out the job with a great deal of pride. Carl, whom I've been training to take over from me, will now only return to SMU when, and if, I become the hospital orderly. And why? An officer has been talking to the press to supplement his income, and among the things he's told them is that I have my own cleaner and a personal assistant. The governor has found it necessary to suspend the two jobs while an enquiry takes place. Mr New is livid, not so much about Carl, but because Mr Clarke has suffered as a direct result of an officer's 'unprofessional conduct'.

The detailed information given to the press has enabled the investigation to narrow the suspects down to two officers. The guessing game in the prison is which two – unfair, because it allows prisoners to put any officer they don't like in the frame.

10.00 am

Labour board. Carl is officially demoted to cleaner, but assured by Mr Berlyn that when my job becomes available, he will take over. Mr Clarke is now sweeping up leaves in the yard. Remember it's December.

12 noon

Over lunch Doug tells me that Mrs Tempest has suggested that his prospective employer come to the prison, where his credentials will be carefully checked, and he'll be questioned as to the job description, which entails driving a lorry from Boston to Birmingham to March and back every day. If all goes to plan, Doug will be able to begin work on Monday morning, I'll go to the hospital as orderly, Carl will move back into SMU and, if the prison shows an ounce of common sense, Mr Clarke will be reinstated as part-time cleaner.

2.00 pm

I spend the afternoon at SMU on my own. There are three prisoners up in front of the sentence planning board, and another who needs advice on HDC (tagging). As he can neither read nor write, I fill in all the forms for him.

Mr New arrives looking frustrated. Another crisis has arisen over prison beds: twelve of the rooms on the south block have no doors. He gives an order that they must be fitted immediately, which in prison terms means next Monday at the earliest.

DAY 139

6.00 pm

I'm called over the tannoy to report to reception. It can only be Mr Daff.

I arrive in front of the Regimental Sergeant Major to find he's on his own. Mr Daff tells me that he has decided to take early retirement because he doesn't like all the changes that are taking place in the Prison Service. 'Far too fuckin' soft,' he mutters under his breath. He adds that because I'm to be the next hospital orderly, I'll be allowed some of my personal belongings. He opens my box and lets me remove a tracksuit, a blanket, two pillowcases, a tablecloth and a dictionary. He fills in the necessary pink form and I sign for them. He then winks as he places them all in a black plastic bin liner. I depart with my swag.

10.00 pm

I leave the hospital, return to my room and settle down to read *The Diving Bell and the Butterfly*, which has been recommended by my son William.

DAY 140   WEDNESDAY 5 DECEMBER 2001

10.00 am

The punishment should fit the crime according to Mr W. S. Gilbert, and I have no quarrel with that. However, shouldn't all inmates be treated equally, whatever prison they are incarcerated? Which brings me onto the subject of wages.

The practice at NSC is just plain stupid and, more important, unfair, because it discriminates in such a way as to be inexplicable to anyone. I have only become fully aware of the disparity because of my twice-weekly contact with the labour board, who not only arbitrarily allocate the jobs, but also decide on the wages. For example, as orderly to the sentence management unit, I am paid £8.50 a week. The library orderlies receive £9.40, the gym orderlies £11.90, reception orderlies £10.50, education orderlies £8.40 and the chapel orderly £9.10. However, a farm worker, who starts at eight in the morning and is out in the cold all day, gets £5.60, and a cleaner £7.20, whereas the prison barber, who only works from six to eight every evening, gets £10 a week.

It's no different in any other prison, but no one seems to give a damn.

Seven prisoners come through reception today. Two of them have been sent to NSC with only eleven and nine days left to serve. Why, when moving to a new prison is a disorientating, frightening and unpleasant experience?*

Why not appoint to the prison board carefully selected prisoners who could tell the Home Office one or two home truths? Here at NSC there are two inmates with PhDs, seven with BAs and several with professional qualifications, all of whom are as bright as any officer I've met, with the exception of Mr Gough, who is happy to discus Sisley, Vanburgh and John Quincy Adams rather than the latest prison regulations.

2.00 pm

Carl takes over from me at SMU because I have a theatre visit. By that I mean that the two people who are coming to see me today are the theatre director David Gilmore, and the producer Lee Menzies. David Gilmore (*Daisy Pulls it Off*) is just back from Australia, where he's been directing *Grease*, and Lee is about to put on *The Island* at the Old Vic.

Currently I'm an investor (angel) with both of them. *Grease*, which is on tour in the UK, has already not only returned my capital investment, but also shown a 50 per cent profit. This is not the norm, it's more often the other way round. I have 10 per cent of *The Island*, which hasn't yet opened. David Ian (who had to cancel his visit at the last minute) has several shows in production in which I have a share: *The King and I* (London and tour), *Chicago* (tour), *Grease* (tour), and he's now talking about a production of the successful Broadway musical, *The Producers*. Once David and Lee have brought me up to date on everything that's happening in the theatre world, we turn to a subject on which I feel they will be able to advise me.

---

* Because the last prison pays the expense of discharging a prisoner.

Mr Daff shouts out in his best Sergeant Major voice that it's time for visitors to leave. Where did the time go?

8.30 pm

Doug tells me that his wife visited him today. She confirmed that he will be offered the haulage job, and therefore I can become hospital orderly next week. I'm going to have to decide which course to take should Spring Hill offer me a transfer.

10.00 pm

Life may be awful, but after watching the ten o'clock news and seeing the conditions in the Greek jail where they've locked up eleven British plane spotters, I count my blessings.

DAY 141   THURSDAY 6 DECEMBER 2001

4.45 pm

After a day of no murders, no escapes, no one shipped out, I meet up with Doug for supper. We sit at a corner table and he brings me up to date on his interview for a job. Having applied to the advertisement in the *Boston Target*, Doug was interviewed in the presence of Ms Tempest. He was offered the job and begins work on Monday as a lorry driver. He will ferry a load of steel coils from Boston to Birmingham, to March, before returning to Boston. He must then report back to the prison by seven o'clock. The job will be for six days a week, and he'll be paid £5 an hour.

Just to recap, Doug is doing a four-and-a-half-year sentence for avoiding paying VAT on imported goods to the value of several millions. He's entitled, after serving a quarter of his sentence – if he's been a model prisoner, and he has – to seek outside employment. This is all part of the resettlement programme enjoyed only by prisoners who have reached D-cat status.

It works out well for everyone: NSC is getting prisoners out to work and in Doug they have someone who won't be a problem or break any rules. Although he has a PSV licence, he hasn't driven a lorry for several years, and says it will be like starting all over again. Still, it's better than being cooped up inside a prison all day.

DAY 142   FRIDAY 7 DECEMBER 2001

9.00 am

I'm asked to report to sister in the hospital for an interview. As I walk across from SMU, I have a moment's anxiety as I wonder if Linda is considering someone else for hospital orderly. These fears are assuaged by her opening comment when she says how delighted she is that I will be joining her. Linda's only worry is that I am keeping a diary. She stresses the confidentiality of prisoners' medical records. I agree to abide by this without reservation.

10.00 am

Mr New confirms that Mr Clarke (theft) has been reinstated as SMU cleaner. What a difference that will make. Carl can now concentrate on the real job of assisting the officers and prisoners and not have to worry whether the dustbins have been emptied.

2.00 pm

Do you recall the two prisoners who were caught returning from Boston laden with alcohol? One attacked an officer with a torch so his friends could escape. The escapee, who managed to slip back to his room and thanks to a change of clothes supplied by a friend, got away with it because it wasn't possible to prove he'd ever been absent. Today, the same prisoner was found to have a roll-on deodorant in his room not sold at the canteen. He was shipped out to a B-cat in Liverpool this afternoon.

6.00 pm

I spend an hour signing 200 'Toad' Christmas cards.

8.15 pm

Doug is having second thoughts about giving up his job. The thought of driving eight hours a day for six days a week isn't looking quite so attractive.

10.00 pm

I return to my room and finish *The Diving Bell and the Butterfly* by the late Jean Dominique Bauby. It is, as my son suggested, quite brilliant. The author had a massive stroke and was left paralysed and speechless, only able to move one eyelid. And with that eyelid he mastered a letter code and dictated the book. Makes my problems seem pretty insignificant.

DAY 143   SATURDAY 8 DECEMBER 2001

8.00 am

Normally the weekends are a bore, but after a couple of hours editing *Sons of Fortune* I start moving my few worldly goods across to the hospital. Although I'm not moving in officially until tomorrow, Doug allows me to store some possessions under one of the hospital beds.

1.00 pm

Among today's letters are ones from Rosemary Leach and Stephanie Cole in reply to my fan mail following their performances in *Back Home*. Miss Leach, in a hand-written letter, fears she may have overacted, as the new 'in thing' is blandness and understatement. Miss Cole thought her own performance was a little too sentimental. I admire them for being so critical of themselves.

I receive seventy-two Christmas cards today, which lifts my spirits greatly. The officers have begun a book on how many cards I'll receive from the public: Mr Hart is down for 1,378, Mr New 1,290 and Mr Downs 2,007. I select three to be put on the ledge by my bed – a landscape by that magnificent Scottish artist Joseph Farqueson, a Giles cartoon of Grandma and a Bellini painting of the Virgin Mother.

2.00 pm

Highlight of my day is a visit from Mary, James and Alison, who between them bring me up to date on all matters personal, office and legal. William returns from America next week, and, along with Mary and James, will come to see me on Christmas Eve. Mary will then fly off to Kenya and attend my nephew's wedding. Mary and I have always wanted to go on safari and see the big cats. Not this year.

DAY 144   SUNDAY 9 DECEMBER 2001

9.00 am

Doug has an 'away day' with his family in March, so I spend the morning covering for him at the hospital.

2.00 pm

A visit from two Conservative front bench spokesmen, Patrick McLoughlin MP, the party's deputy chief whip in the Commons, and Simon Burns MP, the number two under Liam Fox, who covers the health portfolio. They've been loyal friends over many years. I canvassed for both of them before they entered the House, Patrick in a famous by-election after Matthew Parris left the Commons, which he won by 100 votes, and Simon who took over Norman St John Stevas's seat in Chelmsford West where the Liberals had lowered Norman's majority from 5,471 in 1979 to 378 in 1983.

'If you felt the Conservatives might not be returned to power for fifteen years, would you look for another job?' I ask.

'No,' they both reply in unison. 'In any case,' Simon adds, 'I'm not qualified to do anything else.' Patrick nods his agreement. I'm not sure if he's agreeing that Simon couldn't do anything else, or that he falls into the same category.

We have a frank discussion about IDS. Both are pleased that he has managed to downgrade the debate on Europe within the party and concentrate on the health service, education and the social services. They accept that Blair is having a good war (Afghanistan), and although the disagreements with Brown are real, the British people don't seem to be that interested. Patrick feels that we could be back in power the election after next; Simon is not so optimistic.

'But,' he adds, 'if Brown takes over from Blair, we could win the next election.'

'What if someone takes over from IDS?' I ask.

Neither replies.

When they leave, I realize how much I miss the House and all things political.

10.15 pm

This is my last night on the south block. Despite a football match blaring from next door, I sleep soundly.

DAY 145   MONDAY 10 DECEMBER 2001

3.52 am

I wake early, so write for a couple of hours.

6.00 am

Pack up my final bits and pieces and go across to the hospital to join Doug, who's carrying out the same exercise in reverse.

7.30 am

I will describe my new daily routine before I tell you anything about my work at the hospital.

> *6.00 am* Rise, write until 7 am.
>
> *7.00 am* Bath and shave.
>
> *7.30 am* Sister arrives to take sick parade, which lasts until 8 am.
>
> *8.00 am* Deliver 'off work' slips to the north and south blocks, farm, works, education and the front gate.
>
> *8.20 am* Breakfast.

9–10.30 am Doctor arrives to minister to patients until around ten-thirty, depending on number.

11.30 am Sick parade until noon (collecting pills, etc.).

12.00 Lunch.

12.30 pm Phone Alison at the office.

1–2.00 pm Write.

3.00 pm Prisoners arrive from Birmingham, Leicester, Wayland, Lincoln or Bedford, all C-cats, to join us at NSC. They first go to reception to register; after that their next port of call is the hospital, where sister signs them in and checks their medical records. You rarely get transferred to another prison if you're ill.

I check their blood pressure, their urine sample – for diabetes, not drugs; that is carried out in a separate building later – their height and weight, and pass this information onto sister so that it can be checked against their medical records.

4.30–5.00 pm Sick parade. Linda, who began work at 7.30 am, leaves at 5 pm.

5.00 pm Supper. If anyone falls ill at night, the duty officer can open up the surgery and dispense medication, although most are told they can wait until sick parade the following day. If it's serious, they're taken off to Pilgrim Hospital in Boston by taxi, which is fifteen minutes away.

5.30 pm Write for a couple of hours.

7.45 pm Call Mary and/or James and Will.

8.00 pm Read or watch television; tonight, *Catherine the Great*. I'm joined by Doug and Clive (I'm allowed to have two other inmates in the hospital between 7 and 10.00 pm).

10.20 pm After watching the news, I settle down in a bed five
inches wider than the one in my room on the south
block and fall into a deep sleep. It is, as is suggested
by the title of this book – compared with Belmarsh
and Wayland – heaven.

DAY 146   TUESDAY 11 DECEMBER 2001

5.49 am

I am just about getting the hang of my daily routine. It's far more demanding than the work I carried out at SMU. I hope that Linda will be willing to teach me first aid, and more importantly give me a greater insight into the drugs problem in prisons.

7.25 am

I'm standing by the door waiting for Linda to arrive. I prepare her a coffee; one sweetener and a teaspoonful of milk in her pig mug. The five doctors all have their own mugs.

Linda has worked in the Prison Service for over ten years. She has three grown-up children, two sons and a daughter. She was married to a 'nurse tutor', Terry, who tragically died of skin cancer a couple of years ago at the age of fifty-three. She works long hours and the prisoners look on her much as I viewed my prep-school matron – a combination of mother, nurse and confidante. She has no time for shirkers, but couldn't be more sympathetic if you are genuinely ill.

8.15 am

After sick parade, I carry out my rounds to the different parts of the prison to let staff know who will be off work today, before going to breakfast. I ask John (lifer) what meat is in the sausage.

'It's always beef,' he replies, 'because there are so many Muslims in prisons nowadays, they never serve pork sausages.'

10.00 am

The hospital has a visit from a man called Alan, who's come to conduct a course on drug and alcohol abuse. He moves from prison to prison, advising and helping anyone who seeks his counsel. There are 150 such officers posted around the country, paid for by the taxpayer out of the NHS and the Home Office budgets.

Alan is saddened by how few prisoners take advantage of the service he offers. In Bradford alone, he estimates that 40 per cent of inmates below the age of thirty are on drugs, and another 30 per cent are addicted to alcohol. He shows me the reams of Home Office forms to be filled in every time he sees a prisoner. By the end of the morning, only two inmates out of 211 have bothered to turn up and see him.

11.00 am

I have a special visit from Sir Brian Mawhinney MP, an old friend whose constituency is about twenty miles south of NSC. As a former cabinet minister and Shadow Home Secretary, he has many questions about prisons, and as I have not entered the Palace of Westminster for the past six months, there are questions I'm equally keen for him to answer.

Brian stays for an hour, and after we stop going over past triumphs, we discuss present disasters. He fears that the Simon Burns scenario is realistic, a long time in the wilderness for the Conservatives, but 'Events, dear boy events, are still our biggest hope.' Brian runs over time, and I miss lunch – no complaints.

4.00 pm

Mr Hart passes on a message from my solicitors that my appeal papers have not been lodged at court. Panic. I passed them over to the security officer six weeks ago. Mr Hart calls Mr Hocking, who confirms that they were sent out on 29 October. Who's to blame?

5.00 pm

Canteen. Now that I'm enhanced, I have an extra £15 of my own money added to my account each week. With my hospital orderly pay of £11.70, it adds up to £26.70 a week. So I can now enjoy Cussons soap, SR toothpaste, Head and Shoulders shampoo, and even the occasional packet of McVitie's chocolate biscuits.

6.00 pm

I attend a rock concert tonight, performed by the 'Cons and Pros.' The standard is high, particularly Gordon (GBH) on the guitar, who sadly for the band will be released tomorrow.

8.00 pm

Doug returns from his second day at work. He has driven to Birmingham and Northampton in one day. He is exhausted, and fed up with his room-mate, who leaves the radio on all night. I'm in bed asleep by ten-thirty. You will discover the relevance of this tomorrow.

DAY 147   WEDNESDAY 12 DECEMBER 2001

2.08 am

The night security officer opens my door and shines his torch in my eyes. I don't get back to sleep for over an hour.

5.16 am

He does it again, so I get up and start writing.

8.07 am

On my journey around the prison this morning handing out 'off-work' slips, I have to drop into the farm. It's freezing and a lot of the inmates are claiming to have colds. I bump into the farm manager, Mr Donnelly, a charming man who I came to know from my days at the SMU when he sat on the labour board. He introduces me to Blossom, a beautiful creature.

Blossom weighs in at twenty-six stone, and has a broken nose and four stubby, fat hairy legs. She is lucky to be alive. Blossom is the prisoners' favourite pig, so when her turn came for slaughter, the inmates hid her in a haystack. When Mr Donnelly was unable to find Blossom that morning she was granted a week's reprieve. Blossom reappeared the next day, but mysteriously disappeared again when the lorry turned up the following week. Once again Mr Donnelly searched for her, and once again he failed to find her. The inmates knew that it couldn't be long before Blossom's hiding place was discovered, so they put in an application to the governor to buy her, so that she could spend the rest of her days at NSC in peace. Mr Donnelly was so moved by the prisoners' concern that he lifted the death penalty and allowed Blossom to retire. The happy pet now roams around the farm, behaving literally like a pig in clover. (See below.)

Blossom and his friend Blossom

DAY 147

8.30 am

On my way back to the hospital after breakfast, I sense something different, and realize that Peter (lifer, arson) is not on the road sweeping the leaves as he does every morning. A security officer explains that Peter is out on a town leave in Boston; the first occasion he's left prison in thirty-one years. I'll try to have a word with him as soon as he returns, so that I can capture his first impressions of freedom.

9.00 am

The new inductees report to the doctor for their medical check-up. I now feel I'm settling into a routine as hospital orderly.

12 noon

Call Mary to assure her that the courts have now located my papers, and to wish her luck with our Christmas party tomorrow night. She will also be attending Denis and Margaret Thatcher's fiftieth wedding anniversary at the East India Club earlier in the evening. She promises to call me and let me know how they both went. No, I remind her, I can only call you.

4.08 pm

An announcement over the tannoy instructs me to report to reception. I arrive to be told by Sergeant Major Daff that I have been sent two Christmas cakes – one from Mrs Gerald Scarfe, better known as Jane Asher, with a card, from which I reproduce only the final sentence:

194

I'm baking you a cake for Christmas with a hacksaw and file inside.

See you soon, love Jane

– and one from a ladies' group in Middleton. As no prisoner is allowed to receive any foodstuffs in case they contain alcohol or drugs, Mr Daff agrees that one can go to the local retirement home, and the other to the special needs children. So it's all right for the children to be stoned out of their minds and the old-age pensioners to be drugged up to the eyeballs, but not me.

'It's Home Office regulations,' explains Mr Daff.

5.00 pm

I spot Peter (lifer, arson) coming up the drive. He looks in a bit of a daze, so I invite him to join me in the hospital for coffee and biscuits. We chat for nearly an hour.

The biggest shock for Peter on leaving prison for the first time in over thirty years was the number of 'coffin dodgers' (old people) that were on the streets of Boston doing their Christmas shopping. In 1969, the life expectancy for a man was sixty-eight years and for a woman seventy-three; it's now seventy-six and eighty-one respectively. Peter also considered many of the young women dressed 'very tarty', but he did admit that he couldn't stop staring at them. Peter, who is six foot four inches tall and weighs eighteen stone, was surprised that he no longer stands out in a crowd, as he would have done thirty-one years ago. When he visited Safeways supermarket, it was the first time he'd seen a trolley; in the past he had only been served at a counter and used a shopping basket. And as for money, he knows of course about decimalization, but when he last purchased something from a shop there were 240 pennies in a pound, half-crowns, ten shilling notes and the guinea was still of blessed memory.

Peter was totally baffled by pelican crossings and was frightened to walk across one. However the experience he most disliked was having to use a changing room to try on clothes behind a curtain, while members of the public walked past him – particularly female assistants who didn't mind drawing back the curtain to see how he was getting on. He was amazed that he could try on a shirt and then not have to purchase it.

I suspect that the process of rehabilitation – accompanied town visits (six in all), unaccompanied town visits, weekend home visits, week visits, CSV work, followed by a job in the community – will take him at least another three to four years, by which time Peter will qualify for his old-age pension. I can only wonder if he will ever rejoin the real world and not simply be moved from one institution to another.

10.00 pm

I listen to the ten o'clock news. Roy Whiting has been given life imprisonment for the murder of Sarah Payne. Once the sentence has been passed, we discover that Whiting had already been convicted some years ago for abducting a child, and sexually abusing a minor. His sentence on that occasion? Four years.

DAY 148 THURSDAY 13 DECEMBER 2001

6.00 am

Orderlies are the prison's school prefects. They're given their jobs because they can be trusted. In return, they're expected to work for these privileges, such as eating together in a small group, and in my case having a single room with a television.

There are over a dozen orderlies in all. Yesterday both reception orderlies were sacked, leaving two much sought-after vacancies.

Martin, the senior of the two reception orderlies, was due to be discharged this morning, two months early, on tag (HCD). The only restriction was that he must remain in his place of residence between the hours of 7 pm and 7 am. Martin had already completed the 'paper chase', which had to be carried out the day before release. Unfortunately, before departing this morning he decided to take with him a brand-new prison-issue denim top and jeans, and several shirts. A blue and white striped prison shirt apparently sells at around a hundred pounds on the outside, especially if it has the letters NSC on the pocket.

When the theft was discovered, he was immediately sacked and, more sadly, so was the other orderly, Barry, whose only crime was that he wouldn't grass on Martin. It's rough justice when the only way to keep your job is to grass on your mate when you know what the consequences will be for that person – not to mention how the other inmates will treat you in the future. We will find out the punishment tomorrow when both men will be up in front of the governor.

2.00 pm

I am disappointed to receive a letter from William Payne, the governor of Spring Hill, turning down my application for transfer. His reasons for rejecting me are shown in his letter reproduced here. (See opposite.) I feel I should point out that the last five inmates from NSC who have applied to Spring Hill have all been accepted. It's not worth appealing, because I've long given up expecting any justice whenever the Home Office is involved.

3.00 pm

Six new inductees: four on short sentences ranging from three weeks to nine months, and two lifers who, for the past sixteen years, have been banged up for twenty-two hours a day. They are walking around the perimeters of the prison (no walls) in a daze, and can't understand why they're not being ordered back to their cells. Linda tells me that lifers often report at the end of the first week with foot-sores and colds, and take far longer to adapt to open conditions.

One of the short-termers from Nottingham who's been placed in the no-smoking spur on the south block that has mostly more mature CSV workers who only return to the prison at night – tells me with a wry smile that he couldn't sleep last night because it was so quiet.

HM Prisons
Grendon & Springhill
Grendon Underwood
Aylesbury
Bucks HP18 0TL
Telephone   01296 770301
Fax   01296 770756
E mail   governorpayne@hotmail.com

INVESTORS IN PEOPLE

Mr J Archer FF8282
HMP North Sea Camp
Frieston   Ref: 103/2001
Boston
Lincs   Date: 10 December 2001
PE22 0QX

Dear Mr Archer,

APPLICATION TO TRANSFER TO SPRING HILL

Thank you for your application to transfer to HMP Spring Hill.

I have considered your application carefully. You requested a transfer in order that
you may receive visits from your family more easily than you can at North Sea
Camp. While Spring Hill would be suitable, there are currently more vacancies at
HMP Hollesley Bay,*near Woodbridge in Suffolk which is within easy reach of
Cambridge and commuting distance of London. For this reason I am refusing your
request to transfer to Spring Hill.

The Governor of Hollesley Bay has confirmed that he is able to offer you a place
should you wish to request a transfer to that establishment. I hope this provides a
positive alternative to you.

Yours sincerely,

William Payne.

William Payne
Governor

cc: Colin New, HMP North Sea Camp
     Karen Mackenzie-Howe, HMP Spring Hill

---

* Hollesley Bay is further away from Cambridge than North Sea Camp.

DAY 148

6.00 pm

A visit from Mr Hocking. I'm no longer to dispose of personal papers, letters, envelopes or notes in the dustbin outside the hospital, as a prisoner was caught rifling through the contents last night. In future I must hand them to a security officer, who will shred them. NSC does not want to repeat the Belmarsh debacle, where an officer stole a chapter of my book and tried to sell it to the *Sun*.

8.00 pm

I sit in my palace and hold court with Doug, Clive and Carl, or at least that's how it feels after Belmarsh and Wayland.

In London, Mary is hosting our Christmas party.

DAY 149　　FRIDAY 14 DECEMBER 2001

10.00 am

Today is judgment day. Three prisoners are up in front of the governor. Inmates take a morbid interest in the outcome of any adjudication as it's a yardstick for discovering what they can hope to get away with.

Martin, the reception orderly who pleaded guilty to attempting to steal prison clothes on the day he was due to be released, has his tagging privileges removed, and seven days added to his sentence. So for the sake of a pair of jeans and a few prison shirts, Martin will remain at NSC until a couple of weeks before Easter, rather than spending Christmas at home with his wife and family. Added to this, the sixty-seven days will not be spent in the warmth of reception as an orderly, but on the farm in the deep mid-winter cleaning out the pig pens.

Barry is next up. His crime was not grassing on Martin. Although Martin stated clearly at the adjudication that Barry was not party to the offence, he also loses his orderly job, and returns to the farm as a shepherd. For the governor to expect him to 'grass' on his friend (I even doubt if they were friends) seems to me a little rough.

Finding competent replacements will not be easy. The rumour is that Peter (lifer, just had his first day out after thirty-one years) has been offered the job as the next step in his rehabilitation. Peter tells me that he doesn't want to be an orderly, and is happy to continue sweeping up leaves.

The third prisoner in front of the governor this morning is Ali, a man serving three months for theft. Ali has refused to work on the farm and locked himself in his room. For this act of defiance, he has four days added to his sentence. This may not sound excessive, and in normal circumstances I don't think he could complain, as it's the statutory sentence for refusing to work. However, the four days are Christmas Eve, Christmas Day, Boxing Day and 27 December.

Ali arrives in the hospital moments after the adjudication and bursts into tears. The governor decides that I should be punished as well, because Linda puts me in charge of him. It's ten-forty and the governor wants Ali back on the farm by this afternoon. Fortunately, England are playing India. It's the second day of the Test, and Ali knows his cricket. We settle down in the hospital ward to watch the final session of the day. Sachin Tendulkar is at the crease so Ali stops crying. By lunchtime (end of play in Madras), Tendulkar has scored 123 and Ali's tears have turned to smiles.

He's back on the farm at one o'clock.

3.00 pm

Seven new prisoners in from Nottingham today, and as we only released three this morning, our numbers reach 211; our capacity is 220. The weekly turnover at NSC is about 20 per cent, and I'm told it always peaks at this time of year. I'm also informed by one of the lifers that there are more absconders over Christmas, many of whom give themselves up on Boxing Day evening. The governor's attitude is simple; if they return to the gate and apologize, they have twenty-eight days added to their sentence; if they wait until they're picked up by the police, then in addition to the added twenty-eight days, they're shipped out to a B-cat the following morning.

4.00 pm

Linda asks me to take two blood samples down to the gate, so they can be sent to Pilgrim Hospital. On the three-hundred-yard walk, I become distracted by a new idea for how the twins discover their identity in *Sons of Fortune*. When I arrive at the gate, the blood samples are no longer in the plastic packet, and must have fallen out en route. I run for the first time in weeks. I don't want to lose my job, and end up working on the farm. I see Jim (gym orderly) running towards me – he's found the samples on the side of the path. I thank him between puffs – he's saved me from my first reportable offence. Actually, I think I should confess at this stage that some weeks ago I picked up a penny from the path and have kept the tiny coin in my jeans pocket, feeling a slight defiance in possessing cash. I put the samples back in their plastic packet and hand them in at the gate.

Incidentally, the other gym orderly Bell is also the NSC goalkeeper. He used to be at Spring Hill, but asked for a transfer to be nearer his wife. NSC needed a goalkeeper, so the transfer only took four days. Thanks to this little piece of subterfuge we're now on a winning streak. However, I have to report that the goalkeeper's wife has run off with his best friend, which may account for Bell being sent off last week. We lost 5–0.

DAY 150   SATURDAY 15 DECEMBER 2001

7.30 am

I now have to work seven days a week, as there's a surgery on Saturday and Sunday. It's a small price to pay for all the other privileges of being hospital orderly.

Not many patients today, eleven in all, but then there's no work to skive off on a Saturday morning. Sister leaves at ten-thirty and I have the rest of the day to myself, unless there's an emergency.

11.00 am

Spend a couple of hours editing *Sons of Fortune*, and only take breaks for lunch, and later to watch the prison football match.

2.00 pm

The football manager and coach is a senior officer called Mr Masters. He's proud of his team, but when it comes to abusing the referee, he's as bad as any other football fan. Today he's linesman, and should be supporting the ref, not to mention the other linesman. But both receive a tirade of abuse, as Mr Masters feels able to give his opinion on an offside decision even though he's a hundred yards away from the offence, and the linesman on the other side of the pitch is standing opposite the offending player. To be fair, his enthusiasm rubs off on the rest of the team, and we win a scrappy game 2–0.

DAY 151   SUNDAY 16 DECEMBER 2001

7.30 am

Only five inmates turn up for early morning surgery. Linda explains that although the prison has a photographic club, woodwork shop, library, gym and chapel, a lot of the prisoners spend the weekend in bed, rising only to eat or watch a football match on TV. It seems such a waste of their lives.

2.00 pm

My visitors today are Malcolm and Edith Rifkind. Malcolm and I entered the House around the same time, and have remained friends ever since. Malcolm is one of those rare animals in politics who has few enemies. He was Secretary of State for Defence and Foreign Secretary under John Major, and I can't help reflecting how no profession other than politics happily divests itself of its most able people when they are at their peak. It's the equivalent of dropping Beckham or Wilkinson at the age of twenty-five. Still, that's the prerogative of the electorate, and one of the few disadvantages of living in a democracy.

Malcolm and his wife Edith want to know all about prison life, while I wish to hear all the latest gossip from Westminster.

Malcolm makes one political comment that will remain fixed in my memory: 'If in 1979 the electorate had offered us a contract for eighteen years, we would have happily signed it, so we can't complain if we now have to spend a few years in the wilderness.' He and Edith have travelled up from London to see me, and they will now drive on to Edinburgh. I cannot emphasize often enough how much I appreciate the kindness of friends.

8.00 pm

Mr Baker drops in for coffee and a chat. The officers' mess is closed over the weekend, so the hospital is the natural pit stop. He tells me that one prisoner has absconded, while another, on returning from his town visit, was so drunk that he had to be helped out of his wife's car. That will be his last town visit for several months. And here's the rub, it was his first day out of prison for six years.

DAY 152   MONDAY 17 DECEMBER 2001

8.50 am

'Papa to Hotel, Papa to Hotel, how do you read me?'

This is PO New's call sign to Linda, and I'm bound to say that the hospital is the nearest I'm going to get to a hotel while I remain incarcerated in one of Her Majesty's establishments.

It's a freezing morning in this flat, open part of Lincolnshire, so there's a long queue for the doctor. First in line are those on the paper chase, due for release tomorrow. The second group comprises those facing adjudication – one caught injecting heroin, a second in possession of money (£20) and finally the inmate who came back drunk last night. The doctor declares all three fit, and can see no medical reason that might be used as mitigating circumstances in their defence. The heroin addict is subsequently transferred back to Lincoln. The prisoner found with £20 in his room claims that he just forgot to hand it in when he returned from a town visit, so ends up with seven days added. The drunk gets twenty-one days added to his sentence, and no further town visits until further notice. He is also warned that next time, it's back to a B-cat.

Those in the third group – by far the largest – are either genuinely ill or don't feel like working on the farm at below-zero temperatures. Most are told to return to work immediately or they will be put on report and come up in front of the governor.

2.00 pm

I phone Mary, who has some interesting news. I feel I should point out that Mr Justice Potts claimed at the end of my trial that this is, 'As serious an offence of perjury as I have had experience of and as I have been able to find in the books'.

A Reader in Law at the University of Buckingham has been checking sentencing for those convicted of perjury. She has discovered that, in the period 1991–2000, 1,024 people were charged with this offence in the United Kingdom. Of the 830 convicted, just under 400 received no custodial sentence at all, while in the case of 410, the sentence was eighteen months or less. Only four people were given a four-year sentence upheld on appeal. One of these framed an innocent man, who served thirty-one months of a seventeen year sentence for a crime he did not commit; the second stood trial twice for a murder of which he was acquitted, but was later convicted of perjury during those trials. The other two were for false declarations related to marriage as part of a large-scale immigration racket.

7.17 pm

There's a knock on my door, and as the hospital is out of bounds after six o'clock unless it's an emergency, I assume it's an officer. It isn't. It's a jolly West Indian called Wright. He's always cheerful, and never complains about anything except the weather.

'Hi, Jeff, I think I've broken my finger.'

I study his hand as if I had more than a first-aid badge from my days as a Boy Scout in the 1950s. I suggest we visit his unit officer. Mr Cole is unsympathetic, but finally agrees Wright should be taken to the Pilgrim Hospital. Wright reports back an hour later with his finger in a splint.

'By the way,' I ask, 'how did you break your finger?'

'Slammed it in a door, didn't I.'

'Strange,' I say, 'because I think I've just seen the door walking around, and it's got a black eye.'

DAY 153   TUESDAY 18 DECEMBER 2001

10.00 am

In my mailbag is a registered letter from the court of appeal. I print it in full. (See overleaf.) The prison authorities or the courts seem to have been dilatory, as my appeal may be put off until February, rather than held in December. The experts on the subject of appeals, and by that I mean my fellow inmates, tell me that the usual period of time between receiving the above letter and learning the date of one's appeal is around three weeks. It's then another ten days before the appeal itself.

Among my other letters is one from Dame Edna, enquiring about the dress code when she visits NSC.

12 noon

Brian (attempt to defraud an ostrich company) thanks me for a box of new paperbacks that have arrived at the Red Cross office in Boston, sent by my publisher.

1.00 pm

My new job as hospital orderly means I've had to adjust my writing regime. I now write between the hours of 6 and 7 am,

**COURT
SERVICE**

All letters should be addressed to

THE REGISTRAR

JEFFREY HOWARD ARCHER
HMP NORTH SEA CAMP
FREISTON
BOSTON
LINCS
PE22 0QX

THE COURT SERVICE

Criminal Appeal Office

Royal Courts of Justice,
Strand, London, WC2A 2LL
Telephone: 020 7947 7082 (Direct line)
0207 7947 6014 (Enquiries)
(Direct line - between 9.00am and 5.00pm)
Fax: 020 7947 6900   DX 44450 STRAND
Minicom: 020 7947 7594

Date: 12 December 2001

Your ref: FF8282

Our ref: 200104555S2

Dear Sir/Madam,

<u>Regina v JEFFREY HOWARD ARCHER</u>

I acknowledge receipt of the form seeking to renew your application for leave to appeal against conviction.

In due course our List Office will set a date for your application to be considered by the Full Court of Appeal. You will be aware that since leave to appeal was refused, you are not entitled to Legal Aid for counsel to represent you in relation to the application(s). Accordingly, unless you have already informed this office of a different arrangement, the List Office will presume that the matter is to be fixed for consideration without a legal representative to appear on your behalf.

Please note that if your renewal was not filed within the specified time limits and an extension of time to renew is required, the Court will consider that application first. If an extension of time is refused, the matter will be finished and the Court will not go on to consider the main application for leave to appeal.

It is most important for you to be aware that your application(s) may be listed for hearing at very short notice. If, therefore, you have already made private arrangements for legal advisers to represent you or if you make such arrangements before the hearing date, you must inform this office <u>immediately</u>, supplying details of their name(s), address(es) and telephone number(s). You should also ensure that they are aware of any date fixed for consideration of your application(s).

Yours faithfully

Mrs Jushna Chowdhury
For Registrar
A copy of this letter is being sent for information purposes to;
The Governor, HMP NORTH SEA CAMP
MICHCON DE REYA, Solicitors

1 and 3 pm, and 5 and 7 pm. During the weekends, I can fit in an extra hour each day, which means I'm currently managing about thirty-seven hours of writing a week.

6.00 pm

I visit the canteen to purchase soap, razor blades, chocolate, Evian and phonecards, otherwise I'll be dirty, unshaven, unfed and unwatered over Christmas, not to mention uncontactable. The officer on duty checks my balance, and finds I'm only £1.20 in credit. Help!

DAY 154   WEDNESDAY 19 DECEMBER 2001

9.00 am

'Archer to report to reception immediately, Archer to report to reception immediately.'

Now Mr Daff has retired, I'm not allowed the same amount of latitude as in the past.

I've received five parcels today. The first is a book by Iris Murdoch, *The Sea, The Sea*, kindly sent in by a lady from Dumfries. As I read it some years ago when Ms Murdoch won the Booker Prize, I donate it to the library. The second is a silver bottle opener – not much use to an inmate as we're not allowed to drink – but a kind gesture nevertheless. I ask if I can give it to Linda. No, but it can be put in the old-age pensioners' raffle. The third is a Parker pen. Can I give it to Linda? No, but it can be put in the old-age pensioners' raffle. The fourth is a teddy bear from Dorset. I don't bother to ask, I just agree to donate it to the old-age pensioners' raffle. The fifth is a large tube, which, when opened, reveals fifteen posters from the Chris Beetles Gallery, which I've been eagerly awaiting for over a week. I explain that it's a gift to the hospital, so there's no point in putting it in store for me because the hospital will get it just as soon as I am released. This time *they* agree to let me take it away. Result: one out of five.

2.00 pm

I happily spend a couple of hours, assisted by Carl and a box of Blu-Tack, fixing prints by Albert Goodwin, Ronald Searle, Heath Robinson, Emmett, Geraldine Girvan, Paul Riley and Ray Ellis to the hospital walls. With over 900 Christmas cards littered around the beds, the ward has been transformed into an art gallery. (See opposite.)

5.00 pm

I return to the canteen. I'm only £2.50 in credit, whereas I calculate I should have around £18. It's the nearest I get to losing my temper, and it's only when the officer in charge says he's been trying to get the system changed for the past year that I calm down, remembering that it's not his fault. He makes a note of the discrepancy on the computer. I thank him and return to the hospital. I have no reason to complain; I've got the best job in the prison and the best room, and am allowed to write five hours a day. Shut up, Archer.

6.00 pm

I attend the carol service at six-thirty, where I read one of the lessons. Luke 2, verses eight to twenty. As I dislike the modern text, the vicar has allowed me to read from the King James version.

The chapel is packed long before the service is due to begin and the organ is played with great verve and considerable improvisation by Brian (ostrich fraud). The vicar's wife, three officers and four inmates read the lessons. I follow Mr New, and Mr Hughes follows me. We all enjoy a relaxed service of carols

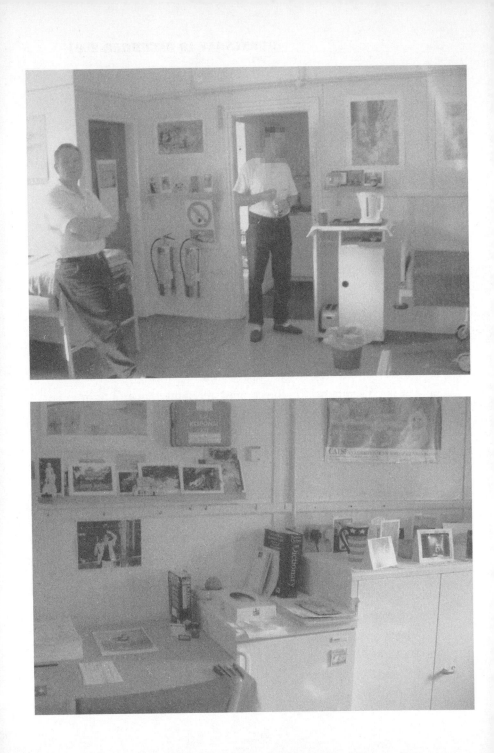

and lessons, and afterwards there is the added bonus of mince pies and coffee, which might explain the large turnout.

After the service, Brian introduces me to Maria, who's in charge of the Red Cross shop in Boston. She has brought along my box of paperbacks and asks if I would be willing to sign them. I happily agree.

DAY 155   THURSDAY 20 DECEMBER 2001

7.30 am

Record numbers report sick with near freezing conditions outside.

11.00 am

The last inmate to see the doctor is a patient called Robinson. He's shaking and trying in vain to keep warm. I've been in prison long enough now to spot a heroin addict at thirty paces. While he waits for his appointment, Robinson confides that he's desperately trying to kick the habit, and has put himself on a compulsory urine test every morning. He's thirty-two years old, and has been in and out of prison for the past fourteen years.

'I'm lucky to be alive,' he says. 'After I got nicked this time, I took the rap and let me mate get off in exchange for a promise he'd send me ten quid a week while I'm inside.'

The 'friend' died a few weeks later after injecting himself from a contaminated batch of heroin.

'If the deal had been the other way round,' Robinson suggests, 'I'd be the dead man.'

12.30 pm

Over lunch I discuss the drug problem in prisons with the two gym orderlies, both of whom abhor the habit. I am shocked – can I still be shocked? – when Jim (burglary, antiques only) tells me that 30 per cent of the inmates at NSC are on heroin. But more depressing still, when Jim was here eight years ago for a previous offence, he says only a handful of the inmates were on drugs. What will it be like in ten years' time?

1.00 pm

As I walk back from lunch, I see Brian and John, the CSV Red Cross workers, heading towards me. They've both been taken off the job and confined to the prison while an enquiry is being conducted. Maria, who runs the Red Cross shop in Boston, has been accused of smuggling contraband (twelve paperbacks) into the prison. Apparently she should have informed the gate staff of her request to have the books autographed by me. Brian tells me they left her in tears, and I am bound to say that what started out as a simple goodwill gesture has ended in turmoil; the Red Cross have been removed as participants in the CSV scheme, and Brian and John have lost their jobs. I resolve to find out if there is more to it – prison has taught me not to automatically take something on trust – and if there isn't, to try to right this injustice.

8.00 pm

Carl suggests we watch *Midnight Express*, a sure way of reminding ourselves just how lucky we all are. And to think Turkey wants to be a full member of the European Union.

DAY 156   FRIDAY 21 DECEMBER 2001

9.00 am

Dr Walling is on duty today. He's full of good cheer, and brings Christmas presents for Linda and myself. Linda gets a box of Ferrero Rocher chocolates, and he presents me with a bottle of Scotch. Linda quickly grabs the bottle, explaining that it's against prison rules to offer prisoners alcohol. If I'd been caught with a bottle of whisky (actually I don't drink spirits) I would have lost my job, and possibly have been sent to a B-cat with added days. Dr Walling looks suitably embarrassed.

12.00 pm

Simon (abduction of his son, mess orderly) drops in to deliver Linda's sandwich lunch. While I make her a coffee, Simon tells me he's moving room today. His room-mate, a married man with two children, asked him last night if he'd ever considered being bisexual. Simon tells me that he jumped out of bed, got dressed, left the room and demanded to be moved, as he didn't want to be locked up with, in his words, 'a raving faggot'.

8.00 pm

I watch *Great Artists* on BBC 2. The subject is Breughel, and all the little Breughels.

10.00 pm

Fall asleep in my chair, exhausted. It must be the combination of writing and hospital duties. Can't complain though, as the days are passing far more quickly.

DAY 157   SATURDAY 22 DECEMBER 2001

9.00 am

Prison life is like a game of cricket; every day you discover a new way of getting out.

The doctor has to pass as fit this morning an inmate by the name of Hal (cat burglar, six months) before he goes up in front of the governor. Last night Hal left the prison and walked into Boston. He dropped into one of the local pubs, had a pint and then purchased a bottle of vodka, a bottle of rum and a six-pack of Fosters. Hal didn't feel like walking the six miles back, so he decided to thumb a lift to the prison. Mr Blackman, one of our younger officers, obliged and happily escorted Hal back, confiscated the contraband and booked him into the segregation block. Hal was due to be released in January, but I fear it's now looking more like February. It turns out that he also suggested to Mr Blackman that if he dropped him off half a mile from the prison, he could keep the bounty. Nice try, Hal.

Among the other inmates who will appear in front of the governor this morning is Simon (abducting his son), but only for a warning. It appears he's been telling anyone who will listen that his cell-mate is 'a raving faggot'. The governor will order him to stop using such inflammatory language otherwise he will lose his job as mess orderly.

I chat to the cat burglar as he waits to see the doctor. Hal says he doesn't care that much what the governor decides. His partner has left him, his mother won't speak to him and he hasn't seen his father in years. When he gets out, he doesn't have anywhere to stay overnight, and only has £37 to his name. He says he needs a job that will earn him enough money to ensure that he doesn't have to revert to stealing again.

I ask him, 'How much is enough?'

'Two hundred quid,' he replies. 'Then I'd have a chance of finding some digs and getting a job.'

11.00 am

Mr Lewis drops into the hospital to wish Linda a happy Christmas. While I'm making him a coffee, he complains that I've thrown away the hospital ashtray, so he can't enjoy a cigar. I reluctantly supply an old saucer. He tells me that he was surprised by the Spring Hill decision and, looking round the hospital, says pointedly, 'If they suggest Hollesley Bay, don't even consider it.'

2.50 pm

Mary and William turn up almost an hour late for their visit because of the snow and ice that caused long hold-ups on the A1. My time with them is cut down to forty minutes.

It's Mary's birthday, and she's wearing the emerald that Sergio purchased for me from the Green Mountains after he returned to Columbia.* I wanted to also give her the pot I made at Wayland, but they told me it shattered in the kiln.

We chat about her forthcoming trip to Kenya for her

---

* See *Volume II – Wayland: Purgatory.*

nephew's wedding. She'll be away for the first ten days of January, but as my appeal won't be heard until mid-February, this isn't a problem. She hopes to see Sir Sidney Kentridge and Godfrey Barker before she leaves. If Godfrey signs an affidavit confirming that Mr Justice Potts discussed me adversely at a dinner party they both attended a year before my arrest, I could be out of here in a few weeks' time. Will isn't optimistic. He feels Godfrey will feel compromised because his wife works for the parole board. As Godfrey has sent me a Christmas card, I can only hope Will's wrong.

Surely justice and truth matter to such a man. We shall soon find out.

DAY 158   SUNDAY 23 DECEMBER 2001

8.35 am

The *Sunday Telegraph* reports that I've written a 300,000-word novel entitled *Sons of Fortune* during the *short* time I've been in prison. It might seem short to them, but it's been 158 days for me.

I actually wrote the first three drafts of the novel before my conviction. I had planned to drive from Boston (Connecticut) to Newhaven via Hartford, where the book is set, and research the final points before Mr Justice Potts intervened. I ended up spending the month of August not in the US, but in Belmarsh writing the first diary.

9.00 am

Five inmates' names are called over the tannoy. They are told to report to the doctor, which means they've been charged and will later be up in front of the governor for adjudication: two for smoking cannabis, one for being drunk, one for secreting £25 in a cigarette tin, and finally Hal, who you will recall thumbed a lift back from Boston, while in possession of a bottle of vodka, a bottle of rum and a six-pack of Fosters. Hal did point out to me that it's a twelve-mile round trip to Boston and back to NSC, and it was 2 degrees below zero. I don't think the governor will consider these to be mitigating circumstances!

Hal loses all privileges, and has twenty-one days added to his sentence.

11.00 am

The governor, Mr Lewis, who has only a few days to go before retirement, pops into the hospital to check on the end of year audit, or was it just to enjoy a cup of coffee with Linda and a cigar during his morning break? As he's leaving, I ask him to tell me a story.

'What about my memoirs?' he protests, but then recounts an anecdote from his time as governor of Oxford Prison: two brothers were charged with a burglary, but the elder did not feel his younger brother would be able to cope with a spell in jail, so he took the rap and was sentenced to six months. As it turned out, the younger brother couldn't cope with being 'on the out' without his elder brother, so he stole a ladder, climbed over the prison wall and broke *into* jail. No one was any the wiser until roll-call that night, when the duty officer reported that they had one more prisoner than was on the manifest. The younger brother was arrested and charged with breaking into a prison. He got three months, and ended up sharing a cell with his brother.

Mr Lewis went on to tell me about two prisoners who escaped from Oxford Crown Court while handcuffed to each other. They ran down the street pursued by the police, but when they came to a zebra crossing, one decided to cross the road while the other kept on going. The handcuffs that bound them together collided with the Belisha beacon at full speed, and they swung round and knocked each other out.

DAY 159   CHRISTMAS EVE

Today is a nightmare for security. First there are the truly stupid inmates who abscond sometime during the morning and then return to the prison on Boxing Day evening. If they are also drunk, they are allowed to sleep it off, with twenty-eight days added to their sentence. Second are the group who slip out to Boston and arrive back with provisions and food. As long as they remain in their rooms and cause no trouble, the officers turn a blind eye. Should they cause any trouble, they also get twenty-eight days. This is known as 'Nelson time', and occurs only at Christmas.

It must seem madness to you, but when you have 211 inmates and only 5 officers on duty, it's no more than common sense. Why aren't there more officers on duty? Because the service is understaffed and underpaid. The average prison officer is paid £17,000 a year, and this year's pay rise was 1.8 per cent. Why not send the offenders back to a closed prison? Because they are all already overcrowded (67,500 in Britain) and if you did, the D-cats would be empty. Then cut down on D-cats? If you did that, you would never rehabilitate anyone. Prisoners in a D-cat used to be released at 8 am (with the exception of lifers) on Christmas Eve and had to return to prison before 8 pm on Boxing Day. But Michael Howard put a stop to that when he became Home Secretary. This little break was more for the staff than the prisoners.

7.30 am

Dave (murder) is among the walking wounded, and comes to surgery doubled up with stomach cramps. Sister gives him painkillers that contain certain opiates. She then has to make out a separate form, which I take across to security because if Dave were to have an MDT he would show up positive. Sister is especially vigilant in these cases, looking out for those prisoners who fake the pain in order to get the drugs, especially when they know they're about to be tested for heroin. In Dave's case, there is no doubt that he's in real pain, and any case, he's been a model prisoner since the day he arrived at NSC. He's desperate to impress the parole board and be released as soon as possible. He's already served twenty-one years, and his wife says she can't wait much longer.

9.00 am

Despite its being Christmas Eve, one inmate will not be able to avoid a nicking because he has pushed his luck a little too far. During an MDT, he attempted to exchange a tube of someone else's urine for his while he was in the loo. It turns out that he got this drug-free sample from another prisoner in exchange for a Mars Bar.

11.00 am

Sue from accounts drops into the hospital to tell me that my private money has run out, and that's why my canteen account only showed £1.20 in credit. Had she let me know a week ago, I could have asked Mary to top it up. However, Sue explains that she is not allowed to let a prisoner know that his money is running low, and can only inform him if he asks directly for his account balance. The reason is that most inmates are penniless, and don't need to be continually reminded of that fact. Fair enough.

8.00 pm

Doug returns from the canteen laden with goodies, and tells me that an inmate has just been nicked for ordering a taxi to take him on a round trip to Boston. The cab company phoned the prison, so two officers were waiting when the inmate returned. He was caught in possession of forty-eight cans of lager and one bottle each of whisky, vodka and brandy. He also had six packets of fish and chips, a melon, a carton of strawberries, a pot of cream and a box of jellied eels.

The prisoner begged to be placed in the segregation cell overnight in case the inmates who had lost their 'Christmas cheer' thought he'd sold the goodies to someone else. The duty officer duly obliged, but he'll still be up in front of the governor on Boxing Day.

DAY 160   CHRISTMAS DAY

Christmas Day for those who are incarcerated can be summed up in one word: dreadful. I have learned during the last 159 days as a prisoner how perverse reality is.

I go to work today, as every other day, and am grateful for something to do. At the seven-thirty surgery, only six prisoners report for sick parade; you have to be really ill to get up at 7.30 am on Christmas morning and troop across to the hospital when the temperature on the east coast is minus two degrees.

At eight-fifteen I go to breakfast, and even though it's eggs, bacon and sausage served by the officers (Mr Hocking, Mr Camplin, Mr Baker and Mr Gough), only around forty of the two hundred inmates bother to turn up.

On returning to the hospital, Linda and I unload bags of food from her car so I can hold a tea party for my friends this afternoon. She also gives me a present, which is wrapped in Christmas paper. I open it very slowly, trying to anticipate what it might be. Inside a neat little box is a china mug, with a black cat grinning at me. Now I have my own mug, and will no longer have to decide between a Campbell's Soup giveaway and a plain white object with a chip when I have my morning Bovril.

10.00 am

Linda leaves me in charge of the hospital while she attends the governor's Christmas party. Frankly, if over half the prisoners weren't still in bed asleep, I could arrange for them all to abscond. When the tabloids claim I have privileges that the other prisoners do not have, in one respect they are right; I am lucky to be able to carry on with the job I do on the outside. While everyone else tries to kill time, I settle down to write for a couple of hours.

12 noon

Lunch is excellent, and once again served by the officers, and shared with a half dozen old-age pensioners from the local village; tomato soup, followed by turkey, chipolatas, roast potatoes and stuffing, with as much gravy as will go on the plate. I don't allow myself the Christmas pudding – several officers have kindly commented on the fact that I'm putting on weight (nine pounds in nine weeks).

After lunch I walk over to the south block and phone Mary and the boys. All things considered they sound pretty cheerful, but I can't hide the fact that I miss them. My wife is fifty-seven, my boys twenty-nine and twenty-seven, and today I'm surrounded by men sitting in their rooms staring at photographs of young children anywhere from six months to fifteen years old. Yes, they deserve to be incarcerated if they committed a crime, but we should remember it is Christmas Day, and it's not their families who are guilty.

As I walk back through the block, I notice that those not in the TV room or on the phone are just lying on their beds willing the day to pass. I have so much food in my fridge that I invite a dozen inmates over to join me in the hospital.

They all turn up, without exception. We watch *The Great Escape* (somewhat ironic) and enjoy Linda's feast – pork pies, crisps, sausage rolls, shortbread biscuits, KitKats and, most popular of all with my fellow inmates, a chunk of my Cheddar cheese. This is accompanied not by Krug, but a choice of lemonade, Evian water, tea, coffee or Ribena.

They laugh, they chat, they watch the film, and when they leave, David (fraud, schoolmaster) pays me a compliment I have never received at any of my champagne and shepherd's pie parties. 'Thank you for getting rid of the afternoon so pleasantly.'

DAY 161   BOXING DAY

7.30 am

For those prisoners who do not return to work, Boxing Day is almost worse than Christmas Day. Very few inmates attend surgery this morning, and certainly none of them have any illness worth reporting.

8.15 am

Over breakfast, I learn another terrible consequence of the drug culture in prisons. Jim (antiques only), the gym orderly, tells me that some inmates who are addicted to heroin often die within a few months of leaving prison. The reason? The heroin they take in jail is always weaker because the dealers add other substances such as caster sugar, talc or flour. So when they are released, they are immediately exposed to a purer substance, which the body can no longer tolerate. Result? They end up dying of an overdose.

11.00 am

The governor drops in to see Linda, and gives me a Christmas present and a birthday present for Mary, neither of which he's allowed to do, as it could compromise him should I ever come up in front of him on report. However, as it's only a few days before he retires, I suppose he feels this is unlikely.

It turns out that the governor is a collector of farthings, and he gives Mary a farthing dated 1944 and I receive one dated 1940 – our respective years of birth. I am touched. He also brings in three volumes of *The World's Greatest Paintings: Selected Masterpieces*, published in 1934 and edited by T. Leman Hare, for me to read over Christmas. He understands what turns me on.

The three volumes are fascinating at several levels, not least because of the one hundred pictures, almost all of them would be in an equivalent compilation circa 2002. The paintings include da Vinci's *Mona Lisa*, Bellini's *Portrait of the Doge Lorendano*, Rembrandt's *Mother*, Landseer's *Shoeing the Bay Mare* (wonderful) and Yeames' *When Did You Last See Your Father?* However, in this 1934 volume, there is no mention of the Impressionists; no examples of Monet, Manet, Van Gogh or even Cézanne. Velasquez is described as the greatest Spanish painter of all time, with Murillo in second place. I wonder if Professor Hare had even heard of Picasso in 1934, and where he would place him in the lexicon of Spanish artists in 2002.

There are only two artists I have never come across before: John MacWhiter and Millet – not Jean-Francois Millet, but an American, Francis David Millet. 'On the out' I visit Tate Britain regularly – I live opposite, on the other side of the river – but I don't remember seeing either MacWhiter's *June in the Austrian Tyrol* (magnificent), or Millet's *Between Two Fires*. I hope Sir Nicholas Serota has them on display, because Tate Britain will be among the first places I visit once I'm released.

In his foreword, Professor Hare writes something that, in my opinion, is even more relevant today than it was in 1934:

There is so much nonsense spoken and written about art today that the average man is, naturally, inclined to be shy of the whole subject, and suspicious of those who practise the Arts. He thinks, if this mass of contradiction and confusing jargon is the result of the love of Art, he had better do without Art altogether. There is no mystery about Art, but there is mystification without end, evolved by certain critics who love to pose as superior persons. Such writers put forward the theory that the enjoyment of fine arts is reserved for a select and exclusive minority, meaning of course, themselves and their disciples. No greater error could be propounded than this, which is a comparatively modern fallacy and one which is so dangerous that if persisted, it must in time bring into contempt everything and everyone connected with Art.

1934.
2002. No comment.

1.00 pm

Linda shuts up shop for the day and goes home for a well-earned rest. She has been on duty for the past nineteen days without a break.

9.00 pm

I confess that, by prison standards, I am in heaven. But I feel I ought to let you know I'm still desperate to get back to earth.

DAY 162   THURSDAY 27 DECEMBER 2001

10.00 am

Governor Lewis has received a call from Sir Brian Mawhinney, and although he can't divulge any details, he suspects the Shadow Home Secretary will be in touch with Mary who in turn will brief me. Mystery.

The governor sips his tea. 'As I'm leaving shortly, I'm going to tell you a story about a present member of staff who must remain anonymous. The officer concerned had a day off, and in the evening he and his wife went to their local for a drink. When they left the pub later, the officer saw a man trying to get his car started, but it sounded as if the battery was flat. The officer asked if he could help by giving a push. The driver said thank you and the officer pushed him out of the car park. The ignition caught, and the driver gave a toot of thanks as he disappeared over the horizon.

When the officer concerned returned to work the following morning, he learned that one of the inmates had absconded. The prisoner had even managed to steal a car from a local pub with the help of an obliging member of the public, who had given him a push start.'

'It can't be true,' I protest. 'Surely he recognized the prisoner?' (To be fair, there are over two hundred inmates at NSC and the turnover is often twenty to thirty a week.)

'You'd think so,' replied the governor, 'especially as the inmate was the only West Indian on the camp.'* He laughs. 'The officer concerned might have even lived it down if it weren't for the fact that neither the prisoner nor the stolen car has been seen since.'

---

* In Belmarsh, around 70 per cent of the inmates were black, in Wayland 30 per cent, and currently at NSC we have four black prisoners out of 207. I'm not sure what this proves: possibly there might be more black prisoners involved in violent crime than in fraud.

DAY 163   FRIDAY 28 DECEMBER 2001

11.07 am

Whenever there's a serious injury in prison, the immediate question always asked is, 'Was another prisoner involved?' So when Linda and I are called over to the north block to check on an inmate who is thought to have broken his leg after slipping on the floor, Linda's first question is, 'Who pushed him?'

By the time we arrive the duty officers, Mr Hughes and Mr Jones, are present, and they are satisfied Ron has had a genuine accident. However, there are several touches of irony in this particular case. The inmate involved is serving a six-week sentence, and is due to be released next Thursday. Last year he broke his left leg in a motorbike accident. This time he has managed to break his right leg, and several of the pins in his left have been dislodged. Linda confirms that an officer must accompany him to hospital; although how he'd abscond with two broken legs is beyond me – and why would he want to try, six days before he's due to be released? However, regulations are regulations.

Normally you can't be released from prison unless you have been given a clean bill of health by the duty doctor, and in Ron's case it will be at least six weeks before the plaster comes off.

'We'll let him go,' Linda says, 'but only if a family member picks him up next Thursday and also agrees to take responsibility for him.'

'And if no one does?' I ask.

'Then he'll stay here until he's fully recovered.'

DAY 164   SATURDAY 29 DECEMBER 2001

2.00 pm

Mary, William and James visit me. We talk mainly of the legal issues surrounding my trial and appeal. The topic of conversation then turns to Baroness Nicholson. Mary has written to her asking for an apology.

Mary is off to Kenya with her sister Janet on Monday, a journey she has wanted to make for some years because of her love of cats, whatever their size.

What happened to our ninety minutes together?

6.00 pm

I'm in my final writing session for the day when there's a knock on the door. This usually means that a prisoner has a headache and needs some paracetamol, which I am allowed to dispense as long as the inmate has a note from the duty officer. If it's something more serious, then his unit officer has to be consulted. I open my door and smile up at an inmate, who looks pretty healthy to me.

'Have you got any condoms, Jeff?' he asks.

'No,' I tell him, aware that Linda keeps a supply for prisoners going on weekend leave, or just about to be released, but even then she only gives them out very sparingly. 'If you report to surgery at seven-thirty tomorrow morning, Linda will . . .'

'It'll be too late by then,' he says. I look surprised. 'It's just that my sister visited me this afternoon and she hasn't got enough money to get home. A few of the lads are willing to pay her ten quid for a blow job, which usually ends up with them going the whole way and ending up paying twenty.'

All of which begs several questions when possession of money in a prison is illegal. Is this an indoor or outdoor activity (it's minus two degrees outside) and is she really his sister?

'Sorry, I can't help,' is my only response, and after he has disappeared into the night. I try hard to concentrate on my writing.

DAY 165   SUNDAY 30 DECEMBER 2001

7.30 am

The security officer on duty today enjoys his job, but never feels fulfilled until he's put someone on a charge. Mr Vessey rushes into surgery to see sister. During the night he's found fourteen empty bottles of vodka at the bottom of the skip by the entrance to the prison. A whispered conversation ensues, not that it takes a lot of imagination to realize that he's asking if any inmates checked into surgery this morning 'a little worse for wear'. Moments later, he rushes off to the south block.

In fact, very few inmates were on sick parade this morning as most of them are sleeping in, or sleeping it off, and the ones that appeared were genuinely ill. He will be disappointed.

10.00 am

During the morning we have visits from Mr Lewis and Mr Berlyn, the new deputy governor, who join Linda for coffee. Mr Hocking is the next to arrive, with the news that five inmates have failed the breathalyser test. Two of them are CSV workers, who could lose all their privileges. For example, they could be put back to work on the farm for the rest of their sentence.* Mr Hocking tells me he doubts if the punishment will be that draconian, but the warning will be clear for the future.

Why would anyone risk losing so much for a couple of vodkas?

12 noon

Linda leaves at midday so I spend four of the next six hours editing *Belmarsh*, volume one of these diaries.

7.00 pm

During the evening I read *Here is New York* by E. B. White, which Will gave me for Christmas. One paragraph towards the end of the essay is eerily prophetic.

> The subtlest change in New York is something people don't speak much about, but that is in everyone's mind. The city, for the first time in its long history, is destructible. A single flight of planes, no bigger than a wedge of geese, can quickly end this island fantasy, burn the towers, crumble the bridges, turn the underground passages into lethal chambers, cremate the millions. The intimation of mortality is part of New York now; in the sound of jets overhead, in the black headlines of the latest edition.

This was written in 1949, and the author died in 1985.

---

* An inmate who completes a quarter of his sentence and proves to be a model prisoner is eligible for outside work. First he must complete two town visits without incident. The next step is to apply for Community Service Volunteers work (CSV), perhaps in an old people's home or an Oxfam shop. Once he's completed a month of CSV without incident, he can move on to a wage-earning job, making perhaps £200–£250 a week. This gives a prisoner the chance to send money back to his wife or partner, and to build up some savings to fall back on once released.

DAY 166 — NEW YEAR'S EVE 2001

11.00 am

Four new prisoners arrive at the hospital from Nottingham, looking lost and a little disorientated. I'm surprised that Group 4 has deposited them before lunch as they don't usually arrive until around four in the afternoon.

'It's New Year's Eve,' explains Linda. 'They'll all want to be home by four.'

12 noon

Linda checks her books and tells me that NSC had a turnover of just over a thousand prisoners during 2001, so after eleven weeks, I'm already something of an old lag.

6.00 pm

Mary and I usually invite eight guest to dinner at the Old Vicarage on New Year's Eve. This year I'll have to settle for a KitKat, a glass of Ribena and hope that Doug and Clive are able to join me.

DAY 167   NEW YEAR'S DAY 2002

6.00 am

The camp is silent, so I begin to go over volume one of these diaries. Reading through those early days when I was so distressed, I can't believe how much I have made myself forget. And this has become even more pronounced since my appointment as hospital orderly, where I have everything except freedom and the daily company of my wife, family and friends; a punishment in itself, but not purgatory and certainly not hell.

10.00 am

Mr New drops into the hospital to say his farewells. He leaves NSC tonight and will, on 8 January, change his uniform for a suit, when he becomes a governor at Norwich Prison. He's taught me a great deal about good and evil during the past three months.

6.00 pm

I miss my wife, I miss my family and I miss my friends. The biggest enemy I have to contend with is boredom, and it's a killer.

For many prisoners, it's the time when they first experiment with drugs. To begin with, drugs are offered by the dealers for nothing, and when they demand more, in exchange for a phonecard and an ounce of tobacco or cash, and finally, when they're hooked, they'll give anything for a fix – including their life.

Tonight, the Lincolnshire constabulary informed sister that a former prisoner called Cole, who left NSC six weeks ago, has been found under a hedge in a quiet country lane.

He died from an overdose.

Happy New Year.

DAY 168   WEDNESDAY 2 JANUARY 2002

6.00 am

I continue to edit *A Prison Diary Volume One – Belmarsh: Hell.*

10.00 am

Mr Berlyn drops in to tell me that he already has plans for my CSV work should my sentence be reduced, and this even before the date of my appeal is known. He wants me to work in an old-age pensioners' home, as it will be out of sight of the press. He also feels I would benefit from the experience. I had hoped to work in the Red Cross shop in Boston, but Mr Berlyn has discounted that option after Maria brought in, without permission, some books for me to sign before Christmas to raise money for their Afghanistan appeal. The Rev Derek Johnson, the prison chaplain, has been to see him to plead their case, explaining that he is in the forgiveness and rehabilitation business. Mr Berlyn's immediate retort was, 'I'm in the punishment and retribution business.' He must have meant of prisoners; I can't believe he wishes to punish a hard-working, decent woman trying to run a Red Cross shop.

DAY 168

4.50 pm

Linda looks very tired. She's worked twenty-one of the last twenty-four days. She tells me that she's going to apply for a job in Boston. My only selfish thought is that I hope she doesn't leave before I do.

8.00 pm

Doug turns up at the hospital for his nightly bath and to watch television. He's now settled into his job as a driver, which keeps him out of the prison between the hours of 8 am and 7 pm. I wonder if, for prisoners like Doug, it wouldn't be better to rethink the tagging system, so he could give up his bed for a more worthy candidate.

DAY 169   THURSDAY 3 JANUARY 2002

7.30 am

Morning surgery is packed with inmates who want to sign up for acupuncture. You must report to hospital between 7.30 and 8 am in order to be booked in for an eleven o'clock appointment. Linda and Gail are both fully qualified, and 'on the out' acupuncture could cost up to £40 a session. To an inmate, it's free of charge, as are all prescriptions.

The purpose of acupuncture in prison is twofold: to release stress, and to wean you off smoking. Linda and Gail have had several worthwhile results in the past. One inmate has dropped from sixty cigarettes a day to three after only a month on the course. Other prisoners, who are suffering from stress, rely on it, and any prisoner who turns up for a second session can be described as serious.

However, back to the present. Eight inmates suspiciously arrive in a group, and sign up for the eleven o'clock session. They all by coincidence reside in the south block and work on the farm, which means that they'll miss most of the morning's work and still be fully paid.

At eight o'clock Linda calls Mr Donnelly on the farm to let him know that the morning's acupuncture session is so oversubscribed (two regular applicants, one from education and one unemployed) so she'll take the eight from the farm at four o'clock this afternoon. This means that they'll have to complete their day's work before reporting to the hospital. It will be interesting to see how many of them turn up.

9.00 am

Young Ron (both legs broken) hobbles in to see the doctor. He's on the paper chase and has to be cleared as fit and free of any problems before he can be released at 8 am tomorrow. After the hospital, he still has to visit the gym, stores, SMU, education, unit office and reception. How will they go about signing out a man with two broken legs as fit to face the world? Linda comes to the rescue, phones each department and then signs on their behalf. Problem solved.

9.15 am

When Dr Walling has finished ministering to his patients, he joins me in the ward. We discuss the drug problem in Boston, sleepy Boston, (population of around 54,000).

Recently Dr Walling's car was broken into. All the usual things were stolen – radio, tapes, briefcase – but he was devastated by the loss of a box of photographic slides that he has built up over a period of thirty years. Because he hadn't duplicated them, they were irreplaceable, and the theft took place only days before he was due to deliver a series of lectures in America. Assuming that it was a drug-related theft (cash needed for a quick fix), Dr Walling visited the houses of Boston's three established drug barons. He left a note saying that he needed the slides urgently and would pay a reward of £100 if they were returned.

The slides turned up the following day.

The true significance of this tale is that a leading doctor knows who the town's drug barons are, and yet the police seem powerless to put such men behind bars. Dr Walling explains that it's the old problem of 'Mr Big' never getting his hands dirty. He arranges for the drugs to be smuggled into the country before being sold to a dealer. Mr Big also employs runners to distribute the drugs, free of charge, mainly to children as they leave school unaccompanied, so that long before they reach university or take a job, they're hooked. And that, I repeat, is in Boston, not Chelsea or Brixton.

What will Britain be like in ten years' time, twenty years, thirty, if the police estimate that 40 per cent of all crime *today* is drug-related?

4.00 pm

No one from the farm turns up for acupuncture.

7.37 pm

Carl rushes in, breathless, to say a prisoner has collapsed on the south block. Linda went home two hours ago, so I run out of the hospital, to find Mr Belford and Mr Harman a few yards ahead of me.

When we arrive at the prisoner's door, we find the inmate gasping for breath. I recognize him immediately from his visit to Dr Walling this morning. I feel helpless as he lies doubled-up, clutching his stomach, but fortunately an ambulance arrives within minutes. A paramedic places a mask over the inmate's face, and then asks him some routine questions, all of which I am able to answer on his behalf – name of doctor, last visit to surgery, nature of complaint and medication given. I'm also able to tell them his blood pressure, 145/78. They rush him to the Pilgrim Hospital, and as he failed his recent risk assessment, Mr Harman has to travel with him.

As Mr Harman is now off the manifest, we are probably down to five officers on duty tonight, to watch over 211 prisoners.

DAY 170   FRIDAY 4 JANUARY 2002

5.00 am

I finish editing *Belmarsh*, and post it back to my publishers.

8.00 am

I leave the hospital to carry out my morning rounds. This has three purposes: first, to let each department head know which inmates are off work, second, in case of a fire, to identify who is where, and third, if someone fails to show up for roll-call, to check if they've absconded.

En route to the farm I bump into Blossom, who had one of the pigs named after him. (See photo page 193.) Blossom is a traveller, or a gipsy as we used to describe them before it became politically incorrect. Blossom tells me that he's just dug a lamb out of the ice. It seems it got its hindquarters stuck in some mud which froze overnight, so the poor animal couldn't move.

'You've saved the animal's life,' I tell Blossom.

'No,' he says, 'he's going to be slaughtered today, so he'll soon be on the menu as frozen cutlets.'

DAY 170

12 noon

I pick up my post from the south block. Although most of the messages continue along the same theme, one, sent from a Frank and Lurline in Wynnum, Australia is worthy of a mention, if only because of the envelope. It was addressed thus:

> Lord Jeffrey Archer
> Jailed for telling a fib
> Somewhere in England.

It is dated Christmas Day, and has taken only nine days to reach me in deepest Lincolnshire.

2.30 pm

The main administration block has been sealed off. Gail tells me that she can't get into the building to carry out any paperwork and she doesn't know why. This is only interesting because it's an area that is off-limits to inmates.

Over the past few months, money and valuables have gone missing. Mr Berlyn is determined to catch the culprit. It turns out to be a fruitless exercise, because, despite a thorough search, the £20 that was stolen from someone's purse doesn't material- ize. Mr Hocking, the security officer in charge of the operation, found the whole exercise distasteful as it involved investigating his colleagues. I have a feeling he knows who the guilty party is, but certainly isn't going to tell me. My deep throat, a prisoner of long standing, tells me the name of the suspect. For those readers with the mind of a detective, she doesn't get a mention in this diary.

DAY 171   SATURDAY 5 JANUARY 2002

7.30 am

A prisoner from the south block checks into surgery with a groin injury. Linda is sufficiently worried about his condition to have him taken to the local hospital without delay. Meanwhile she dresses his wounds and gives him some painkillers. He never once says please or thank you. This attitude would be true of over half the inmates, and nearer 70 per cent of those under thirty. Although it's a generalization, I have become aware that those without manners are also the work shy amongst the prison population.

2.30 pm

Among the thousands of letters I've received since I've been incarcerated, several are from charities that continue to ask for donations, signed books and memorabilia, and occasionally for a doodle, drawing, poem or even a painting. Despite my life-long love of art, the good Lord decided to place a pen in my hand, not a paintbrush. But I found an alternative when I came across Darren, an education orderly. Darren has already designed several imaginative posters and signs for the hospital. The latest charity request is that I should produce a sunflower, *in any medium*. I came up with an idea which Darren produces. (See overleaf.)

DAY 172   SUNDAY 6 JANUARY 2002

8.00 am

As it's Twelfth Night, I spend a couple of hours taking down my Christmas cards (1,712), and packing them up so I can hand them over to Will when he visits me this afternoon.

10.30 am

Linda tells me that a nurse at the Pilgrim Hospital phoned urgently about the prisoner with the groin injury. An officer is dispatched immediately to keep an eye on him until he's safely back in his room at NSC. Not a bad idea to get yourself transferred to the local hospital if you plan to escape, but it's not that bright to ask a nurse where the exits are.

2.00 pm

Will visits me, accompanied by my Christmas present. Neither he nor James have heard a word from their mother since she landed in Kenya. Will reassures me by suggesting she's either having a good time, or she's been eaten by a lion.

DAY 172

8.00 pm

Doug arrives at the hospital with the news that five prisoners who were out on a town leave have failed to return. As none of them are murderers, only the local police will be alerted. If a murderer absconds, the Home Office has to brief the national press within twenty-four hours.

North Sea Camp has been told to increase its bed space. Now that almost every room has a TV set, the large television rooms can be converted into three dormitories, giving the prison another thirteen beds. I don't think this will go a long way to solving the problem of overcrowding in prisons.

11.00 am

When Mr Berlyn drops into the hospital, Linda tells him that she's applying for a job at the coroner's office in Boston. He assures me later that he doesn't believe she'll ever leave. He seems surprised, and frowns when I tell him that she's already completed an application form.

He then reveals that, of the five prisoners who failed to check back in by seven the previous evening, two turned up late and will be in front of the governor this morning, two were caught drunk in an amusement arcade in Skegness and have already been shipped out to Lincoln, where they'll complete their sentence with a further twenty-eight days added, and one is still on the run.

'It can't be worth it,' I declare when discussing the absconders with Jim (antiques only) over lunch.

'It may not be worth it for you, Jeffrey, but we don't know their domestic situation. Has the wife run away with his best mate? Are the children OK? Are they all being turfed out of their home? Are they...'

I agree with Jim. I can't begin to imagine such problems.

DAY 174   TUESDAY 8 JANUARY 2002

10.00 am

This statement is publicly displayed in every prison in England, and I must admit that I have never witnessed an officer showing any racial prejudice at any time. On the contrary, I have witnessed several prisoners play the race card to their advantage.

'You're only saying that because I'm black...'

'You're picking on me because I'm a Muslim...'

Unfortunately, I've not seen a black or Asian officer at either Wayland or North Sea Camp, otherwise I might have tried, 'You're only picking on me because I'm white...'

Can you name one country on earth that has a race relations

_____
* Interesting grammatical error.

policy to protect the whites? Certainly not Zimbabwe, which is in the headlines again today. I mention this only because a circular was sent to all departments today, which clearly shows how seriously the Prison Service takes minority rights.

12 noon

Mr Belford drops into the hospital and reports a conversation he heard between two elderly ladies standing at a bus stop in Boston:

First lady: 'Did you see Jeffrey Archer in the pub last night?'
Second lady: 'No, I thought he was in jail.'
First lady: 'No, he's down at our local almost every night, drinking pint after pint, before he's driven back to the prison by his chauffeur in a Rolls Royce.'
Second lady: 'It's a disgrace.'

The officer pointed out to the ladies that I have never once left the NSC since the day I arrived, and I don't drink.

'That's what you think,' came back the immediate reply.

DAY 175   WEDNESDAY 9 JANUARY 2002

5.14 am

I wake and consider the future.

Everything rests on the result of my appeal. I currently have a four-year sentence. In present circumstances, assuming I remain a model prisoner, I'll serve two, subject to my parole board report being positive, which means I will be released on 19 July 2003. However, I am appealing against sentence and conviction, and if my conviction is overturned, then I'll be released the same day. If not, all will depend on my sentence being reduced. If the three appeal judges were to lower my sentence from four years to three, I would no longer be subject to the parole board, and would be eligible for automatic release in eighteen months. If my record remains unblemished, I will be released on a tag two months before that, after sixteen months – on 17 November 2002. Ten months' time. If the appeal court judges reduce my sentence to two years, I will be released on 17 May, which is only another four months. If my sentence is reduced to the common length for perjury, i.e. eighteen months, I will be released on 17 March – in six weeks' time.

Perhaps now you can understand why I am so anxious about my appeal, and wait daily to hear from the courts when I will appear before them.

DAY 175

10.00 am

A trainee nurse joins us. Simon will spend three weeks at NSC on secondment from the Pilgrim Hospital. He will quickly discover that prisoners are treated far better than the general public. At seven, you can pick up your paracetamol, aspirins, lozenges, mouthwash and prescribed medication. At nine, you can see the doctor, and you never have to wait for more than twenty minutes. At eleven, if you are stressed or want to give up smoking or come off drugs, you can attend an acupuncture course. At twelve, you can come back and get some more medication. At two-thirty you can attend a talk on giving up smoking; nicotine patches are handed out when the talk is over. At four-thirty you can come back for more medication. After 5 pm, the orderly can supply aspirin or paracetamol to any prisoner who has a slip from an officer. If you are seriously ill, an ambulance will have you tucked up in the Pilgrim Hospital within the hour.

In any one day, a determined prisoner can spend hundreds of pounds of taxpayers' money, whereas in truth, I doubt if 10 per cent of them would visit a doctor 'on the out' and certainly wouldn't go to a chemist if it meant parting with a penny of their own cash. So what, our new intern will learn is that if you are ill, it's better to be in prison than an infirm old-age pensioner or a sick child.

DAY 176   THURSDAY 10 JANUARY 2002

1.15 pm

Although the fire alarm is tested every day at one o'clock, today it sounds for a second time at one-fifteen. Security are carrying out a full-scale fire drill.

All staff, prison officers and inmates have to report to the farmyard, where we line up in separate pens. I go to the one marked hospital, and join Linda, Gail and Simon. On my left is north block one, on my right the lifers' unit – a score of murderers gathered together.

Everyone from the governor to the most recently arrived inmate is on parade. We wait to be checked off by Mr Hocking, the senior security officer. It's the first time I've seen the whole community in one place, and it highlights how disproportionate the numbers of staff are to prisoners. This is fine in a D-cat where everything is based on trust, but would be impossible in closed conditions. If you had a fire drill in an A- or B-cat, you could only hope to carry it out spur by spur, in a C-cat perhaps block by block, unless you wanted a riot on your hands or a mass escape.

DAY 176

1.45 pm

Two hundred and eleven prisoners, and thirty-eight staff (including clerical) return to work.

8.00 pm

I watch *Raiders of the Lost Ark*. The last time I saw this film was with my two sons – Will was then nine and James seven. It was produced by one of my oldest friends, Frank Marshall.*

---

* Frank flew from LA to London to appear in my trial to deny a statement by Angie Peppiatt that I had been in Rome with a mistress when in fact I had been with Frank attending the World Athletics Championships. Not that I think Mr Justice Potts gave a damn, as by then he had already made up his mind that I was guilty.

6.03 am

I'd like to bring you up to date on a couple of matters you may wish to have resolved.

Six prisoners have absconded in the past ten days, and I have already accounted for five of them. But not McGeekin. McGeekin had a town visit, which allowed him to leave the prison at eight in the morning, as long as he reported back to the gate by seven the same night. He did not return, so the matter was placed in police hands. 'He's already back in custody,' the gate officer was informed by the local desk sergeant. He'd reported to his nearest police station and told them he wanted to be sent back to HMP Wayland in Norfolk, rather than return to North Sea Camp.

It's not uncommon for an inmate to want to return to the more regulated life of a closed prison. Some will even tell you they feel safer with a wall around them. Lifers in particular often find the regime of an open prison impossible to come to terms with. After fifteen years of being banged up, often for twenty-two hours a day, they just can't handle so much freedom. Within hours of arriving, they will apply to be sent back, but are told to give it a month, and if they then still feel the same way, to put in a transfer application.

Frankly they'd have to drag me back to Wayland and I'd abscond rather than return to Belmarsh.

DAY 178   SATURDAY 12 JANUARY 2002

10.00 am

The hospital bath plug has been stolen which is a bit of a mystery, because it's the only bath in the prison available to inmates, so the plug can't be of much use to anyone else. However, I have a reserve one, which makes me king, because I am now 'controller of the bath plug'. I will still have to make an application for a new one, which will mean filling in three forms and probably waiting three months.

2.00 pm

The camp is playing football against the local league leaders. When our team runs out onto the pitch, I hardly recognize any of them. Mr Masters, gym officer and coach, points out that the rapid turnover of inmates has meant he's put fifty-four players on the pitch since the opening match of the season. That's something even Man United couldn't handle. Added to this is the fact that our star goalkeeper, Bell, has been suspended for one match after using foul and abusive language when the referee awarded a penalty to the opposition. He was a little unlucky that an FA official was assessing the referee that afternoon, and therefore the ref couldn't pretend not to have heard Bell. Indeed they could have heard, 'Get some glasses, you fuckin' muppet,' in the centre of Boston.

Our reserve goalkeeper is Carl (fraud), the SMU orderly who took over from me and comes over most evenings to watch TV in the hospital. He gamely agreed to stand in for the one fixture, while Bell watches from the sidelines.

I felt it nothing less than my duty to turn up and support the team in such dire circumstances. I left at half time, when we were trailing 7–1, just after our prison reporter, Major Willis (stabbed his wife with a kitchen knife – two years), told me that the *Boston Standard* had given him so little space to report the match that he would only be able to list the names of the scorers. I was also amused by his chivvying from the touchline: 'Well played, Harry,' 'Good tackle, David,' and 'Super shot, Reg,' as if he were a house master addressing the 3rd XI of a minor public school.

5.00 pm

I join Carl for supper, but he doesn't look too happy.

'What was the final score?' I ask.

'We had a better second half,' he offers.

'So what was the final score?' I repeat.

'15–3.'

The only man who has a big smile on his face is the suspended Bell, whose position as 'first choice goalkeeper' remains secure.

DAY 179   SUNDAY 13 JANUARY 2002

11.00 am

Once Linda has closed the surgery for the morning, I settle down to read *The Sunday Times*. The lead story is about Prince Harry, and the revelation in the *News of the World* that he's tried marijuana and has also been involved in heavy drinking, despite the fact that he's still under age. Some of us are old enough to remember the shocking revelation that Prince Charles was caught drinking cherry brandy when he was still at Gordonstoun.

2.00 pm

My visitors this week are Stephan Shakespeare, my former chief of staff for the London mayoral campaign, Robert Halfon, senior adviser to Oliver Letwin MP, the Shadow Home Secretary, and my son Will.

The general view is that IDS is doing better than expected. I warn them that if the inmates and the prison staff are anything to go by most people simply don't know who he is.

Will tells me that he won't be returning to the States until after the appeal. He also reports that Godfrey Barker has had a change of heart and is no longer willing to help and may even leave the country rather than be forced to give evidence about the dinner party conversation that took place with Mr Justice Potts. His wife Anne has said she will divorce him if he does.*

8.00 pm

A lifer has absconded. He was out on an unaccompanied town visit and didn't return for check-in by 7 pm. If he's still absent in twenty-four hours' time, the Home Office will release the name and his record to the press. When a young hooligan escapes, it rarely makes even the local paper, but the public has a right to know if a murderer is on the loose.

Doug fills me in on the background. It seems that the inmate failed an MDT (heroin) a few weeks ago and was moved out of the lifers' unit back onto the north block. The result of his latest test last week is also expected to be positive. As this will be a second offence, he would automatically be transferred back to a B-cat, and have at least another eighteen months added to his sentence. This is a man who began with a twelve-year tariff, and has already served seventeen years.

If he'd been a model prisoner, he could have been released five years ago.

---

* Mr and Mrs Barker are now separated. Mrs Barker stood down from the parole board in September 2001.

DAY 180   MONDAY 14 JANUARY 2002

9.00 am

When the doctor arrives each morning, he first signs the discharge papers of any prisoner due to be released. He then signs applications for a five-day leave, showing a clean bill of health. His next task is to see all the new prisoners who have just arrived from another jail. Finally, the doctor handles 'nickings': prisoners who have been put on a charge, and again must be passed fit both mentally and physically before punishment can be administered. Once all these inmates have been dealt with, the doctor moves onto the genuinely sick.

Today we have three 'nickings'. Two are commonplace, but the third even took the governor by surprise. The first was for swearing at an officer, and that has to be pretty extreme for the prisoner to end up in front of the governor. The second was an inmate found to have £20 in his room. The first ended up with four days added to his sentence, the second seven days, but the third . . .

All prisoners out on town leave have to report back to the gate sober before 7 pm. This particular inmate was a few minutes late and was, to quote the gate officer, legless. Out there you can be breathalysed if you're driving, in here we are when we're walking.

When charged with being drunk, the prisoner claimed that he'd swallowed half a bottle of mouthwash thirty minutes before returning to the prison. It is true that a bottle of mouthwash contains alcohol, and it will register on the breathalyser at 0.5 per cent. The trouble was that the breathalyser was showing 3.5 per cent. Next, they checked his medical records, and as the prisoner had not visited the surgery for over a month, and never requested a mouthwash, he was asked to explain why he suddenly drank half a bottle.

'Because I was giving my partner a blow job,' he replied.

When the officer recovered from this revelation, he thumbed through the rule book and came up with a winner. 'Did you sign the trust agreement for prisoners who are on a town visit?' he asked innocently.

'Yes,' came back the immediate reply.

'And who did you select as the person who would be responsible for you at all times?'

'My mother,' the prisoner replied.

'And did your mother witness the action you have just described?'

The inmate paused for a moment, pleaded guilty, and had twenty-eight days added to his sentence.

11.00 am

Linda leaves the hospital and walks across to reception, where two prisoners have just been taken from their rooms without warning, as they are to be shipped out to Lincoln (B-cat). They have both failed an MDT and came up positive for heroin.

Prisoners are never given any warning they are on the move in case they decide to abscond rather than be transferred back to closed conditions.

DAY 181   TUESDAY 15 JANUARY 2002

9.00 am

The Derby Five are on the paper chase, and each of them comes to the hospital to say goodbye. Eamon, who shared a room with me for a short time, is particularly friendly and says he hopes we will meet again. I nod.

5.00 pm

Over supper I sit next to John (murder) who makes an interesting point about Chris (murder) who is still on the run. If he's managed to escape to certain European countries (Sweden, Portugal or Italy) whose governments do not approve of our tariff system for lifers, it's possible that the authorities in that country may turn a blind eye, especially after the Home Office announced today that they did not consider Chris to be a danger to the public.

8.30 pm

I'm going over today's script when an inmate staggers into the hospital. He's sweating profusely, and badly out of breath.

I take his blood pressure, 176/109, and immediately brief the unit officer, but not until I've taken my own (130/76) to check the machine is not faulty.

Mr Downs (who replaced Mr New as PO) is on duty and I tell him that Gail has been keeping an eye on this patient for the past four days, and told me that if the monitor went over 105 again, he was to be taken straight to Pilgrim Hospital for a full check-up.

'It's not quite that easy,' explains Mr Downs. 'I've only got five officers on duty tonight, and this inmate hasn't been risk assessed, so one of us would have to accompany him.'

Mr Downs sighs, phones for a taxi, and instructs an officer to travel with the inmate to Pilgrim Hospital (cost £20).

That means tonight we have 191 prisoners being guarded by four officers – one of them a young woman who's recently joined the service.

Good night.

DAY 182   WEDNESDAY 16 JANUARY 2002

10.00 am

Martin, the inmate who lost two months for attempting to steal some prison clothes on the morning he was due to be released, has had another twenty-five days added to his sentence, this time for being caught with marijuana in his room. He was originally due to leave NSC on 14 December, and now he won't be released until 14 March. At this rate I might even get out before him.

It's not uncommon for inmates to end up serving a longer period than their original sentence. However it will take Martin a number of 'knock backs' before he can beat a prisoner in Wayland (*A Prison Diary*, Volume II) who started with a three-year sentence for possession of heroin and is still a resident of that establishment eight years later.

3.00 pm

Among the new inductees are a policeman and a man who was sentenced to five years for attempting to kill his mother-in-law. The rest are in for the usual tariff – burglary, driving offences, drugs, drugs and drugs. Still, I sense one or two stories among this lot.

7.00 pm

I have a visit from Keith (class B drugs), which is a bit of a surprise as he was on the paper chase last Monday, and should have been discharged yesterday. I can't believe he's committed another crime in the last twenty-four hours. No. It turns out that the parole board, having informed the prison that he could be released on Monday, have now told him he must wait until one or two more pieces of paper are signed. Why couldn't they tell him that last Monday rather than unnecessarily raise his hopes?

I tell Keith about a prisoner who was transferred from Leicester yesterday and is being returned to that prison today. The authorities forgot to send all his parole details. The man travelled to NSC in a sweat box, spent the night here, and now has to go back to Leicester Prison. By the way, we expect him to return to NSC next week. This bureaucratic incompetence will be paid for out of taxpayers' money.

DAY 183   THURSDAY 17 JANUARY 2002

After a month of being hospital orderly, I have my work schedule mastered.

5.00–7.00 am Write first draft of previous day's events.

7.00–7.30 am Draw curtains, make bed, put on kettle, shave, bathe and dress.

Prepare lists and make coffee for Linda – dash of milk, one sweetener.

7.30–8.00 am Surgery, usually twenty to thirty inmates who collect prescriptions or need to make an appointment to see the doctor at nine.

8.00–8.30 am Deliver slips for absentees from work to the farm, the works, stores, mess, education department, north and south blocks and the gate.

8.30–8.45 am Breakfast in the dining room.

9.00–10.30 am Doctor's surgery.

11.00 am Acupuncture, usually three or four inmates.

11.10–11.40 am Read this morning's draft of this diary.

11.50 am Wake up patients having acupuncture; Linda removes needles.

12 noon Lunch.

12.40 pm Phone Alison at the penthouse, and collect my mail from south unit office.

1.00–3.00 pm Continue second draft of yesterday's work.

3.00–4.00 pm Check in arrivals from other prisons. Give short introductory talk, then take their blood pressure and weight, and carry out diabetes test (urine).

4.30–4.50 pm Evening surgery. Those inmates who ordered prescriptions this morning can pick them up as they'll have been collected from a chemist in Boston during the afternoon.

4.50 pm Linda leaves for the day.

5.00 pm Supper.

5.30–7.00 pm Final writing session, totalling nearly six hours in all.

7.00 pm Unlock the end room for use by outside personnel, e.g. Listeners, Jehovah's Witnesses, drug and alcohol counselling sessions and prison committees.

7.10–8.00 pm Read through the day's mail, make annotated notes and post to Alison.

8.00–10.00 pm Doug and Carl join me for a coffee, to chat or watch a film on TV.

10.30 pm Read until I feel sleepy.

The hospital orderly has the longest and most irregular hours of any prisoner. It's seven days a week. On Saturday and Sunday after Linda and Gail have left I sweep the hospital ward, lobby, lavatory and bathroom before mopping throughout. (Although I can't remember when I last did any domestic chores, I find the work therapeutic. I wouldn't, however, go so far as saying I enjoy it.)

I then check my supplies, and restock the cupboards. If I'm short of anything, I make out an order form for the stores (memo pads, lavatory paper and today for a new vacuum cleaner – the old one has finally given up).

Some prisoners tell me that they would rather work in the kitchen or the officers' mess because they get more food. I'd rather be in the hospital, and have a bath and a good night's sleep.

DAY 184   FRIDAY 18 JANUARY 2002

5.26 am

The night security guard has just walked in and tells me with a smile that I can abscond. I put my pen down and ask why.

'We've got one too many on the manifest.'

'How did that happen?' I ask.

'A lad who was released yesterday arrived home and no one wanted him, so he crept back in last night and dossed down in his old room.'

'So what did you do?' I ask.

'Marched him back to the gate and threw him out for a second time.'

I feel sorry for a man who has nowhere to go, and can only wonder how long it will be before he reoffends.

8.00 am

I bump into Keith ('knowingly concerned' with a class B drug) on his way back from breakfast. He must still be waiting for his missing papers to be signed before they can release him. You might be – as I was – puzzled by what his charge means.

Keith ran a small transport company, and one of his lorries

had been fitted with spare fuel tanks. When the driver came through customs, the spare fuel tanks were found to contain 249 kilos of marijuana. Keith was sentenced to nine years.

Whenever a judge passes a sentence on drugs, there's a tariff according to the class of the drug – A, B or C. Also relevant is whether you are considered to be 'in possession of' or a supplier, and the amount involved.

Drugs' classification:

Class A heroin, ecstasy, cocaine, opiates

Class B cannabis (marijuana) (now Class C), amphetamines

Class C anabolic steroids, keratin, amyl nitrite (poppers)

Here's a rough guide to the *maximum* penalties:

Class A	possession, seven years (fine or both)	supplier, life (fine or both)
Class B	possession, five years	supplier, fourteen years
Class C	possession, two years	supplier, five years

Many of the inmates feel unjustly treated when sentences can vary so much from court to court, and as over 50 per cent of prisoners are in on drug-related charges, comparisons are made all the time. A few admit to having got off lightly, while most feel hard done by.

5.00 pm

The man who was sentenced to five years for attempting to murder his mother-in-law turns out to be another unusual case. This particular inmate hit his mother-in-law when she refused to allow him access to visit his children. She collapsed and was taken to hospital. As she didn't die, and the police didn't have proof that he intended to murder her, the charge was dropped to aggravated burglary and he was sentenced to five years. It would take a trained legal mind to understand how the second charge came about. The prisoner explains that when he went in search of his children, he entered his mother-in-law's house when she had not invited him in – and this offence is aggravated burglary.

DAY 185 SATURDAY 19 JANUARY 2002

2.00 pm

I was hoping to see Mary, Will and James today, but the authorities have decreed that I've used up all my visits for this month, and therefore can't see them until the beginning of February.

3.00 pm

This week's football match has also been cancelled, so once again I come face to face with the prisoner's biggest enemy, boredom.

DAY 186   SUNDAY 20 JANUARY 2002

10.51 am

Mr Hart (an old-fashioned socialist) visits the hospital to tell me that there's a double-page spread about me in the *News of the World*. It seems that Eamon (one of the Derby Five) is the latest former inmate to take his thirty pieces of silver and tell the world what it's like to share a room with Jeff.

I am surprised how many prisoners visit me today to tell me what they think of Eamon. Strange phrases like 'broken the code', 'not the done thing' come from men who are in for murder and GBH. After Belmarsh, Fletch, Tony, Del Boy and Billy said nothing, while Darren, Jimmy, Jules and Sketch from Wayland also kept their counsel. Here at NSC, I trust Doug, Carl, Jim, Clive and Matthew. And they would have stories to tell.

4.00 pm

I've started a prison tea club as I love to entertain whatever the circumstances. Admittedly it would have been impossible at Belmarsh or Wayland, but as I now reside in the hospital, I am even able to send out invitations. Membership is confined to those over the age of forty.

My guests are invited to attend 'Club Hospital' on Sunday between the hours of 4 pm and 6 pm. They will be served tea, coffee, biscuits and scones supplied by Linda. The current membership is around a dozen, and includes David (fraud, schoolmaster), John (fraud, accountant), John (fraud, business-man), Keith (knowingly in possession of drugs), Brian (ostrich farm and chapel organist), Doug (importing cigarettes), the Major (stabbed his wife), the Captain (theft, drummed out of the regiment), Malcolm (fraud) and Carl (fraud).

The talk is not of prison life, but what's going on in the outside world. Whether the IRA should be given rooms in Parliament, whether Bin Laden is dead or alive, the state of the NHS and the latest from the Test Match in India. All of my guests keep to the club rules. They remove their shoes and put on slippers as they enter the hospital, and no smoking or swearing is tolerated. Two of them will be leaving us next week, Keith will have served five years, and Brian nearly three. We raise a cup to them and wish them luck. Carl and David stay behind to help me with the washing-up.

DAY 187   MONDAY 21 JANUARY 2002

7.30 am

I'm becoming aware of the hospital regulars: five prisoners who turn up every morning between 7.30 and 8 am to collect their medication. I couldn't work out why these five need the same medication for something most of us would recover from in a few days. Sister has her suspicions, but if a prisoner complains of toothache, muscle sprain or arthritis, they are entitled to medications that are opiate based – for example codeine, co-codamol or dextropropoxyphene. These will show up as positive on any drugs test, and if a prisoner has been on them every day for a month, they can then claim, 'It's my medication, guv.' However, if an inmate tests positive for heroin, the hospital will take a blood sample and seek medical advice as to whether his daily medication would have registered that high. Several prisoners have discovered that such an element of doubt often works in their favour. Doug tells me that some addicts return to their rooms, flush the pills down the lavatory and then take their daily dose of heroin.

11.20 am

A lifer called Bob (twelve years, murder) is due to appear in front of the parole board next week. He's coming to the end of his tariff, and the Home Office usually recommends that the prisoner serves at least another two years before they will consider release. This decision has recently been taken out of the hands of the Home Office and passed to the parole board. Bob received a letter from the board this morning informing him he will be released next Thursday.

Try to imagine serving twelve years (think what age you were twelve years ago) and now assume that you will have to do another two years, but then you're told you will be released on Thursday.

The man is walking around in a daze, not least because he fell off a ladder yesterday and now has his ankle in a cast. What a way to start your re-entry back to Earth.

DAY 188   TUESDAY 22 JANUARY 2002

11.00 am

Andrew Pierce of *The Times* has got hold of the story that Libby
Purves will be interviewing Mary tomorrow. The BBC must have
leaked it, but I can't complain because the piece reads well, even
if Mr Pierce is under the illusion that NSC is in Cambridgeshire.
I only wish it were.

4.00 pm

Among my afternoon post is a Valentine's card, which is a bit
like getting a Christmas card in November, one proposal of
marriage, one offer of a film part (Field Marshall Haig), a request
to front a twelve-part television series and an invitation to give
an after-dinner speech in Sydney next September. Do they know
something I don't?

8.00 pm

An officer drops in from his night rounds for a coffee. He tells
me an alarming story about an event that took place at his last
prison.

It's universally accepted among prisoners that if one particular officer has got it in for you, there's nothing you can do about it. You can go through the complaints procedure, but even if you're in the right, officers will always back each other up if a colleague is in trouble. I could fill a book with such instances. I have experienced this myself at such a petty level that I have not considered the incident worth recording. On that occasion, the governor personally apologized, but still advised me not to put in a complaint.

However, back to a prisoner from the north block who did have the temerity to put in a written complaint about a particular officer. On this occasion, I can only agree with the prisoner that the officer concerned is a bully. Nevertheless, after a lengthy enquiry (everything in prison is lengthy) the officer was cleared of any misdemeanour, but that didn't stop him seeking revenge.

The inmate in question was serving a five-year sentence, and at the time he entered prison was having an affair that his wife didn't know about, and to add to the complication, the affair was with another man. The prisoner would have a visit from one of them each fortnight, while writing to both of them during the week. The rule in closed prisons is that you leave your letters unsealed in the unit office, so they can be read by the duty officer to check if you're still involved in any criminal activity, or asking for drugs to be sent in. When the prisoner left his two letters in the unit office, the officer on duty was the same man he had made a complaint about to the governor. The officer read both the love letters, and yes, you've guessed it, switched them and sealed the envelopes and with it, the fate of the prisoner.

How do I know this to be true? Because the officer involved has just told me, and is happy to tell anyone he considers a threat.

DAY 189   WEDNESDAY 23 JANUARY 2002

9.00 am

Mary is on *Midweek* with Libby Purves.

12.15 pm

I call Mary. She's off to lunch with Ken Howard RA and other artistic luminaries.

2.00 pm

My visitors today are Michael Portillo and Alan Jones (Australia's John Humphreys). I must first make my position clear on Michael's leadership bid. I would have wanted him to follow John Major as leader of the party. I would also have voted for him to follow William Hague, though I would have been torn if Malcolm Rifkind had won back his Edinburgh seat.

It is a robust visit, and it serves to remind me how much I miss the cut and thrust of Westminster, stuck as I am in the coldest and most remote corner of Lincolnshire. Michael tells us about one or two changes he would have made had he been elected leader. We need our own 'Clause 4' he suggests, which

Tony Blair so brilliantly turned into an important issue, despite it being of no real significance. Michael also feels that the party's parliamentary candidates should be selected from the centre, taking power away from the constituencies. It also worries him how few women and member of minority groups end up on the Conservative benches. He points out that at the last election, the party only added one new woman to its ranks, at a time when the Labour party have over fifty.

'Not much of an advertisement for the new, all-inclusive, modern party,' he adds.

'But how would you have handled the European issue?' ask Alan.

Michael is about to reply when that red-hot socialist (local Labour councillor) Officer Hart tells us that our time is up.

Politics is not so overburdened with talent that the Conservatives can survive without Portillo, Rifkind, Hague, Clarke and Redwood, all playing important roles, especially while we're in opposition.

When the two men left I was buzzing. An hour later I wanted to abscond.

5.00 pm

I call Mary. She has just left the chambers of Julian Malins QC, and is going to dinner with Leo Rothschild.

DAY 191   FRIDAY 25 JANUARY 2002

8.15 am

I'm called out of breakfast over the tannoy and instructed to return to the hospital immediately. Five new prisoners came in last night after Gail had gone home. She needs all the preliminaries carried out (heart rate, weight, height) before Dr Walling arrives at nine. One of the new intake announces with considerable pride that although this is his fifth offence, it's his first visit to NSC.

10.30 am

Once surgery is over, Dr Walling joins me for a coffee on the ward. 'One of them was a nightmare,' he says, as if I wasn't 'one of them'. He doesn't tell me which of the twenty patients he was referring to, and I don't enquire. However, his next sentence did take me by surprise. 'I needed to take a blood sample and couldn't find a vein in his arms or legs, so I ended up injecting his penis. He's not even half your age, Jeffrey, but you'll outlive him.'

2.00 pm

The new vacuum cleaner has arrived. This is a big event in my life.

4.00 pm

I call Mary at Grantchester. She has several pieces of news; Brian Mawhinney has received a reply to his letter to Sir John Stevens, the commissioner of the Metropolitan Police, asking why I lost my D-cat and was sent to Wayland. A report on the circumstances surrounding that decision has been requested, and will be forwarded to Brian as soon as the commissioner receives it.

Mary's next piece of news is devastating.

Back in 1999, Julian Mallins had kindly sent a note he had retained in his files (see overleaf), sent to him by Geoffrey Shaw, junior to Michael Hill for the defence in the libel trial. In the note, Shaw asks Julian for my two diaries for 1986 (an A4 diary and an Economist diary) 'in case Michael asks to look at them'. Julian passed the diaries to Shaw and Hill for inspection, and told Mary he is pretty sure that they would have gone through them thoroughly – and clearly found nothing worthy of comment in them, since they were not an issue in the libel trial. Julian added that it would be 'absolute rubbish' to suggest that the *Star*'s lawyers could not have examined these two diaries (which Angela Peppiatt had claimed in the criminal trial were almost entirely blank) in court for other entries.

Later Julian wrote to Mary: 'English law in 1986 was not an ass. If it had been Michael Hill's suggestion that the alibi evidence was all true, except for the date, neither Lord Archer in the witness box nor the judge, still less Lord Alexander nor I,

Tuesday morning

Dear Julien,

Could you have Mr. Archer's
diaries in court in case Michael
asks to look at them?

I wanted to ask you
this last night. I'm sorry I
forgot to do so!

love

[signature]

could have objected to Michael Hill going through the rest of the diary to find the same dinner date with the same companion at the same restaurant but on another date.'

None of us had known anything of Peppiatt's pocket diary for 1986, in which she noted both her own and my engagements, kept as her own property for over ten years, but produced in court as my 'true' diary for that year.

Mary also tells me that she has written to Godfrey Barker about his earlier reference to dining with Mr Justice Potts some time before the trial, when the judge might have made disparaging remarks about me. She now fears Godfrey will disappear the moment the date of the appeal is announced.

DAY 192   SATURDAY 26 JANUARY 2002

10.00 am

I weigh myself. Yuk. I'm fourteen stone two pounds. Yuk. I lost eleven pounds during my three weeks at Belmarsh, falling to twelve stone seven pounds. At Wayland I put that eleven pounds back on in ten weeks, despite being in the gym every day. At NSC the food is better, but because of my job I don't have time to go to the gym (poor excuse). On Monday I must stop eating chocolate and return to the gym. I am determined to leave the prison, whenever, around twelve stone eight pounds.

1.00 pm

I have a visit from an inmate who was sentenced to three months, which means he'll serve around five or six weeks. His crime? The theft of £120 while in a position of trust. He was a policeman. I am not going into much detail about his crime, as I'm more interested in the problems a police officer faces when being sent to jail. He's remarkably frank.

On his arrival, he was placed in the north block, and within minutes recognized a drug dealer he'd arrested in the past. He reported this to Mr Hughes, the unit officer, and was immediately placed in segregation overnight. The duty governor had to make a decision the following morning as to which one to ship out. He chose the drug dealer, as he had recently proved positive for an MDT. The policeman was put back on the north block, given a job in the kitchen and told to keep his head down. That was a week ago. So far no one else has recognized him, but he still has two weeks to serve.

Incidentally, he was originally charged with stealing £1,000, which, by the time the case came to court, had dwindled to £120. However, that was three years ago, and during that time he was suspended on full pay (a little over £60,000).

The police and Prison Service don't seem to care how much taxpayers' money they spend. If either service were a private company, they would be declared bankrupt within a year. I'm not suggesting he shouldn't have been charged, but I am saying it ought not to have cost over £100,000 and taken three years to discover if he'd stolen £120.

2.00 pm

I stand in the drizzle watching the prison football team do a little better than last week. However, one of our best strikers, Jean-Noel, is called off when Mr Masters (our coach) receives a call over the intercom to say that Jean-Noel has a young lady waiting for him in the visits hall. He runs off the pitch, quickly showers and changes, and joins his girlfriend.

At the time we are 1–0 in the lead. We lose 5–1.

5.00 pm

At tea I felt I had to chastise Jean-Noel for getting his priorities wrong and letting the team down. After all, surely the match was more important than seeing his girlfriend, and in any case, how could he forget that she was coming? He laughed, and explained that they'd had a row during the week, and she told him she wouldn't be turning up. She did, and we lost.

6.00 pm

Another pile of letters awaits me in the hospital, including a long handwritten missive from John Major, who among other things mentions that he's heard that I'm writing a prison diary. He suggests that reporting the facts will be both interesting and informative, but he also wants to hear about my personal feelings on the issues and the people involved. He adds that he's not surprised that the public have been so supportive; he says he got far more sympathy and backing when he lost an election than when he won one.

DAY 193   SUNDAY 27 JANUARY 2002

4.00 pm

The members of Club Hospital meet for tea and biscuits. However, as Brian (ostrich farm), Keith (knowingly, etc.) and John (fraud) were released this week, and David (fraud) and Malcolm (fraud) are on town leave, our little band of miscreants has dwindled to five. We discuss whether we should ask anyone else to join the club, as if we were all attending a Conservative committee meeting; and let's face it the Conservative party seem to be suffering from a similar problem. Some of them have been released, and several more are on temporary leave. But just like prison, one must wonder just how many will in time return.

6.00 pm

I spend a quiet evening reading and bringing the diary up to date.

DAY 194   MONDAY 28 JANUARY 2002

12.45 am

The duty night officer wakes me and asks for an ice pack. I take one out of the fridge and ask if he needs any help.

'No,' he says without explanation, and dashes off.

2.15 am

The same officer wakes me again when he returns accompanied by a prisoner called Davis who has a large swelling on his forehead and cuts over his face. Mr Hayes explains that the inmate has been in a fight, and the window in his door has shattered, leaving glass all over the floor. The prisoner can't remain in his room, because if he were to be injured by a piece of broken glass he could sue the Prison Service for negligence (can you believe it?).

While we make up his bed Davis tells me that the other prisoner involved in the fight was his cell-mate Smith (one of eleven Smiths currently at NSC), who has now been moved to the south block. They have shared a pad for eight months, a sort of forced marriage. Smith, who works in education, often needs to borrow cigarettes. Davis got sick of this and refused to hand over his tobacco, so Smith took a swipe at him. Davis claims he didn't retaliate, as he'd recently been up on a charge of taking marijuana and didn't need to be 'nicked' again. Once Smith had calmed down, Davis decided to leave the room. As he opened the door, Smith picked up a table leg that had broken off during the fight, and took a swipe at Davis – hence the shattered glass and the cuts and bruises.

It doesn't add up, and I feel sure Davis will have refined his story by the time he comes up in front of the governor. Mind you, I'd like to hear Smith's version of what took place.

9.00 am

Both prisoners involved in last night's fracas have to be passed as fit before they come up for adjudication at ten o'clock. They sit chatting to each other like bosom buddies in the corner of the waiting room.

12 noon

Over lunch I learn that the two fighting inmates have both had a fortnight's wages deducted from their pay packets to cover the damage they caused to the furniture and the broken window in their room. They also have had seven days added to their sentence. This is significant for Smith, because he was due to be released in two weeks' time. I'm told the reason they didn't get a tougher punishment was because both apologized to the governor and then to each other. They left almost holding hands.

DAY 194

7.00 pm

I go off to the canteen to buy some Oxo cubes, Evian water, two phonecards and a tin of Princes ham. No chocolate.

Mr Blackman (the officer on duty) asks me if I want a Valentine card and produces a large selection for me to consider. They are all about a foot high in size and contain some of the worst rhyming couplets I have ever come across; more interesting is that there are just as many cards for men as for women. I obviously don't mask my surprise because Mr Blackman sighs and says, 'If I didn't supply them in equal numbers, I'd be accused of discrimination.'

DAY 195   TUESDAY 29 JANUARY 2002

9.00 am

Ten new prisoners who arrived from Leicester last night are waiting to see the doctor. While they sit around, one of them boasts
that he can always beat any drugs test, even fool the breathalyser.
Although Lee is well aware I'm writing a diary, he's still quite
willing to reveal his secrets. Lee is in his mid-twenties, good looking and well built. However, after one look at the inside of his
arm, there's no doubt that he's on drugs, and heaven knows what
state he'll be in in ten years' time.

'How can you beat an MDT?' I ask.

'Easy,' he says, and produces a tiny bar of soap from his jeans
pocket – the kind you find in the washbasin of any small hotel.
He breaks the soap in half, puts it in his mouth and begins to
suck it as if it were a hard-boiled sweet.

'What difference does that make?' I enquire.

'If I'm tested in the next few hours, my urine sample will
be so cloudy that they won't be able to charge me, and they're
not allowed to test me again for another twenty-eight days. By
then I will have had enough time to wash everything out of
my system. I can even go on taking heroin up until the twenty-
fourth day; it's only cannabis that takes a month to clear out of
the blood stream.'

'But that can't apply to the breathalyser?'

'No,' he says, laughing, 'but I've got two ways of beating the breathalyser.' He produces three pennies from another pocket and begins to suck them. After a few moments he removes them and claims that the copper neutralizes the alcohol, and it therefore won't register.

'But what happens if the police don't give you enough time to put the coins in your mouth?'

'I can still beat them,' says Lee, 'using my special breathing technique.' Every prisoner in the waiting room is now hanging on his every word, and when the next patient is called in to see the doctor, he doesn't move, for fear of missing the final instalment.

'When the police hand you the machine to blow into,' Lee continues, aware of his captive audience, 'you pump out your chest, but you don't take a deep breath. For the next four seconds you blow in very little air, until the machine registers orange. You hand back the machine and gasp as if you've given everything. You'll get away with it because green is negative and orange is still clear. It's only the red you have to worry about, and they can't charge you once you've registered orange. And,' he goes on, 'if your eyes are blurred or vacant, I also have a way of getting over that problem. There's a product you can buy over the counter from any chemist called Z1 which was developed for clubbers to stop their eyes getting irritated by smoke. A combination of the copper, careful breathing and Z1, and you'll never be charged.'

11.00 am

One of the inmates has been put on suicide watch. He's a lad of twenty-one, five foot five, seven and a half stone and terrified of his own shadow. He's in for driving while disqualified, and will be released in two weeks' time.

He turns up at eleven to collect two new sheets and hands over two in a plastic bag because he wet them last night. While I go off to the cupboard to collect new sheets, he walks around in small circles, muttering to himself.

Gail can't be sure if it's all an act, because he's currently working on the farm and some prisoners will go to any lengths to get themselves off that detail. In fact, when he learns that he will be granted a change of job, he smiles for the first time. However, Gail can't afford to take any risks so she writes out a detailed report for the unit officer.

Suicide watch in this particular case means that an officer (Mr Jones) will have to check on the inmate every hour until all concerned are confident he is back to normal. This usually takes two to three days. I'll keep you informed.

7.00 pm

Doug has the flu and Carl is at singing practice with the 'cons and pros,' so I'm on my own for the evening.

I read a paper on the effects of heroin on children, written by Dr Simon Wills. I never imagined that Dr Wills would replace Freddie Forsyth as my bedtime reading.

DAY 196   WEDNESDAY 30 JANUARY 2002

.

9.00 am

Two new inductees arrive from Nottingham (A-cat). A young man serving four months for a driving offence tells me that on his block at Nottingham they had three suicides in three weeks, and all of them prisoners who had not yet been convicted.

The other inmate nods and tells me that he was made to share a cell with a man who was injecting himself with vinegar because he couldn't afford heroin.

DAY 197   THURSDAY 31 JANUARY 2002

10.00 am

Mr Lewis drops in to see Linda, as it's his last official day as governor. He's handed in his keys, handcuffs, whistle, torch, identity card and everything else that denoted his position of authority. An experience he obviously didn't enjoy. He jokes about suddenly becoming aware of afternoon television, and endless advertisements for comfortable chairs that move with the press of a button, beds that change shape when you turn over and baths that you can easily get out of.

Mr Lewis smiles, says goodbye and we shake hands. I suspect that we will never meet again as we both head towards the world of zimmer frames.

11.00 am

Mr McQuity, the National Health inspector, pays a visit to NSC, and leaves Linda in no doubt that he's well satisfied with the way she is running the prison hospital.

DAY 197

2.30 pm

The press is full of stories about the problems the Prison Service is facing because of overcrowding. There are currently a maximum of 71,000 bed spaces, and just over 70,000 of them are taken up. The Home Secretary David Blunkett has the choice of releasing people early or building more prisons. He's just announced that tagging will be extended from two months to three, with effect from 1 April. This would get me out three months early if, on appeal, my sentence is lowered by even a day.

4.00 pm

Among this afternoon's inductees is a prisoner from Lincoln who has only three weeks left to serve. He hasn't stopped complaining since the moment he arrived. He's demanding a single room with a TV, and a bed-board because he suffers from a bad back. All prisoners start life at NSC in a double room, and there are several inmates who have been around for some months and still don't have a TV. And as for the bed-board, all four are out at the moment.

Within an hour of leaving the hospital, the inmate was discovered lying on his back in the car park next to the governor's car. When Mr Leighton was called to deal with the problem, he said he could see no reason why the prisoner shouldn't sleep in the car park and drove away. The inmate returned to his allocated room within the hour. He's been no trouble since.

DAY 198   FRIDAY 1 FEBRUARY 2002

9.00 am

Among those on the paper chase today is a young man who has not yet celebrated his thirtieth birthday, but has been to jail *eighteen* times. He's a small-time burglar, who has – and this is the important point – no fear of prison. For him it's a temporary inconvenience in his chosen career. Because he has no record of violence or involvement with drugs, he's rarely sentenced to more than six months. He spends a few days in an A-cat, before being transferred to a D-cat, open prison. NSC provides him with three meals a day, a room and the company of fellow profession-als. When he leaves, he will go on stealing until he is caught again. He will then be arrested, sentenced and return to NSC, the nearest D-cat to his home in Boston.* He earns between fifty and a hundred thousand a year (no taxes), according to how many months he spends 'on the out' in any particular year.

Mr Hocking (head of security) tells me that this young man has a long way to go before he can beat Greville the cat burglar, who left NSC last year at the age of sixty-three, declaring he now had enough to retire on. During a full-time career of crime,

---

* He was very distressed to learn last year that the Home Office was considering closing the prison.

Greville was sentenced on thirty-one occasions (not a record) and preferred NSC, where he was always appointed as reception orderly within days of checking back in. So professional was he at his chosen occupation that if there was a burglary in his area, with absolutely no trace of entry, fingerprints or any other clues, the local police immediately paid a visit to Greville's home. Greville has since retired to a seaside bungalow to live off his profits, and tend his garden. And thereby hangs another tale, which Mr Hocking swears is true.

Greville was the prime suspect when some valuable coins went missing from a local museum. A few days later, the police received an anonymous tip-off reporting that Greville had been seen burying something in the garden. A team of police arrived within the hour and started digging; they were there for five days, but found nothing.

Greville later wrote and thanked the chief constable for the excellent job his men had done in turning over his soil, particularly for the way they'd left everything so neat and tidy.

2.30 pm

I have my hair cut by the excellent prison barber, Gary (half a phonecard). I want to look smart for my visitors on Sunday.

3.00 pm

Friday is kit change day for every inmate. The hospital has its own allocated time because we require twenty new towels, six sheets, twelve pillowcases and several different items of cleaning equipment every week. While the chief orderly, Mark (armed robbery, ten years), selects a better class of towel for the hospital, he tells me about an inmate who has just come in for his weekly change of clothes.

This particular prisoner works on the farm, and never takes his clothes off from one week to the next, not even when he goes to bed. He has a double room to himself because, surprise, surprise, no one is willing to share a pad with him. Mark wonders if he does it just to make sure he ends up with a single room. I find it hard to believe anyone would be willing to suffer that amount of discomfort just to ensure they were left alone.

Before you ask, because I did, the Prison Service cannot force him to wash or shave. It would violate his human rights.

DAY 199 SATURDAY 2 FEBRUARY 2002

9.24 am

Mr Berlyn drops by. He's agreed to Linda's suggestion that a drug specialist visit the prison to give me an insight into the problems currently faced by young children in schools. But Mr Berlyn goes one step further and tells me about an officer from Stocken Prison who regularly visits schools in East Anglia to tell schoolchildren why they wouldn't want to end up in prison, and it may be possible for me, once I've passed my FLED, to accompany him and learn about drugs first-hand. If my sentence is cut, I would be allowed to visit schools immediately, rather than going through the whole learning process after my appeal.

11.00 am

Sister is just about to close surgery, when a very depressed-looking inmate hobbles in.

'I've caught the crabs,' he says, his hand cupped around the top of his trousers.

Sister unlocks the door to the surgery and lets him in. He looks anxious, and Linda appears concerned. He slowly unzips his jeans, in obvious pain, and places his hands inside. Linda and

I stare as he slowly uncups his hands to reveal two small, live crabs, which he passes across to Linda. She recoils, while I burst out laughing, aware that we will be the butt of prison humour for some weeks to come.

'Oh my God,' says Linda, as she stares down at his unzipped jeans, 'I don't like the look of that. I think I'll have to take a blood sample.'

The inmate rushes out of the door, his jeans falling around his knees. Honour restored, except that he has the last laugh, because it's the hospital orderly (me) who ends up taking the two crabs back down to the sea.

2.00 pm

An inmate was caught in the visitors' car park in possession of two grammes of heroin. On the outside, two grammes of heroin have a street value of £80. Inside prison, each gramme will be converted into ten points, and each point will be made into three sales. Each sale will be one-third heroin and two-thirds crushed paracetamol, which can be picked up any day from the hospital by a prisoner simply claiming to have a headache. Each sale is worth £5, so the dealer ends up with £300 for two grammes, almost four times the market price.

Some dealers are happy to remain in prison because they can make more money inside than they do 'on the out'. The inmate concerned claims a man who was visiting another prisoner handed him a packet in the car park. The head of security is aware who the visitor was, but can't charge him because he wasn't caught in the act. He also knows which prisoner the heroin was destined for, but he's also in the clear because he never received it.

DAY 200   SUNDAY 3 FEBRUARY 2002

5.00 am

I rise early and write for two hours.

2.00 pm

My visitors today are my son Will and Chris Beetles. Will takes me through the preparations for my appeal on sentence, which are almost complete as both pieces of research on perjury and an attempt to pervert the course of justice show that eighteen months would historically be a high tariff for a first offender. Chris brings me up to date on everything that's happening in the art world.

4.00 pm

At Club Hospital's Sunday afternoon tea party, David (fraud, schoolmaster) reveals that Brian (ostrich farm fraud) and John (fraud) are both having trouble since being released. Brian is waking in the middle of the night, sweating because he's frightened he won't make it back in time for the 7 pm check-in and John is stressed because he hasn't been able to find a job.

6.00 pm

Once the club members have left, I settle down to make myself some supper. In a large soup bowl (a gift from William), I place the contents of a tin of Princes ham, two packets of Walkers crisps and an Oxo cube; hot water is then poured on top. What a combination. I eat while reading *Street Drugs* by Andrew Tyler, which is my set text for the week.

The food is wonderful, the book harrowing.

DAY 201 — MONDAY 4 FEBRUARY 2002

9.00 am

A young lad from the north block, who only has two weeks to serve of a three-month sentence, has been found in his room with his head in a noose made from a sheet hanging from the end of his bed. The slightly built lad, who must be about twenty-one, reminds me of the boy having sand kicked into his face in those Charles Atlas advertisements I saw when I was a child. He is taken to the hospital to be interviewed by Mr Berlyn, Dr Harris and sister behind closed doors. He's certain to be placed on red suicide watch, with an officer checking on him every thirty minutes.

Mr Berlyn tells me that they've never had a suicide at NSC because if a prisoner is that desperate, he usually absconds. The real problem arises in closed prisons from which there is no escape. There were seventy-three suicides in prisons last year and not one of them was at a D-cat.

Just as Mr Berlyn leaves, the lad who wets his bed reappears with a black bag containing two more sheets. I supply him with two clean sheets and he leaves looking even more helpless than the suicide case; you'd never think this was a men's prison.

2.00 pm

I watch four videos on the subject of heroin. I'm slowly gaining more knowledge about drugs through reading, videos and my day-to-day work as hospital orderly, but I still have no first-hand experience. I go over to see David in the CARAT (Counselling, Assessment, Referral, Advice, Through-care) office. He is willing to let me attend one of his drug counselling sessions, as long as the other participants agree, because I'll be the only one who isn't currently, and never has been, an addict.

6.00 pm

I attend the drug rehab discussion in the CARAT office. David asks the five other inmates if any of them object to my presence. They all seem pleased that I've taken the trouble to attend.

David opens the discussion by asking if they feel that once they are released they'll be able to resist going back on drugs, and in particular heroin. One of them is adamant that he will never touch a drug again. His relationship with those he loves has been ruined, and he wonders if anyone will ever be willing to employ him. He tells the group that he had reached the stage where he would steal from anyone, including his own family, to make sure he got his fix, and just before he was arrested, he needed four fixes a day to satisfy his addiction.

The next participant says that his only thought on waking was how to get his first fix. Once he'd begged, borrowed or stolen the £20 needed, he'd go in search of a dealer. As soon as he'd got his half gramme of heroin, he'd run back to his house and, often with his wife and two children in the next room, he would place the powder in a large tablespoon, to which he would add water and the juice from any citrus fruit. He would then stir the mixture until he had a thick brown liquid, which he would pour onto a piece of aluminium foil and then warm it with a match. He would then sniff it up through a straw. One of the inmates butts in and adds that he preferred to smoke it. However, all of them agree that the biggest kick came when you injected it. The lad from Scarborough then lifts the sleeve of his denim jacket and his trouser leg, and declares, 'That gets difficult when there are no veins left to inject.'

The one who so far hasn't said a word chips in for the first time. He tells us that he's been off heroin for five weeks and still can't sleep, and what makes it worse is that his room-mate snores all through the night. The dealer jumps in. 'You'll start getting to sleep after about eight weeks, and then it gets better and better each day until you're back to normal.'

I ask what he means by that.

'Once you're an addict, you don't need a fix to make you feel good, you need one just so you can return to normal. That's when you become a "smack head" – in between fixes you start shaking, and the worse you are the more desperate you become to return to normal. And, Jeff,' he adds, 'if you're planning to talk about the problem in schools, you should start with the eleven year olds, because by fourteen, it's too late. In Scarborough, good-looking, well-brought-up, well-educated fourteen-year-old girls approach me all the time for their daily fix.'

The last person to participate is another dealer, who claims he only dealt because the profits allowed him to finance his own drug addiction. From eight in the morning to ten at night, his mobile would ring with a non-stop flow of requests from customers. He assures me that he's never needed to solicit anyone. He tells the groups that he's been off heroin for nearly seven months, and will never deal in, or take drugs, again. I don't feel that confident after he adds that he can earn £1,000 a day as a seller. He ends the session with a statement that takes me – but no one else in the room – by surprise. 'Nearly all my friends are in jail or dead.'

He's thirty-one years old.

DAY 202   TUESDAY 5 FEBRUARY 2002

7.00 am

I put my pen down after a couple of hours of writing to switch on the *Today* programme. Britain is in the middle of a rail strike. There's no station at North Sea Camp.

9.00 am

Two of the inmates who attended last night's drugs counselling meeting are up on a 'nicking'. Once the doctor has pronounced them fit, they will attend an adjudication chaired by Governor Leighton. One of them tested positive for cannabis on his latest MDT, and adds ruefully that he expects to be shipped out to a B-cat prison later today. Now I know why he hardly spoke at yesterday's meeting. He also looks as if he didn't sleep last night.

1.00 pm

The newspapers are full of stories about David Blunkett's proposed prison reforms, which seem no more than common sense. Anyone with a non-custodial sentence for a non-violent first offence will be placed on immediate tagging, with weekend custody, and possibly having to report to a police station every evening. For lesser offences, they would be tagged immediately, with a curfew of 7 pm to 7 am. A second offence and they would be sent to prison.

As of 1 February, the prison population stood at 67,978 and the prediction is that already overcrowded prisons will be under additional pressure following Lord Chief Justice Woolf's recent pronouncement on mobile phone muggers.

4.00 pm

Three more manuscripts arrive in the post today with letters asking if I could critique them. Four publishers have turned one down; another says his wife, who is his sternest critic, thinks it's first class, and the final one seeks my advice on vanity publishers.*

4.20 pm

One of today's inductees is a Mr T. Blair. He has been sentenced to six months for disturbing the peace, but with remission and tagging, expects to be released after only eight weeks. The other Mr T. Blair looks set to serve at least eight years.

4.37 pm

I still marvel at what prisoners will have the nerve to ask sister for. Today, one inmate has demanded a bottle of aftershave because he has a skin problem. I'm about to burst out laughing,

---

* So-called vanity publishers are only too happy to publish your book – if, along with the script, you enclose a cheque for £3,000.

when Linda hands him a bottle and he leaves without another word.

'Why can't he buy one in the canteen?' I ask.

'You can't buy aftershave in the canteen,' Linda reminds me, 'it contains alcohol, and several inmates would happily drink it.'

'But you've just given...'

'Non-alcoholic aftershave supplied especially for prison hospitals. On your day of release,' Linda reminds me, 'any prisoner can demand a free needle to inject himself with heroin, as well as a packet of condoms.'

DAY 203 WEDNESDAY 6 FEBRUARY 2002

9.00 am

I can't believe how stupid some people can be.

On Monday I attended a CARAT meeting where one of the participants told everyone present that he had given up drugs. On Tuesday the same man comes up in front of the governor for failing an MDT for cannabis. Seven days were added to his sentence, and he told me he considered himself lucky not to be shipped out. Last night the same man was caught on his way back from Boston in possession of a plastic bag full of drugs that included cannabis and heroin. He was locked up in the segregation cell overnight, and will be shipped out this morning to a B-cat with a further twenty-one days added to his sentence.

His stupidity is not the only aspect of this incident worth considering. If he'd been caught with such an assignment of drugs 'on the out' he would have been sentenced to at least seven years, but as his sentence is already fourteen, he gets away with twenty-one days added. It's just another pointer to the drugs problem this country is currently facing.

11.00 am

Mary has a piece in *Peterborough* that she came across on the Web. It makes me laugh so much it's simply better to reproduce it rather than attempt any precis. (See below.)

Woman of substance

Lady Archer's sense of humour is alive and well. The fragrant chemist has just submitted a "hazardous materials data sheet" to the *Chemistry at Cambridge* newsletter. "**Element**: woman. **Symbol**: Wo. **Discoverer**: Adam. **Atomic mass**: accepted as 55kg but known to vary from 45kg to 225kg. **Occurrence**: found in large quantities in urban areas, with trace elements in outlying regions. **Physical properties**: boils at absolutely nothing, freezes for no apparent reason. Melts if given special treatment, bitter if used incorrectly. **Chemical properties**: affinity to gold, silver, platinum and all precious stones. The most powerful money-reducing agent known to man. **Common use**: highly ornamental, especially in sports cars. Can be a very effective cleaning agent. **Hazards**: highly dangerous except in experienced hands. Illegal to possess more than one, although several can be maintained at different locations as long as specimens do not come into direct contact with each other."

The *Telegraph* also publishes the results of a poll on Mr Blunkett's recent pronouncements that non-violent, first-offence prisoners should be able, where possible, to continue their work while reporting into jails in the evenings and at weekends; 83 per cent say 'keep them locked up', while only 12 per cent feel the Home Secretary is right to consider legislation along these more realistic lines. I must confess that before I'd been to prison, I would have been among the 83 per cent.

7.00 pm

I phone Mary, who tells me before I can get beyond 'Hello' that Baroness Nicholson has finally issued a statement in which she offers a grudging apology. (See below.)

Baroness Nicholson wishes to make it quite clear that at no time did she intend to suggest that Lord Archer had personally misappropriated money raised by the Simple Truth appeal. Indeed, it had not occurred to her to think that it might have been possible for Lord Archer to gain access to funds raised by the British Red Cross. If the inference was drawn that she was accusing Lord Archer of having stolen Simple Truth money from the British Red Cross, she regrets the misunderstanding and regrets any upset that may have been caused to Lord Archer's family.

DAY 204   THURSDAY 7 FEBRUARY 2002

9.00 am

Mr Berlyn strides in at a brisk pace. After a few minutes ensconced with sister in her office, he emerges to tell me that the Home Office has issued an 'overcrowding' draft, as all the prisons in the north of England are fully occupied. Result: we will be getting ten new inmates today, and will be 'surplus to our manifest' of 213. Here at NSC we are already seeing those overcrowding statistics translated into reality.

Mr Berlyn has directed that two inmates will have to be billeted in the hospital overnight. I fear I will be experiencing a lot of this during the next few weeks, and I may without warning have to share heaven with some other sinners. However, as six inmates are being released tomorrow, this might be only temporary.

12.07 pm

Linda and Gail charge out of the hospital carrying an oxygen cylinder and two first-aid boxes. All I'm told is that a staff member has fallen off a ladder. On the intercom it's announced that all security officers must report to the south block immediately. It's like being back in an A-cat where this was a daily occurrence. Prisoners tell me that in Nottingham ambulances were more common than Black Marias.

A few minutes later Linda and Gail return with a shaven-headed officer covered in blood. It seems that he leaned back while climbing a ladder and overbalanced, landing on the concrete below. No prisoner was involved.

I quickly discover that a small head wound can spurt so much blood that it appears far worse than it is. When Linda has finished cleaning up her patient and I've given him a cup of tea (only the English), he's smiling and making light of the whole episode. But Linda still wants to dispatch him to the Pilgrim Hospital for stitches to the scalp wound, and both she as hospital sister, and Mr Hocking, head of security, have to fill in countless forms, showing that no prisoner was responsible.

6.00 pm

I read another chapter of *Street Drugs*, this time to learn more about crack cocaine, its properties and its consequences. It's quite difficult not to accept the argument that some young people, having experimented with one drug and got a kick out of it, might wish to progress to another, simply to discover if the sensation is even more exciting.

10.00 pm

Only one of the extra two inmates allocated to spend the night in the hospital appears at my door, a blanket and sheet under his arm. It seems they found a bed for the other arrival. He's very quiet, despite the fact that he's being released tomorrow. He slips into bed and simply says, 'Goodnight, Jeff.'

Am I that frightening?

DAY 205   FRIDAY 8 FEBRUARY 2002

5.30 am

'What do you think you're doing, you fucking dickhead?'

I'm about to explain to my overnight companion that I write for a couple of hours every morning, but when I turn to face him, I realize he's still fast asleep. It's the first occasion someone's sworn in front of me for a long time, even in their sleep, and it brings back memories of Belmarsh and Wayland. I continue writing until seven, when I have to wake him.

'Morning, Jeff,' he says.

By the time I emerged from the bathroom, he's disappeared – his sheets and pillowcases folded neatly at the end of the bed. By now he'll be in reception, signing his discharge papers, and by eight-thirty will be on his way, a free man.*

2.00 pm

Our two new inductees today are somewhat unusual, and not just because they're both lifers (we now have 23 lifers out of 210 occupants). The first one tells me that he's been in jail for

---

* The prison is entitled to keep you until midnight on the day of your release, but you're usually off the premises by nine o'clock.

twenty-three years and he's only thirty-nine. The second one limps into the hospital and spends a considerable time with sister behind closed doors.

Later, when I take his blood pressure and check his weight, he tells me that he's already served fourteen years, and two years ago he contracted encephalitis. Once I've filled in his chart and handed it to Linda, I look up encephalitis in the medical dictionary. Poor fellow. Life imprisonment he may deserve, encephalitis he does not.

DAY 206   SATURDAY 9 FEBRUARY 2002

2.00 pm

Mary and James visit me today, and it's far from being a social event. Mary even has a written agenda. I do adore her.

On the domestic front, she has purchased a small Victorian mirror for the hall, and seeks my approval. She goes on to tell me that Baroness Nicholson has written saying that she wants to end the feud, claiming that she never intended anyone to think that I had misappropriated any funds in the first place. In which case, how did I end up in a cell three paces by five, banged up for fourteen hours a day at Wayland, if the police and Prison Service misunderstood her?*

As for the prejudice of Mr Justice Potts, it remains to be seen whether Godfrey Barker is still willing to make a witness statement. He has confirmed, on many occasions, in the presence of

---

* Baroness Nicholson wrote to Sir John Stevens, Commissioner of the Metropolitan Police, in July 2001, demanding 'an investigation into the involvement of Jeffrey Archer in funds raised and spent through the Simple Truth Appeal'. This precipitated not only a police enquiry, but a lengthy and expensive investigation by KPMG on behalf of the Red Cross. Baroness Nicholson's insinuation that I had stolen money from the Appeal was irresponsible and wholly without foundation, and on 23 January 2002, the police closed their enquiry 'in view of . . . the lack of any evidence from the informant'.

several witnesses, that Potts, at a dinner party he and his wife attended, railed against me for some considerable time.

4.00 pm

When my name is called over the tannoy to report to reception, I assume that James has left something for me at the gate. I've been expecting a dozen *West Wing* tapes that will first have to go to the library before I can take them out. My gift turns out to be eight tapes, twelve CDs and three DVDs, not from James, but from an anonymous member of the public, so I can't even write to thank them.

Someone else has sent seven books of first-class stamps and a packet of stamped envelopes, after hearing how many letters I'm receiving every day. Mr Garley, the duty officer, explains that I can't have the stamps (could be exchanged for drugs), but I can have the stamped envelopes (prison logic). Shouldn't the rule be universal to all prisons? At Belmarsh, a category A prison, stamps are permitted. I make no comment. It's not Mr Garley's fault, and he can't do anything about it.

DAY 207   SUNDAY 10 FEBRUARY 2002

7.21 am

Gail is angry. She's recently bought a smart new dark green
Peugeot, which she parks outside the hospital. Yesterday, one of
the prisoners put matchsticks in her locks, so that when she
tried to open the door, she pushed the matchstick further in and
jammed the lock.

4.00 pm

Club Hospital meets for tea and biscuits. One of our new members, who has only been with us for a month, will be released
tomorrow. He was charged with road rage and sentenced to
three months. He will have spent six weeks in prison. I've
watched him carefully at our get-togethers and as he goes about
his business around the prison. He is well educated, well mannered and looks quite incapable of swatting a fly.

He tells the group that he stopped his car to go to the aid
of a woman who was being attacked, but for his troubles, got
punched to the ground by what turned out to be her boyfriend.
The two of them then drove off. He returned home, but was
later arrested for road rage as the woman bore witness that *he*

attacked her. Had he gone to the police station first and reported them for assault, the other man would now be in jail, not him. He has lost his job with the pharmaceutical company he's been with for twenty-one years, and is worried about getting another one now he has a criminal record. His wife has stuck by him, and she hopes that one of his old firm's rivals will want to take advantage of his expertise.* This brings me onto the subject of wives.

Of the seven married Club members present today, two of their wives have had to sell their homes and move to smaller houses in another area; two have had to go out to work full time while trying to bring up children (three in one case, two in the other), and the other two have received divorce petitions while in jail. I'm the seventh.

I make no excuse for the crimes committed, but I feel it bears repeating that it's often the wives who suffer even more than the husbands – for them there is no rehabilitation programme.

---

* He later wrote to tell me that his old firm took him back the day he was released, and treated the six weeks absence as holiday on full pay.

DAY 208   MONDAY 11 FEBRUARY 2002

9.00 am

One of the prisoners waiting to be seen by Dr Walling this morning is a regular attendee. Today he somehow managed to get a nail stuck in his head. It only grazed the surface of his skull, but produced a lot of blood. Once Gail has cleaned and bandaged him up, he asks, 'Could I have rust on the brain?'

2.00 pm

The prison is jam-packed; 211 at lock up last night. Two inmates have been released this morning, and three new prisoners arrived this afternoon from Leicester. They couldn't be more different. One is eighteen, and serving a six-week sentence for a road-traffic offence. He has only two more weeks to serve before taking up a place at Leicester University in September to read mathematics. The second is around twenty-four – he is doing six months for punching someone in a pub. He requests counselling for his drink problem; drink is considered by the prison authorities to be just as much a drug as cannabis or heroin. The third is serving six years for GBH, a year of which he spent in Belmarsh.

6.00 pm

I attend the weekly CARAT meeting, but one of the prisoners objects to my presence, so I leave immediately.

The drugs counsellor tells me later that because I've never been an addict myself and am writing a diary, he doesn't feel free to express himself while I'm there – fair enough.

I settle down to read the latest booklet on the subject of addiction, *Is Your Child on Drugs?* No, thank God. However, it's a fascinating read. It is not uncommon for a child to start smoking at seven – eleven is the norm – so it's no surprise that some children are hooked on heroin by the age of fourteen.

DAY 209   TUESDAY 12 FEBRUARY 2002

9.00 am

We have a full surgery this morning: three for release, two for a week's temporary release and eleven with imagined or real illnesses. Dr Allwood, a thorough and conscientious man, always takes his time. In fact, after forty minutes, one of the inmates in the waiting room complains about how long he's taking. Gail leaps out of the surgery and tells the prisoner that her husband visited his GP last week and had to sit around for three hours, and that was after having to wait a week before he could make an appointment. The inmate snarls.

Chris, a lifer (murdered his wife), rolls up his sleeve and shows me a faded scar on the inside of his arm. 'I did that,' he says, thrusting it under the gaze of the complaining prisoner, who looks surprised. 'Yeah,' he continues, 'stabbed in the middle of the night by my pad-mate, wasn't I, and when I pressed the emergency button no screws came to help me because I was on the top floor.' Chris now has the full attention of the rest of the surgery. 'No doctor at Gartree to come to my aid, so I sewed it up myself.' I look at his faded scar in disbelief, but Gail nods to confirm she's seen many examples of amateur stitching over the years.

'Just a needle and thread was all I needed,' he adds.

10.40 am

Mr Berlyn marches into the hospital and says he needs an urgent word with me. We go into the ward. He has been in touch with Mr Le Sage at HMP Stocken about my accompanying him when he gives his talk to schools on the problems of young people becoming involved in drugs and ending up in prison. The good news is that Mr Le Sage is looking for a new prisoner to assist him, and has agreed to travel up to NSC next Monday to talk about the possibility of my working alongside him. This is the best news I've had since being appointed hospital orderly.

Escaping the confines of NSC, visiting schools and feeling I'm doing something worthwhile must be the next step on this particular journey. I thank Mr Berlyn and once again have something to look forward to. Next Monday.

3.00 pm

Only two new inductees today because the prison is full. When I check my board, I note one of them is called Blackburn. We already have a Blackburn, I tell the young lad sitting in front of me.

'Yeah, that's my dad,' he says. 'He was my co-defendant.' I smell a story. 'You'll never believe what we're in for, Jeff,' he adds. I remain silent. 'We were caught stealing Lion Bars, and got three and a half years.'

'That sounds a bit rough,' I venture foolishly.

'Yeah, well, I have to admit, Jeff, it was forty-six tons of 'em with a street value of nearly two hundred grand.'

'But how do you fence chocolate bars?'

He laughs. 'We already had a buyer.'

'At what price?'

'Forty grand.'

'So how did you get caught?'

'One of the night watchmen who was part of our team grassed us up, didn't he.'

'Why?'

'He was up for a minor charge of burglary and did a deal with the scum.'

'Did he get off?'

'Yeah, they dropped the charge, didn't they, but nicked him for somethin' else a couple of months later and then they banged him up in the Scrubs ... with my father.'

4.07 pm

Mr Hocking drops in to say that he's pleased I might be going out to assist a prison officer with his drugs talk. He's already informed the governor that I am not considered a security risk. He's only been with me a couple of minutes when his radio intercom asks him to report back to the security office immediately.

'We've had another one,' are the only words I clearly hear. I look suitably inquisitive.

'We've got a serial informer,' he explains, 'he writes every day telling us who the drug dealers are and where we'll find the next drop. So far he's been on the button every time.'

'Do you know who the informer is?' I ask.

'No idea, don't want to know,' he replies. 'All I can tell you is that the handwriting is the same every time.'

DAY 210   WEDNESDAY 13 FEBRUARY 2002

5.43 am

I dreamed last night about a lovely man called John Bromley –
Brommers to his friends – who died of cancer a few days ago. I
had the privilege of working with him – you didn't work *for*
John, even though he was the head of ITV's sport. He had an
amazing gift of making even the tea lady feel part of the team. If
you had a love of sport, good humour, fine wine and beautiful
women, he was quite simply the best company a man could ask
for. I predict that his memorial service will be as well attended
as any prime minister's. I only hope I'm out in time to be there.

9.30 am

A beautiful black Labrador called Bessie saunters into the hospital accompanied by two officers from the drug squad. I am told
to wait in the lobby while Bessie goes about her work. Through
the closed door, I can hear her padding around sniffing for drugs
among my personal possessions. If Bessie can read, she'll find
several books, pamphlets and papers on drugs, but until you can
fail an MDT for Ribena, Bovril or Evian, not much else.

The other prisoners sitting in the lobby waiting to see the

doctor can't mask their surprise. A few moments later, the door is opened and Bessie reappears, and as she passes by, ignores me – a good sign, because if Bessie starts to sniff you, you're in trouble. If she licks you, you'll be up on a charge. I ought to be pleased, but when I return to the ward, Bessie's paw-prints are everywhere, and I scrubbed the floor only yesterday.

11.00 am

Mr Hocking explains that the drug search had a purpose. They are about to make a big swoop, following another tip-off, and he wanted the other inmates to see that I was not exempt from being searched. By now everyone in the prison will know, and some might even wonder if I'm about to be shipped out. I suspect the real search will take place later today.

3.00 pm

I have a legal visit from my solicitors Tony Morton Hooper and Lord Mishcon, now aged eighty-four – it's kind of him to endure the seven-hour round trip. We spend the next two hours preparing for the upcoming appeal, not that a date has yet been fixed.

6.00 pm

Doug tells me that we are to have a new governing governor called Mr Beaumont. As he was governor of Leicester Prison, there will be a lot of inmates who can brief us about him.

DAY 211   THURSDAY 14 FEBRUARY 2002

8.15 am

I no longer have breakfast in the main hall because Linda supplies me with a box of cornflakes once a week and a half pint of milk every day. Today she added a new luxury – a banana.

9.00 am

One of the prisoners in surgery this morning needs a weekend leave form signed by the doctor, to show he is fit to be out of prison. Yesterday his leave was revoked because he drew out a large sum of money from his canteen account, leaving a balance of only £3.72. You cannot take weekend leave unless you have at least £4 in your account. It is assumed that if you empty your account, then you're probably going to abscond. This seems unlikely in this case as the prisoner has only two weeks of his sentence left.

Mr Berlyn shows some common sense, allows the prisoner to put 28p back into the account and signs his weekend leave pass.

DAY 211

12 noon

Lunch in the canteen. Potato bake and cabbage, followed by sponge cake covered, and I mean covered, in custard. I never eat the second course, but take it, because Carl can always eat two portions.

3.00 pm

Dr Harris is on duty and his first responsibility is to sign the discharge papers for eight prisoners who will be released tomorrow. All of them have been granted tagging status, which allows them to leave two months early as long as they remain in their homes between the hours of 7 pm and 7 am. These hours can be flexible if it affects their job.

When I first arrived at NSC and worked as the orderly in the sentence management unit, the tagging board of Mr Berlyn and Mr Simpson used to agree to about 50 per cent of those eligible for this privilege. Now all eight are granted on the same day,* including a twenty-three-year-old who's already been to prison four times. Lee admits that he was shocked when the board granted him tagging status, as his offence was punching someone on the nose in a pub brawl and in any case he looks upon prison as a way of life. In fact, his last comment to Linda before leaving us was, 'See you towards the end of the year, if not before.' He turns to me and adds, 'Let's hope you're out by then, Jeff.'

---

* Caused by the problem of overcrowding.

4.15 pm

I sweep out the ward and mop the floor. On alternate days I vacuum Linda's little office removing Bessie's paw prints. All very therapeutic.

5.00 pm

I call Mary. She thanks me for the flowers that I asked Alison to send her yesterday. She then brings me up to date on Angie Peppiatt and Mr Justice Potts.

5.30 pm

I collect my post. Eleven Valentine cards, which I display in the ward for all to see, plus several letters, including one from John Major and another from Billy Connolly.

Many years ago when John was Chancellor of the Exchequer, I asked him to open the extension to our new folly at the Old Vicarage at our annual summer party. John described the building as 'Mary's second folly'. Billy spoke next and immediately closed it.

DAY 212   FRIDAY 15 FEBRUARY 2002

5.23 am

I've only just worked out why it's the same five inmates who appear at the front of the queue every morning for medication; Linda as hospital sister will only allow them one day's supply of drugs, whereas in a surgery 'on the out', she would prescribe enough for a week, and in some cases even a month. Why, you may ask.

a) If a prisoner were given a month's supply he might well take it all on one day.

b) He could also trade his medication for other drugs.*

c) They could be lost or stolen.

Result, we have a long queue every morning for one day's supply of medication, so they will all be back tomorrow.

---

* The analgesic the inmates most commonly ask for is Kapake which is a mixture of paracetamol and codeine. The reason is that codeine will show up in MDT as an opiate, and thus disguise illegal opiates. The user can then protest, 'But I'm taking Kapake which the doctor prescribed.' Prison doctors are now trying to limit the use of Kapake and diazepam when a prisoner has a record of taking drugs.

7.30 am

Mr Beaumont the new governor has hit the ground running. He's demanded that his office be repainted and all the furniture be replaced, and it all has to be completed by the time he gets back from a visit to the Home Office tomorrow.

8.30 am

Mr Vessey, a security officer, marches into the hospital. His appearance usually means that a prisoner is about to be nicked for some offence. I can't think of any offence I've committed recently, other than being in possession of a bottle of Ribena (smuggled in by Doug). Mr Vessey, who never makes any attempt to be friendly, asks me to accompany him, and takes considerable pleasure in marching me out of the hospital and across the camp. Several prisoners stare in disbelief. He eventually tells me my name has come up on the computer for a random MDT test.

He escorts me into a Portacabin, where I am locked in a room with five other prisoners. Three of them look relaxed and are happily chatting, while the other two are silent, twitchy and look distinctly nervous. A few minutes later I hear a key turning in the lock and another officer joins us.

Four of us came up on the computer for a random test, while two others are here on 'reasonable suspicion'. The serial grasser has undoubtedly offered up their names. The officer then reads his authority to carry out such a test (see overleaf) before asking who would like to be tested first.

I stand up and follow him into an adjoining room. The procedure is then explained to me (see page 349), and I am requested to sign a form saying I agree to the test. I am then

MANDATORY DRUG TEST AUTHORISATION FORM

Prisoner Name: .... *ARCHER* .... Number: *FF 8282*

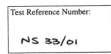

Test Reference Number:

NS 33/01

For allocation when sample is collected

1. The governor has authorised that in accordance with Section 16A of the Prison Act 1952 any prisoner may be required by a prison officer to provide a sample of urine for the purposes of testing for the presence of a controlled drug.

2. You are now required under the terms of Section 16A to provide a fresh and unadulterated sample of urine for testing for the presence of controlled drugs.

3. Authority for this requirement was given by: .... *GOVERNOR* ....

4. Reason for requirement: (only one box to be ticked)

    [✓] **Random test:** You have been selected for this test on a strictly random basis.

    [ ] **Reasonable suspicion:** You have been selected for this test because staff have reason to believe that you have misused drugs. This test has been approved by a senior manager.

    [ ] **Risk assessment:** You have been selected for this test because you are being considered for a privilege, or a job, where a high degree of trust is to be given to you.

    [ ] **Frequent test programme:** You have been selected for more frequent testing because of your previous history of drug misuse.

    [ ] **On reception:** You have been selected for testing on reception on a random basis.

5. The procedures used during the collection and testing of the sample have been designed to protect you and to ensure that there are no mistakes in the handling of your sample. At the end of the collection procedure you will be asked to sign a statement confirming that the urine sealed in the sample bottles for testing is fresh and your own.

6. Your sample will be split at the point of collection into separate containers which will be sealed in your presence. In the event of you disputing any positive test result, one of these containers will be available, for a period of up to 12 months, for you to arrange, if you so wish, for an independent analysis to be undertaken at your own expense.

7. You will be liable to be placed on report if you:

    (a) provide a positive sample;
    (b) refuse to provide a sample; or,
    (c) fail to provide a sample after 4 hours of the order to do so (or after 5 hours if the officer believes that you are experiencing real difficulty in providing a sample).

Consent to Medical disclosure

* (i)   During the past 30 days I have not used any medication issued to me by Health Care.

Signature of Prisoner : .... *J. Archer* .... Date: *15 . 2 . 02.*

FRIDAY 15 FEBRUARY 2002

PRISON SERVICE CHAIN OF CUSTODY PROCEDURE

Prisoner Name: ...... *ARCHER* ...... Number: FF8282

RANDOM TESTING PROGRAMME
This form is to be used only for tests conducted as part of the MDT random programme
(i.e. where prisoners have been selected by the LIDS computer)

Test Reference Number: NS 33/01

Checklist for sample collection - tick boxes as you proceed. Refer to guidance notes if in doubt.

1 [✓] Only **One** sample collection kit present.
2 [✓] Check identity of prisoner. Complete details above and in sample collection register.
3 [✓] Carry out search and handwashing procedures. (No soap).
4 [✓] Show the prisoner that the collection cup and bottles are empty.
5 [✓] Ask prisoner to provide enough urine to be split **equally** between the two sample bottles.
6 [✓] *Take temperature using the temperature strip. If temperature is out of range (32-38C) (90-100F), make note in comment section and refer to guidance notes.*
7 [✓] **Watched by prisoner,** transfer urine **equally** between the two bottles. Fill each **above 15ml line and below 30ml line.** Press caps on securely.
8 [✓] Ask prisoner to initial and date both bottle seals.
9 [✓] **Watched by prisoner,** place a seal over each bottle cap.
10 [✓] Dispose of any surplus urine and the cup.
11 [✓] Pack two bottles in mailing container and then in chain of custody bag - **Do not seal bag.**
12 [✓] **Watched by prisoner,** fix barcode labels and enter test reference number on all copies of this form.
13 [✓] Ask the prisoner to sign and date the Prisoner's Declaration below.
14 [✓] Complete Chain of Custody Report, tear off and place in chain of custody bag facing outwards.
15 [✓] Seal bag, ask prisoner to initial bag where indicated.
16 [✓] Place sealed bag in secure refrigerator until ready for despatch to laboratory.
17 [✓] Allow prisoner to leave.

Prisoner Declaration

I confirm that (i) I understand why I was required to provide the sample and what may happen if I fail to comply with this requirement;
(ii) the urine sample I have given was my own and freshly provided;
(iii) the sample was divided into two bottles and sealed in my presence with seals initialled and dated by me;
(iv) the seals used on these bottles carry a barcode identical to the barcode attached to this form.

Signature of prisoner ...... *Jeffrey Archer* ...... Date 15.2.02.

asked to strip and put on a dressing gown. Mr Vessey hands me a plastic beaker, and asks me to go to the lavatory next door and fill it with at least 60 ml of urine. Having managed this, I hand the beaker back to Mr Vessey, who unseals two plastic tubes in my presence and then pours half the urine into each tube. After I have initialled both, he seals them and places them in a plastic bag, which he also seals. The bag is then deposited in the fridge. He points out that my name is not on the bag, only my number, FF8282.

Having completed this procedure, I sign another form to

349

confirm that I am satisfied with the way the test has been conducted. I am then released to return to the hospital.

Despite this being a humiliating experience, it's one I thoroughly approve of. Although I've never got on with Mr Vessey, he is a professional who cannot hide his contempt for anyone involved in drugs, especially the dealers.

9.00 am

One of the inmates up in front of the governor this morning has been charged with illegal possession of marijuana – but with a difference. When his room was raided they found him trying to swallow a small plastic packet. They wrestled him to the ground and extracted the evidence from his mouth. Had he swallowed the contents, they would not have been able to charge him. The packet was one of those we supply from the hospital containing six paracetamol pills. This one had an ounce of marijuana inside, and the inmate ended up with seven days added to his sentence.

3.00 pm

Mr Hocking appears in the hospital carrying a large attaché case and disappears into Linda's office. A few minutes later they both come out and join me on the ward. The large plastic case is placed on a hospital bed and opened to reveal a drugs kit: twenty-one square plastic containers embedded in foam rubber show the many different drugs currently on the market. For the first time I see heroin, crack cocaine, ecstasy tablets, amphetamines and marijuana in every form.

Linda and Mr Hocking deliver an introductory talk that they give to any prison officer on how to recognize the different drugs and the way they can be taken. Mr Berlyn and his security team are obviously determined that I will be properly briefed before I am allowed to accompany Mr Le Sage when we visit schools.

It's fascinating at my age (sixty-one) to be studying a new subject as if I were a first-year undergraduate.

5.00 pm

The new governor, Mr Beaumont, is making a tour of the camp and spends seven minutes in the hospital – a flying visit. He has heard the hospital is efficiently run by Linda and Gail, and as long as that continues to be the case, gives them the impression that he will not be interfering.

DAY 213   SATURDAY 16 FEBRUARY 2002

8.45 am

Yesterday I was frog-marched off to do an MDT. Today there's an announcement over the tannoy that there are voluntary drugs tests for those with surnames beginning A–E. These are known as dip tests, because once again you pee into a plastic beaker, but this time the officer in charge dips a little stick into the beaker and moments later is able to give you a result.

I walk across to the Portakabin, supply another 60ml of urine and I'm immediately cleared, which makes yesterday's test somewhat redundant.

I later learn that one of the Bs came up positive, and he had to call his wife to let her know that he won't be allowed out on a town visit this weekend. As it was a voluntary test, I can't work out why he agreed to be tested.

10.00 am

Surgery is always slow at the weekend because the majority of inmates who appear with various complaints during the week in the hope that they will get off work remain in bed, while all those who are fit never visit us in the first place.

11.00 am

Carl and an inmate called Jason who is only with us for two weeks (motoring offence) turn up at the hospital. Together we remove all the beds from the ward and push them into the corridor, before giving the hospital a spring clean.

Jason tells me that 'on the out' he's a painter and decorator, and could repaint the ward during his two-week incarceration. I shall speak to the governor on Monday, because at £8.20 a week this would be quite a bargain. You may well ask why Carl and Jason helped me with the spring clean. Boredom. The spring clean killed a morning for all of us.

2.00 pm

I watch the prison football team lose 7–2, and witness two more pieces of unbelievable stupidity by fellow inmates. Our goal-keeper, who was sent off by the same referee the last time we played, shouts obscenities at him again, and is surprised when he's booked. I fear he will be back in prison within months of being released. But worse, our centre forward is a prisoner who's just come out of the Pilgrim Hospital after a groin injury, and has been told to rest for six weeks. He will undoubtedly appear at surgery on Monday expecting sympathy. It's no wonder the NHS is in such crisis if patients behave so irresponsibly after being given expert advice.

DAY 214   SUNDAY 17 FEBRUARY 2002

6.01 am

If I had been given the same sentence as Jonathan Aitken, I would have been released today. Jonathan was sentenced to eighteen months, and because he was a model prisoner, only had to serve seven (half minus two months on tag). Tomorrow I will not be returning home to my wife and family because Mr Justice Potts sentenced me to four years. Instead I will be meeting Mark Le Sage, an officer from Stocken Prison who visits schools in Lincolnshire, warning children of the consequences of taking drugs.

I will remain at NSC until I know the result of my appeal, but for the first time in seven months (since my mother's funeral) I will be able to leave the prison and return to the outside world.

DAY 215   MONDAY 18 FEBRUARY 2002

10.00 am

Mr Le Sage does not turn up for our meeting.

The governor of HMP Stocken has decided that they should not have to bear the cost of my accompanying Mr Le Sage on any school visit, as it would no longer be a voluntary activity that Mr Le Sage would normally pursue in his off-duty time.

As so often is the case in prisons, someone will look for a reason for *not* doing something rather than trying to make a good idea work. I cannot pretend that I've become so used to this negative attitude that I am not disappointed. Mr Berlyn is also unable to mask his anger, and seems determined not to be thwarted by this setback. He has decided that NSC will send its own officer (Mr Hocking) as my escort, so that I might still attend Mark Le Sage's lectures. As I won't know if this suggestion will be vetoed until Mr Berlyn has spoken to the Stocken's governor, I will continue in my role as hospital orderly.

11.30 am

Alan Purser, the prison drugs counsellor, comes across to the hospital to give me a copy of *The Management of Drug Misuse in*

Prisons by Dr Celia Grummitt. Dr Grummitt will become my new bedtime companion.

4.00 pm

Mr Vessey has charged Chris (lifer, murder) and David (lifer, murder) with being on the farm in possession of four potatoes and a cabbage. In normal circumstances this would have caused little interest, even in our self-contained world. However, this will be the new governor's first adjudication, which we all await with bated breath.

DAY 216　　TUESDAY 19 FEBRUARY 2002

10.00 am

Mr Beaumont dismissed the charges against Chris and David as a farm worker came forward to say he'd given them permission to take the potatoes and the cabbage.

2.07 pm

As part of my preparation for talking to children about the dangers and consequences of drugs, I have a visit from a police officer attached to the Lincolnshire drug squad. Her name is Karen Brooks. She's an attractive, thirty-five-year-old blonde, and single mother of two. I mention this only to show that she is normal. Karen has currently served two and a half years of a four-year assignment attached to the drug squad, having been a member of the force for the past fourteen years: hardly the TV image of your everyday drug officer.

She gives me a tutorial lasting just over an hour, and perhaps her most frightening reply to my endless questions – and she is brutally honest – is that she has asked to be transferred to other duties as she can no longer take the day-to-day strain of working with drug addicts.

Karen admits that although she enjoys her job, she wishes she'd never volunteered for the drugs unit in the first place, because the mental scars will remain with her for the rest of her life.

Her son, aged twelve, is a pupil at one of the most successful schools in Lincolnshire, and has already been offered drugs by a fourteen-year-old. This is not a deprived school in the East End of London, but a first-class school in Lincolnshire.

Karen then tells a story that brings her almost to tears. She once arrested a twelve-year-old girl from a middle-class, professional family for shoplifting a pair of socks from Woolworth's. The girl's parents were horrified and assured Karen it wouldn't happen again. Two years later the girl was arrested for stealing from a lingerie shop, and was put on probation. When they next met, the girl was seventeen, going on forty. Three years of experimentation with marijuana, cocaine, ecstasy and heroin, and a relationship with a twenty-year-old drug dealer, had taken their toll. The girl died last month at the age of eighteen. The dealer is still alive – and still dealing.

As Karen gets ready to leave, I ask her how many officers are attached to the drug squad.

'Five,' she replies, 'which means that only about 10 per cent of our time is proactive, while the other 90 per cent is reactive.' She says that she'll visit me again in two weeks' time.

DAY 228   SUNDAY 3 MARCH 2002

6.30 am

Yesterday I read Celia Grummitt's pamphlet on the misuse of drugs in prisons and the following facts bear repeating·

a) Seven million people in Britain take drugs on a regular basis (this does not include alcohol or cigarettes).

b) Sixteen million people in Britain smoke cigarettes.

c) Drug-related problems are currently costing the NHS, the police service, the Prison Service, the social services, the probation service and courts – the country – eighteen *billion* pounds a year.

d) If Britain did not have a drug problem, and by that I mean abuse of Class A drugs such as heroin and crack cocaine, we could close 25 per cent of our jails, and there would be no waiting lists on the NHS.

e) In 1975, fewer than 10,000 people were taking heroin. Today it's 220,000, and for those of you who have never had to worry about your children, just think about your grandchildren.

DAY 231   WEDNESDAY 6 MARCH 2002

10.00 am

Mark Le Sage, the young prison officer from HMP Stocken, visits me at the hospital. He's been in the Prison Service for the past twelve years, and for the last eight, has spent many hours as a volunteer addressing schools in the Norfolk area.

Mr Berlyn joins us, as it was his idea that I should attend a couple of Mark's talks before I venture out on my own. As I have not yet passed my FLED, I'll have to be accompanied by Mr Hocking, who has also agreed to carry out this task in his own time, as NSC do not have the funds to cover the extra expense (£14 an hour). Mr Berlyn says that he'll write to the governor of HMP Stocken today, as Mr Le Sage comes under his jurisdiction.

11.00 am

Blossom (traveller, see page 193) is at the High Court today for his appeal. He's currently serving a five-and-a-half-year sentence for stealing cars and caravans. He's grown his beard even longer, as he's hoping that the judge will think he's a lot older than he is, and therefore shorten his sentence. He intends to shave the beard off as soon as he returns this evening.

6.00 pm

Blossom returns from his appeal and announces that a year has been knocked off his sentence. It had nothing to do with the length of his beard, because he was only in the dock for a couple of minutes and the judge hardly gave him a second look. He had clearly read all the relevant papers long before Blossom showed up.

7.00 pm

Blossom has already shaved off the beard.

The other interesting piece of information to come out of Blossom's visit to the High Court was that three cannabis dealers had their sentences halved from seven to three and a half years. A sign of things to come?

DAY 234   SATURDAY 9 MARCH 2002

8.00 am

Blossom comes in to see sister. He's in a dreadful state. His wife has written to let him know that his oldest son (aged twenty-nine) is on heroin. He asks me to fill out a form so that he can apply for compassionate leave. He tells me that he's already got hold of a pair of handcuffs and he plans to chain the boy to a water pipe until he comes off the drug. He's quite serious.

Linda tells him firmly that his plan is neither legal or practical, nor of much value to his son.

6.00 pm

Blossom has been granted two days compassionate leave. He is such a strange mixture of high moral values and low life. He's quite happy to steal caravans and cars, which has been the reason for several of his family ending up in prison, but is devastated when he discovers his son is on heroin. This is a man who has been married for thirty-six years, has eleven children and countless grandchildren, and until now, none of his offspring has ever been involved in drugs.

DAY 235   SUNDAY 10 MARCH 2002

2.00 pm

My visitors today are Ed Streator, the former US minister to the Court of St James's and later American ambassador to NATO, and Quentin Davies MP, who is currently Shadow Secretary of State for Northern Ireland. The ninety minutes fly by, as both men have so much to tell me about what's happening where you all are.

I had forgotten that Quentin was PPS to Kenneth Baker when he was Home Secretary. During that period, he developed strong views on the reform of our penal system after becoming aware of the drug problem both inside and outside of prison. He talks with refreshing frankness and honesty about both subjects.

Ed adds a view from the other side of the Atlantic, and when we debate smoking cannabis he reminds me that California has recently passed a law to prevent anyone under the age of twenty-one purchasing tobacco, let alone cannabis. In fact, he adds, in California it's virtually illegal to smoke anywhere except in your own home. Quentin suggests that if tobacco was discovered today, cigarettes would be illegal – possession two years, tobacconists five years.

4.00 pm

Stephen is the latest member to join Club Hospital (Sundays, 4 pm to 6 pm). He's currently serving a two-year sentence for theft, perverting the course of justice and false accounting. But there are several twists.

He is a former captain in the Adjutant General's Corps, and after being court-martialled, was sent to Colchester Prison (an army establishment) for the first month. But because his sentence was more than twenty-eight days, he was automatically transferred into the prison system to complete his term.

And now for the second twist. A European Court ruling has recently determined that the armed forces disciplinary system is invalid, and all prisoners serving a sentence resulting from a court martial must be released.

Not only might Stephen be set free, but he will also be entitled to £60,000 in compensation, as well as being reinstated as a captain. Our masters in The Hague have decided that you should not be arrested, charged, tried and convicted *by your peers*.

Stephen tells me that there are 600 such prisoners currently in British jails, and he hopes to learn the outcome of this ruling in the next few weeks.

The final twist – just before he was arrested, Stephen received a letter from his commanding officer to tell him that he was being considered for promotion to major.

DAY 236   MONDAY 11 MARCH 2002

9.00 am

A man comes into surgery whom I despise.

Drink drivers are the staple diet of NSC. Of the 220 prisoners currently resident, around 20 per cent have been sentenced with driving offences. Sadly, Tony is not untypical.

Tony is in his early fifties, the father of five children by four women. He currently lives with another woman on a caravan park in Scunthorpe. He pleaded guilty to his latest charge, of driving whilst being disqualified and uninsured (surely the time has come for all motorists to display – as they do in France – an insurance disc, as well as a road fund licence). For this, his latest offence, Tony was sentenced to twelve months, which in real terms means that if he is granted a tagging facility, he will be released after four. Now here is the rub: during the past twenty years, he has been charged with twelve similar offences, and sent to jail on seven separate occasions. He's been banned from driving for four years, and happily tells anyone who will listen that as soon as they release him he'll be back behind the wheel.

It gets worse. He's currently employed by a local garage as a second-hand car dealer, and therefore has access to a variety of vehicles, and admits he likes to get 'tanked-up' at the pub across the road once he's closed a sale. He displays no remorse, and has no fear of returning to prison. He considers NSC to provide a slightly higher standard of living than the one he currently enjoys on a Scunthorpe caravan park.

Perhaps the time has come to change the offence for those who are regularly convicted of drink driving to one of 'potential manslaughter', carrying with it a custodial sentence of four years in a closed prison, and treat such people like any other violent criminals.

12 noon

Alison tells me that the BBC has been in touch about a pro-gramme on best-selling authors called *Reading the Decades*. While accepting the fact that I can't appear on camera, they ask if I could do a telephone interview. They already have contributions from King, Grisham, Le Carre, Forsyth, Cooper and Rowling. I ask Governor Leighton for a view, and he says that he'll seek advice from the Home Office.*

4.00 pm

Mr Beaumont sent a circular to all the officers at NSC a few days before he arrived which I obtained recently. It gives you a flavour of the man. (See opposite.) I can't believe his secretary ever checked the piece for grammatical mistakes. Even an eleven-year-old would have spotted the error in the last line. I can't wait to meet him.

---

* Mr Leighton is unable to make the decision himself. He reports back the following day that the BBC had already been in touch with the Home Office, and they have been turned down.

HM PRISON NORTH SEA CAMP

STAFF INFORMATION NOTICE NO. 62/2002
(Not to be displayed in inmate areas)

APPOINTMENT OF NEW GOVERNOR
NORTH SEA CAMP

The following message has been received from Keith Beaumont, who has been appointed as Governor of North Sea Camp with effect from Monday, 18 March 2002:

"By now you will all know that I am appointed as your new Governor and I have no doubt that there are a thousand and one opinions as to why I am coming to North Sea Camp and why I have left Nottingham. The truth is very simple. I am coming to North Sea Camp to take over as its Governor and to help develop it for the future. The new units give it a chance to re-emphasise and re-focus itself so that it can establish itself as a place of excellence.

This will require hard work from us all but, as you have already demonstrated so far, keeping North Sea Camp open was not just about staying there but about offering reasons why the place should remain open and demonstrate that to one and all. This you have clearly done in order to get the new development.

I have no doubt equally, that you have heard much rumour, some of it true, some of it malicious, about my person, about my styles and about how I like to operate. Again, I am an honest person who believes in honesty and together we will be able to move forward.

I look forward to the chance of working with you and trust, over the months to come, we will get to know one and other well."

KEITH BEAUMONT
Governor designate

New Units = Quick Build this next 3 months for one or two blocks holding 40 inmates !

R LEIGHTON
Acting Governor

13 March 2002

DAY 238   WEDNESDAY 13 MARCH 2002

7.22 am

Gail rushes in, slightly flushed. She's been door-stepped by a woman from the *News of the World* who has discovered (from an inmate) that she's leaving NSC to take up another post. The journalist is looking for stories and asked, 'Are you leaving because of Archer?'

Gail replied that I am working as a hospital orderly, and that I take the job very seriously, am popular with both the officers and the other prisoners and am learning about drugs and their relevance in prison. Gail innocently asked how much they would pay for a story, to which the journalist replied a couple of thousand pounds – more if it was a big story that would show Archer in a bad light.

10.11 am

I am called in for a voluntary drugs test. You can refuse, but should you do so your privileges – town visits, canteen cash and weekend leave – are likely to be rescinded. I discover that two prisoners have come up positive, one for amphetamines, the other for cannabis.

By the end of the morning, that number had risen to five; all will appear in front of the governor for adjudication tomorrow.

12 noon

An officer comes into the hospital and tells me that he once worked on the sex offenders' unit at Whitemoor Prison and he could tell me enough stories to fill another volume.

'Give me an example,' I ask, topping up his coffee.

He pauses for a moment. 'We once had a young prisoner on B block who used to keep a budgerigar in his cell, and the little bird became the most important thing in his life. Another prisoner living on the same wing, sensing the lad's vulnerability, threatened to kill the budgie unless he gave him a blow job. The prisoner reluctantly agreed. Within days, the first prisoner had become a prostitute, and the second his pimp. The pimp would charge two phonecards for the prisoner to give a blow job and three to be buggered. The pimp ended up making a hundred pounds a week, and the budgie survived. That was until an inmate grassed on him in the hope that the pimp would be transferred to another prison and he could take over his lucrative position. Both prisoners were moved to separate establishments the following day.

That morning the budgie was strangled.'

DAY 247   FRIDAY 22 MARCH 2002

Governor Berlyn comes to the hospital this morning and tells me that despite his efforts, I will not be allowed to accompany Mark Le Sage whenever he addesses school on the problem of drugs. The governor of HMP Stocken has told Mr Le Sage that he will not permit such excursions even if an NSC security officer accompanies me.

The nation is currently in the grip of a massive drug epidemic, with children of twelve being offered heroin in our playgrounds. As part of my rehabilitation, I have volunteered to visit schools in the Lincolnshire area and talk to them about the problem. To date I have had assistance from the local police drug squad, the Lincolnshire education authority and the medical team at NSC, lead by Dr Walling. So I can only wonder why the governor of Stocken would want to stop such a worthwhile project.

Perhaps the Home Office knows the answer?

DAY 249   SUNDAY 24 MARCH 2002

4.00 pm

It's been a week for visitors: last Sunday, Henry Togna and David Watson, Monday, Gilly Gray QC, Wednesday, Lords Hayhoe and Denham – Bertie, my old Chief Whip.

So now I'm up to date on the Lords reform bill, foxhunting and the state of Margaret Thatcher's health. Not to mention the euro, and when the planned referendum might or might not be.

I put an idea to Bertie on the Lords reform bill, when to my horror he withdrew from an inside pocket, a small memo recorder. I glance over to the desk to see the duty officers chatting to each other. I was relieved when Bertie put the recorder back in his pocket. We don't need another member of the House of Lords as a resident of North Sea Camp.

DAY 250   MONDAY 25 MARCH 2002

10.00 am

The papers are full of stories about the model Naomi Campbell, who has been awarded £3,500 against the *Daily Mirror* and its then editor, Piers Morgan, for breaching her privacy. However, the judge also states that she had deliberately lied when in the witness box.

Norman Tebbitt has asked through the press if she will be tried for perjury, or do these laws only apply to Conservative politicians?

4.00 pm

Mr Belford comes to the hospital clutching the results of my MDT. (See opposite.)

6.00 pm

Peter (arson, set fire to a police station) has so far served thirty-one years; you may recall that I earlier reported his first town visit. This morning, two officers arrived outside his room and took him down to the segregation cells, which can only mean one thing: he's going to be shipped out to a closed prison today.

HM PRISON SERVICE

H M PRISON NORTH SEA CAMP

MANDATORY DRUG TEST

NAME: ARCHER   **NUMBER:** FF8282   **LOCATION:** HOSP.

I am pleased to inform you that the urine sample you gave under the Mandatory Drug Test Programme has tested **negative** and no further action will be taken.

You will, however, still be liable to be tested again, if need be, at a later date.

DRUG TEST CO-ORDINATOR   DATE: 20 / 2 / 02 .

I suspect that one trip to Boston will be the last time he ever sees the outside world.

When I first came to NSC some months ago, Peter swept the main road that runs from the gate through to the office block; some 300 yards away. With a six-foot-four-inch frame, Peter had a presence you could not easily avoid, but zero social skills, and thirty-one years in prison (twenty-eight of them behind bars) ensured that it was never going to be easy for him to settle.

Every morning he would break away from his sweeping and open car doors for members of the female staff. He would then engage them in long conversations. Harmless enough, you may say, but several of the younger girls felt harassed and didn't complain for fear it might harm Peter's parole prospects. Unfortunately, these episodes continued, despite several warnings from officers. Governor Berlyn, who is in charge of the lifers, was left with little choice but to take action to allay the staff's fears.

He took Peter off his job as a road sweeper and asked him to be a reception orderly. Peter made the tea and helped officers with minor tasks. It was beyond him. He lasted a fortnight. They next moved Peter to the officers' mess, to assist with cleaning and occasional serving. He lasted ten days before being transferred to the farm as a shepherd, where he survived less than a week before being sent to the kitchen. This was no more successful, and he has ended up in segregation prior to being moved back to the B-cat.

Peter is in his sixties, and has no hope of returning to a D-cat in under five years, if ever. This case highlights a bigger issue. Don't we have some duty to a human being other than to lock him up for the rest of his life? Peter failed to come to terms with the system, so the system has failed him.

When I am eventually released, I am going to be asked so many questions to which I do not know the answer.

10.30 am

I listen to an announcement over the tannoy.

'Anyone wanting to assist with the special needs group trip to Skegness, please report to the bus at the front gate.' The word 'please' should have given it away. Prison officers rarely, if ever, say please. However, two inmates still report to the gate in the hope of boarding the non-existent bus to Skegness.

The April Fool prank played on me took a different form. Mr Hewitt, the head of the works department, purchased a jigsaw puzzle of the House of Lords at a car-boot sale, and told me he expected me to finish it by the end of the week as part of my anger management programme.

It took me two hours just to finish the border. I intend to draft in all the members of Club Hospital to assist me with this 1,000-piece monster.

DAY 262   SATURDAY 6 APRIL 2002

Dr Susan Edwards, Reader of Law at Buckingham University, has completed her independent study showing the harshness of my four-year sentence.*

> Jeffrey Archer, former deputy chairman of the Conservative party and best-selling author, was convicted of perjury and perverting the course of justice arising from a libel action over whether he spent a particular night with a Monica Coghlan, for which, following a 'not guilty' plea, he received a prison sentence of four years. As Jeffrey Archer's prison sentence is the longest passed in any case of civil perjury and the sentence length is comparable to prison sentences passed in the gravest cases of criminal perjury including murder and police corruption it requires some rather more detailed consideration.

Gilbert Gray QC has already warned Mary that he'll be able to predict the outcome of my appeal as soon as he knows the make-up of the three-judge panel. What a dreadful condemnation of British justice – that my future will not be decided on whether I'm innocent or guilty, but on who judges me.

---

* The full report was published in the *Criminal Law Review* of August 2003.

NSC, like most prisons in Britain, is badly understaffed. We have over 200 inmates, and only 27 full-time officers, meaning that there are never more than 12 officers on duty at any one time. The following advertisement appears in several local papers *every week*, and elicits few replies. (See overleaf.)

I'm told it's no different for any of the other 137 prisons in Britain. It's hardly an appealing career, other than for the truly dedicated believers in justice – or someone not quite tall enough to get into the police force.

HM PRISON SERVICE

HMP NORTH SEA CAMP
OPERATIONAL SUPPORT GRADE VACANCIES

HM Prison North Sea Camp has vacancies for operational support grades (OSG). The posts will involve the supervision of prisoners: applicants should be able to communicate clearly and effectively and want to be an effective part of the prisoner rehabilitation process. Duties may include security, working in the gate lodge, driving escorts, switchboard, canteen and stores.

Hours:	39 hours per week
Annual leave:	22 days a year rising to 25 after one year
Salary:	starts at £12,651 rising annually to the maximum of the grade by annual increments
	A full clean driving licence is essential
	A PSV licence would be an advantage but is not essential

Application forms may be obtained from the Boston Job Centre, West Street, Boston, Lincs. Tel: (01205) 883000.

For further information please contact Mrs Carole Pattinson in the personnel office at North Sea Camp. Tel (01205) 760481 ext 2 28.

Application forms should be returned to the Boston Job Centre by Friday, 22 March, 2002.

Applicants will be required to declare whether they are a member of a group or organisation which the Prison Service considers to be racist.

The Prison Service is an equal opportunities employer. We welcome applications from candidates regardless of ethnic origin, religious belief, gender, sexual orientation, disability or any other relevant factor. Members of the ethnic minorities are currently under-represented at North Sea Camp and applications from them would be welcome. All applications will be considered and appointments made on merit.

DAY 268   FRIDAY 12 APRIL 2002

9.07 am

Dr Walling arrives a few minutes late. When Stephen Sherbourne (Margaret Thatcher's former political secretary) visited me, I told him that if you reported sick between 7.30 and 8 am any morning, Monday to Friday, you were guaranteed to see a doctor at nine o'clock the same day.

Stephen asked if I could think of a crime for which he would be sentenced to two weeks, so he could get all his medical problems sorted out.

11.11 am

MURDERER WEDS PRISON PSYCHIATRIST is the sort of headline one might expect to read in the *Sun*.

Today Andy, a lifer who has served twelve years, has been granted a week's leave. He has been a model prisoner and expects to be released some time next year. While he was in his previous prison, Ashwell, part of his rehabilitation course included regular meetings with the prison psychiatrist, and as the months passed, they struck up a relationship. I think it right to point out at this stage that Andy is thirty-five, six foot one, with the dark swarthy looks of an Italian film star. When he was transferred to NSC, the psychiatrist visited him regularly. A report of her visit was passed back to her own prison, and she subsequently had to resign from the service. She found a new job in Loughborough and her relationship with Andy continued to blossom. Today they were married at a ceremony in Boston attended by five officers and nine prisoners.

NSC currently has twenty-three resident murderers, and I think I've met every one of them. Three of them, including Andy, are among the gentlest people I have ever come across.

3.30 pm

One of the inmates is refusing to take an MDT. It's well known that he's a heroin addict, and has found yet another way to beat the system. If he refuses to take the test, the governor can only add twenty-eight days to his sentence, whereas if he agrees to take it and then proves positive for heroin, he could be sentenced to fifty-six extra days and even be shipped out to a B-cat. However, Mr Vessey points out that should he refuse a second time, they can ship him out the same day.

The new chapel orderly committed an unusual crime. 'On the out' he was an accounts executive for a well-known furniture company. He became head of the complaints department, whose responsibility it was to ensure that when customers returned goods they received a refund and the article was returned to the store's seconds department.

One Christmas, the chapel orderly purchased a sofa for his mother, but she didn't like it. He returned the sofa and applied for a refund, giving his own name and address. The money was refunded quite legally. It was then that the man realized that only he and the computer were aware of the transaction. Using a false name but his own address, he authorized and presented a bogus claim and the computer happily credited his account. By changing the name every time, he could make a claim once a week, and during the following year, he supplemented his income by over £200,000. The chapel orderly and his girlfriend (she unwittingly) lived in comfort, as he became more and more confident, upping the sums on a weekly basis, and even giving himself a bonus over the Christmas rush.

So how was he caught? A secretary mistakenly opened a random file on her computer, and was surprised by what she found – how could 127 people living at the same address all require a refund for 127 different pieces of furniture they'd ordered over the past year?

The accounts executive pleaded guilty and was sentenced to three years. He is now the chapel orderly at NSC.

As part of his rehabilitation into society, one of the lifers (Malcolm, armed robbery) has just started an outside job as a cleaner at Haven High School.

The first day turned out to be a bit of a culture shock when he discovered how mature and self-confident modern young women have become. He repeated a conversation he'd had this morning with a fourteen-year-old who approached him in the corridor.

'Are you a convict?'

'Yes, I am.'

'What are you in for?'

'Armed robbery.'

'How many years have you served?'

'Fourteen.'

'Fourteen years without sex?' the girl said in mock disbelief.

'Yes,' he repeated, to which the girl lifted up her skirt, and said, 'Well you must be up for it.'

Malcolm ran out of the building. Had she reported him for even talking about sex, he probably would have been transferred back to a B-cat the same day.

DAY 287   WEDNESDAY 1 MAY 2002

10.30 am

Strange goings-on in the camp today. Tony, a well-known drug dealer, has collapsed after taking an overdose only hours before he's due to be released. What kind of problems can he have on the outside, that he considers suicide a better way out than the front gate?

Tony has been a regular at the hospital over the past few weeks, so there's no way of knowing if he's been storing up pills, and how many he swallowed today. Rather than wait for an ambulance, Tony's been rushed into the Pilgrim Hospital in the prison mini-bus, accompanied by two officers. I'll know more tonight.

6.00 pm

Tony has just returned to the camp to spend his final night in jail. They pumped out his stomach, so he'll still leave us at 8 am tomorrow. But how long will he survive on the outside?

7.08 pm

I have just returned from an hour's walk around the playing field with the intention of watching Hendry vs. Doherty in the quarter-final of the World Championship snooker,* when there's a knock on my door.

It's Tony clutching a letter that he wants me to hand to sister, but he asks me to read it first. It's a two-sided handwritten missive, apologizing for his behaviour over the past few weeks, and thanking sister for her kindness and understanding. I promise to give it to her tomorrow morning. Tony is just about to leave when I ask him if he'd be willing to answer a few questions about drugs. I quite expect him to tell me what I can do with myself, using the usual prison vernacular, but to my surprise he takes a seat in the waiting room and says, 'Ask me anything you want, Jeff. I don't give a fuck, I'm out of here first thing in the morning.'

During the next hour, I ask him question after question, all of which he answers with a brutal frankness.

'Did you try to commit suicide?'

'No, I just OD'd.'

'How often do you take heroin?'

'While I've been here, usually four times a day. When I wake in the morning, just after dinner, then again after tea and just before I go to bed.'

'Do you inject it, sniff it or smoke it?'

'Smoke it,' Tony replies. 'Only fuckin' morons inject it. I've seen too many crack-heads get HIV or hepatitis B by injecting themselves with someone else's needle. While I've been in jail,

---

* I was president of the World Snooker Association until I was arrested, when the board asked me to resign. Two other bodies expelled me, the Royal Society of Arts and the MCC.

I've seen needles used by a hundred different inmates. Don't forget, Jeff, 235,000 people in Britain are regular heroin users, and if you consider their families, over a million people must be involved. Heroin costs the NHS three billion a year.'

'How do you get the heroin into prison?'

'There are several ways, but the most common is to pick it up from a dealer when you're out on a weekend leave, and then pack a couple of ounces in a condom and stuff it up your rectum. No officer enjoys checking up there.'

'A couple of ounces?'

'That was all I could afford this time. My record "on the out" was coming back from Holland with seven ounces of marijuana.'

'How much would that be worth?'

'If it's pure, the best, you could be talking around a hundred grand.'

'So when you bring the drugs back into the prison, are they just for you?'

'No, no, no, I have to pay my supplier "on the out". I'm only a dealer. Dealers are either kings or pawns. I'm a pawn. A king rarely takes drugs, just brings them in from abroad and distributes them among his pawns, most of whom only deal so they can satisfy their own craving.'

'So how many of the two hundred inmates at NSC are on heroin?'

He pauses to consider the question. 'Thirty-nine that I'm aware of,' he says.

'But that's around twenty-five per cent.'

'Yeah,' he replies, matter-of-factly.

'How do you pay back the king dealer while you're on the inside?'

'Easy,' says Tony. 'I only sell to those inmates who have

someone on the outside who will hand over cash direct to my dealer. I never supply until the money has been received.'

'But that could take days, and if you're in the grip of a craving . . .'

'It only takes one phone call, and an hour later I check with the dealer and if he's received the cash, then I supply.'

'If you were on the outside and not a dealer, how much would you need to cover your own addiction?'

'Three hundred quid a day.'

'But that's a hundred thousand pounds a year – cash.'

'Yeah, but as a dealer I can earn twice that, and still get my fix four times a day.'

Tony goes on to talk about his fears after he's released tomorrow morning. His parents will come to pick him up at eight o'clock. They believe he's kicked the habit following a spell in special prison in Devon, where they weaned him off heroin for fifteen months. But, once he was considered cured, they transferred him to a D-cat, in this case NSC, where it was 'in his face', and within weeks he was addicted again.

'I won't live to see fifty,' Tony says. 'I'll have been in jail for over half my life.' He pauses. 'I wish I'd never taken that first freebie when I was fifteen. You'll pass ten of us in the street every day, Jeff, and you won't have been aware. Perhaps you will from now on.'

Tony left the hospital at 7.28 pm.

I handed his letter to sister the following morning.

DAY 294   WEDNESDAY 8 MAY 2002

9.00 am

Today's list of new inductees to see the doctor includes Patel, Patel, Patel and Patel. It's hard to believe that there isn't a story there somewhere. When the prisoners appear, it soon becomes clear we are dealing with a father and three sons. I later discover that the mother is also in jail at Holloway; all five were charged with the same offence.

The Patels are Sikhs, and have very strong family values, so that when they discovered that their daughter/sister was earning her living as a prostitute, they formed a plan to kidnap her (the law's views)/ rescue her (the Patel family's value). The first part of this plan was not too difficult to carry out for a bright, reasonably determined team of Sikhs – they simply bundled the girl into a car and whisked her off to the family home. However the pimp/lover/friend – I can't be sure which – set out to *rescue* her, so that she could be put back to work. Unfortunately for him, he had not taken into account the resolution of the Patel family, so he ended up with a broken arm and nose after being beaten up.

The pimp reported the incident to the police, which resulted in the father and three brothers being sentenced to two years for kidnapping and ABH, and the mother to eighteen months as an accomplice. All five went to jail, while the daughter was set free to continue to ply her trade. As a novelist, I can come up with a dozen scenarios as to what might happen when the Patel family are all released in 2003.

10.30 am

Among the prisoners who will be released today is Daryl, who is serving twelve months for burglary. He has been a model prisoner, no sign of any drugs, never on report, and whenever he visits the hospital, he's always courteous and considerate, so I was not surprised he had been granted his tag and would be leaving us after only four months. Once the doctor has checked him out and signed him off, Daryl thanks sister and shakes hands with me.

'Good luck,' I offer, and add, 'I hope we never meet again,' – the traditional goodbye to those you consider unlikely to reoffend. Imagine my surprise when I learned this evening that Daryl was back in jail. It happened thus.

He was driven to Boston station on the prison bus, where he was handed a rail voucher for Manchester and £40 in cash. Every prisoner who is not picked up at the front gate is a travel voucher and £40 if they have a known address to go to. If they are of no fixed abode (NFA) they are handed £90, and the address of a hostel in the area they are heading for. After fourteen days, if they have been unable to find a job they can go on the social service register and collect unemployment benefit. Back to Daryl.

He boarded the train at Boston, but had to change at Birmingham to catch another train to Manchester. During the stopover at Birmingham, he picked up some fish and chips before making his way over to platform six. But as the train was not due to arrive for a few minutes he popped into W. H. Smith and picked up a magazine to read on the journey. The magazine rack is situated next to the bookshelf, and his eye lighted on the A section. He left a few moments later with a magazine and three paperbacks by the same author. He was about to board the train when a station policeman arrested him for shoplifting.

When the police learned that Daryl had been released from jail that morning on a tag, he was immediately taken to Gartree Prison in Birmingham, where he will spend the next two months completing his sentence, and whatever period of time is added because of the shoplifting.

Daryl, however, does not hold the record for being back in custody the quickest following his release. Mr Belford assures me that that distinction belongs to Fingers Danny of Pentonville.

Danny was released from Pentonville at 8 am on a cold November morning. Clutching his £90, he headed off on foot to Islington, not in search of the nearest hostel, but the nearest Sainsbury's. He arrived just as they were opening the front doors. He proceeded to fill a trolley with products, and then walked slowly out of the shop without making any attempt to pay. When the store detective approached him on the pavement, Danny made a dash for it, but not too quickly.

Danny was arrested, and appeared in front of the magistrate at ten o'clock that morning. He pleaded guilty. Before sentence was passed, Danny threw in a few choice observations concerning the magistrate's bald head, his lack of charisma and his doubtful parentage, ensuring that he was back in his cell at Pentonville by midday.

However, the difference between Danny and Daryl is that the Irishman had planned the whole operation weeks before he was released. After all, it was November, and where else could Danny be guaranteed a bed in a warm cell, three meals a day and the companionship of his friends during the festive season?

He put his £90 release money in his canteen account.

DAY 311   SATURDAY 25 MAY 2002

Three inmates absconded yesterday; it's an hour to Boston on foot, about an hour and a half to Skegness. The first, Slater (GBH) had a six-year sentence and had only been at NSC for four days. Even more inexplicable is the fact that he was due for parole in September, and having been transferred to a D-cat, could expect to have been released. Slater was rearrested four hours after departing and taken off to HMP Lincoln, a B-cat, where he will spend the rest of his sentence – two more years plus twenty-eight days for absconding. Madness.

I am informed by an officer that the second inmate, Benson (ABH), was anticipating a positive MDT back from the Home Office, and as it was his second offence in three months, the governor would have been left with little choice but to ship him out to a B-cat. So he shipped himself out. He was picked up in Boston early this morning, and is now on his way to Nottingham (A-cat) with twenty-eight days added to his sentence.

The third inmate, Blagdon (pub stabbing), is a more interesting case. He was due out in July, having already served nine years. He walked into a police station this morning, and gave himself up after being on the run for only seven hours. He is also now safely locked up in an A-cat. However, in Blagdon's case, he never intended to make good his escape. His cell-mate tells me that he didn't think he could handle the outside world after nine years in jail – eight of them in closed conditions (banged up for twenty-two hours a day) – so now he'll return to those conditions for at least a further five years, at the end of which he will have to come up with another way of making sure he isn't set free, because he'll never return to a D-cat.

10.00 am

Every day this week, an inmate called Jenkins has been popping into hospital to ask me how many new inductees we were expecting that day, and added 'Are any of them from HMP Lincoln?' I assumed Jenkins was hoping that one of his mates was being transferred to NSC. On the contrary, he is fearful of the imminent arrival of an old enemy.

Yesterday morning the hospital manifest showed that six prisoners were due in from Lincoln, and when Jenkins studied the list of names, he visibly paled before quickly leaving the hospital. That was the last I saw of him, because he missed the 11.45 am roll-call. Three hours later he gave himself up at a local police station. He was arrested and shipped off to Lincoln.

I sat next to Jenkins's room-mate at lunch, who was only too happy to tell me that Jenkins had been sleeping with the wife of another prisoner called Owen whenever he was out on a fortnightly town leave. He went on to tell me that Owen (manslaughter) had recently found out that his wife was being unfaithful, and she had even told him the name of her lover. Owen, who had just been given D-cat status after eight years in jail, immediately applied to be sent to NSC and is due to arrive this afternoon. Now I understand why Jenkins absconded.

2.00 pm

A group of five prisoners arrive from Lincoln, but Owen is not among them. When they walk through the door, I report to sister that we seem to have lost one.

'Oh yes, Owen,' she says, looking down at her list. 'He committed some minor offence this morning and had his D-cat status taken away. So he'll be remaining at Lincoln for the foreseeable future.'

DAY 313   MONDAY 27 MAY 2002

9.07 am

A letter from the High Court informs me that my appeal date is set for Monday 22 July – in eight weeks' time.

10.07 am

A prisoner called Morris arrived this morning. He is thirty-six years old and serving a four-year sentence for credit-card fraud. Morris has stolen over £500,000 since leaving school, and shows no remorse. He tells me with considerable pride that he still has just under £100,000 in cash safely stashed away, and that he and his co-defendant lead 'the good life'. They share a large flat in London, drive a Mercedes, enjoy a wardrobe full of designer clothes and only stay at the best hotels. They fly first class, and work even while on holiday. He is a career criminal for whom prison is a temporary inconvenience, and as the authorities always transfer him to a D-cat within three weeks of being sent down, not *that* much of an inconvenience.

Morris has been found guilty of fraud four times in the last ten years, and received sentences of six months, eight months, twelve months and four years. However, he will have served less than three years in all by the time he's released next January.

In 2003, he anticipates that he and his partner will have cleared over a million pounds in cash, and if they are caught, he will be happy to return to NSC.

In Dickens's time Morris would have been known as 'a dip'. While the artful dodger stole handkerchiefs and fob watches, Morris purloins credit cards. His usual method is to book into a four-star hotel which is holding a large weekend conference. He then works the bars at night when many of the customers have had a little too much to drink. After a good weekend, he can leave the hotel in possession of a dozen or more credit cards. By Sunday evening, he's sitting in first class on a plane to Vienna (one card gone) where he books into a five-star hotel (second card). He then hires a car, not with a credit card, but with cash, because he needs to travel across Europe without being apprehended. He will then drive from Vienna to Rome, spending all the way, before returning to England in a car loaded with goods. He and his partner then take a short rest, before repeating the whole exercise.

Morris has several pseudonyms, and tells me that he can pick up a false passport for as little as a thousand pounds. He intends to spend another ten years rising to the top of his profession before he retires to warmer climes.

'It's a beautiful way of life,' he says. 'I can tell you more, Jeffrey.'

But I don't want to hear any more.

11.45 am

A prisoner comes in asking to see the doctor urgently. I explain that he left about an hour ago, and sister is over at the administration block, but he could see the doctor tomorrow. He looks anxious, so I ask if I can help.

'I've just come back from home leave,' he explains, 'and while I was out, I had unprotected sex, and I'd like to check that I haven't caught anything.'

'Did you know the girl?' I ask.

'I didn't know any of them,' he replies.

'Any of them?'

'Yes, there were seven.'

When I later tell sister, she doesn't bat an eyelid, just makes an appointment for him to see the doctor.

12 noon

Among the new receptions today is a prisoner called Mitchell (drink driving, three months). While I'm checking his blood pressure, he tells me he hasn't been back to NSC since 1968, when it was a detention centre.

'It's changed a bit since then,' he adds. 'Mind you, the hospital was still here. But before you saw the doctor, they hosed you down and shaved your head with a blunt razor, to make sure you didn't have fleas.'

'How about the food?' I ask.

'Bread and water for the first fortnight, and if you spoke during meals an officer called Raybold banged your head against the wall.'

I had to smile because I know one or two officers who'd still like to.

2.30 pm

The director-general, Martin Narey, has issued a directive requiring all prison officers to address inmates with the prefix Mr.

When an officer bellows across the car park, 'Get your

fuckin' arse over here, Archer,' I courteously point out to her that she must have missed the director-general's missive.

'I don't give a fuck about the director-general,' she replies, 'I'll fuckin' well call you what I like.'

One prisoner found an unusual way around this problem a few years ago. He changed his name by deed poll to Mister Rogers, but then he did have a twenty-year sentence.

3.00 pm

If you work outside the prison, you can earn up to £300 a week, which allows you to send money back to your wife, partner and family, which you certainly can't do on the amount you are paid working inside. An added bonus is that some companies offer full-time work on release to any prisoner who has proved himself while in their employ.

Once you're qualified to work outside, you must first complete a month of CSV (Community Service Volunteer) work, partly as retribution, and also to prove you are both fit and safe to work in the community. Once this has been completed, you can then spend the rest of your sentence working outside, so that when you're released, in the best scenario, it's a seamless progression. In the worst . . .

Mike was only a few weeks away from that seamless progression when two prison officers turned up at his place of work, and accompanied him back to NSC. It seems that a young lady who worked at the same factory could do nothing to deter his unrequited advances. Her mother also worked there, and reported him to the management. The management, quite rightly, were not willing to condemn the prisoner simply on the mother's word, and carried out their own investigation. A few days later they sent a full report to the prison governor.

Mike has subsequently been shipped out of NSC back to Lincoln Prison, a tough B-cat. He was only a few weeks away from parole, and the factory had already offered him a full-time job on release. He has now lost his D-cat status, lost his job, lost his income and possibly lost any chance of parole.

I am reminded of Robin Williams's classic remark: 'God gave man a penis and a brain, but not enough blood to work both at the same time.'

Few prisoners turn down the opportunity to have weekly visits, or the chance to be tagged and released two months early. Gary is the rare exception.

Gary was sentenced to two years for theft of a motor vehicle (BMW), and because of good behaviour will only serve twelve months. But why does no one visit him, and why won't he take up his two-month tagging option and serve only ten months?

None of Gary's family or friends knows that he is in prison. His mother believes that he is working with his friend Dave on a one-year contract on an oil rig in Mexican waters. When he arrived in Mexico, Dave sent Gary a large selection of Mexican scenic postcards. Gary pens a weekly card to his mother, sends it back to his friend Dave in Mexico, who then stamps it and forwards the missive to England.

Gary will be released next week, and seems to have got away with his little subterfuge, because Dave will fly back from Mexico on the same day, when they will meet up at Heathrow and return to Wolverhampton together. During the journey, Dave will brief Gary on what it's like to work and live on a Mexican oil rig.

Now that's what I call a friend.

DAY 316　　　THURSDAY 29 MAY 2002

North Sea Camp has five doctors who work a rota, and one of them, Dr Harris, is also responsible for the misuse of substances unit in Boston. Dr Harris arrives at the hospital today, accompanied by a male nurse. Nigel, who is in his early thirties and is dressed in a black T-shirt, blue jeans, with a ring in his ear, has come to visit me because he is currently working with young people aged twelve to nineteen who have a heroin problem. I can see why they would feel at ease with him.

Nigel explains that he can only work with youngsters who want to work with him. He listens to their questions, offers answers, but never judges. They've had enough of their parents telling them to grow up, behave themselves and find a job. He outlines the bare statistics – they are terrifying.

There are currently 220,000 heroin addicts in Britain, of which only 3,000 (11 per cent) are involved in some form of detox programme. One of the problems, Nigel explains, is that if you apply to your local GP for a place on one of these programmes, the wait can be anything up to six weeks, by which time 'the client' has often given up trying to come off the drug. The irony is that if you end up in prison, you will be put on a detox programme the following day. Nigel knows of several addicts who commit a crime hoping to be sent to jail so that they can wean themselves off drugs. Nigel works directly with a small group of seven addicts, although he reminds me, 'You can't save anyone; you can only help those who want to help themselves.'

He then guides me through the problems the young are facing today. They start experimenting with cannabis or sniffing solvents, then progress to ecstasy and cocaine, followed by crack cocaine, ending up on heroin. He knows several seventeen year olds who have experienced the full gamut. He adds ruefully that if the letter of the law were adhered to, seven million Britons would be in jail for smoking cannabis, as possession currently has a two-year tariff. A gramme of an A-class drug costs about £40. This explains the massive rise in street crime over the past decade, especially among the young.

The danger is not just the drugs, but also the needles. Often, drug users live in communes and share the same needles. This is the group that ends up with HIV and hepatitis B and C.

Today, for example, Nigel has appointments with two girls addicted to heroin, one aged nineteen and the other seventeen, who both want to begin a detox programme. His biggest problem is their boyfriends, who are not only responsible for them being on drugs in the first place, but are also their suppliers, so the last thing they want is for their girlfriends to be cured of the craving. Nigel tells me that there is only a 50–50 chance they will even turn up for the appointment. And if they do, addicts on average make seven attempts to come off heroin before they succeed.

Nigel's responsibility is to refer his cases to a specialist GP so that they can be registered for a detox programme. He fears that too many addicts go directly to their own GP, who often prescribes the wrong remedy to cure them.

Nigel displays no cynicism as he takes me through a typical day in his life, and reminds me that he's not officially funded, something he hopes the NHS will sort out in the near future. He suddenly brings the problem down to a local level, highlighting the national malaise. Nigel has seven heroin addicts on his books, in a county that has 10,000 on the drug. It's not a chip, not a dent, not even a scratch, on the overall surface.

Nigel leaves me to keep his appointment with a seventeen-year-old boy who has, for the past four years, been visiting caravan sites so that he can feed his addiction; he cuts the rubber hose and sniffs calor gas. He's not even breaking the law, other than by damaging property.

2.00 pm

Gail is searching for a bed-board for a new inmate with a back problem. There are twelve boards out there somewhere. The problem is that once you've allocated them, you never get them back, because when an inmate is released, the last thing on his mind is returning a bed-board.

Gail calls the south block unit, only to discover that a replacement officer from Lincoln is holding the fort. She throws her hands in the air in despair, but nevertheless tells him about her problem. By cross-referencing with the prisoners' files, she can check those who are in genuine need, and those who have just come into possession of a bed-board by default. To her surprise, the officer returns an hour later accompanied by seven of the offending bed-boards.

I offer him a cup of coffee and quickly discover that his whole life is equally well organized. He tells me about work at Lincoln, and one sentence stops me in my tracks.

'I've developed a system that ensures I only have to work five months a year.'

The officer has been in the Prison Service for just over seven years, and has, along with five other colleagues, developed an on-off work schedule so he only needs to be on duty for five months a year for his £23,000 salary. He assures me that the system is carried out in most jails with slight variations. He would be happy to work extra hours if he could get paid overtime, but currently few prisons can afford the extra expense except for accompanied visits (hospitals, court or transfer). This is the bit where you have to concentrate. Officers work the following shifts:

Shift A: the early shift, 7.30–12.30 or Shift B: a main shift (day), 7.30–5.30.

Shift C: the late shift, 1.30–8.30 or Shift D: the evening shift, 5.00–9.00.

Shift E: a main shift (night), 9.00–7.00.

The officer and his colleagues swap shifts around and, as there is no overtime, they take time off in lieu. Every officer should work thirty-nine hours per week, but if they swap shifts with colleagues, they can end up doing A+C or B+D or D+E, and that way notch up nearly seventy hours per week, while another colleague takes the week off. Add to this the twenty-eight days holiday entitlement per year, and they need work only five months while taking off seven. Three of his colleagues also have part-time jobs, 'on the out' and the officer assures me that a large percentage of junior officers supplement their income this way.

I can only assume this does not come as a surprise to Martin Narey, currently the director-general of the Prison Service. I'm bound to say if my secretary, housekeeper, agent, accountant, publisher or doctor took seven months per year to do another job, I would either reorganize the system or replace them.

DAY 320   MONDAY 3 JUNE 2002

As from today, the Home Office have recategorized NSC as a resettlement prison. In future all prisoners having served one quarter of their sentence and passed their FLED will be eligible to move into one of the recently built blocks and start working outside the prison. The thinking behind this is that by allowing prisoners to earn a living, they will be less likely to reoffend when released. Two new blocks (Portakabins) of forty rooms have been constructed on the playing fields near the gate for this purpose. From today, sixty-two prisoners will be eligible to leave NSC from 7.30 am, and need not return until 7 pm.

But, and there are always buts in prison, Mr Berlyn has posted a notice in both new blocks, making it clear that this is to be considered a privilege, and anyone who fails to keep to the guidelines will be suspended and put to work on the farm at £5.60 a week.*

---

* Two prisoners absconded during their first week at work. Both were caught and transferred to a B-cat in Nottingham. Two were found in a pub and are back working on the farm; while three were sacked for inappropriate behaviour – unwanted advances to the female staff. And that was in the first week.

DAY 325　　　FRIDAY 7 JUNE 2002

Mr Beaumont (the governing governor) has just marched into the hospital, accompanied by Mr Berlyn. Dr Walling, David and I are watching England play Argentina in the World Cup, and Beckham has just scored from a penalty to put us in the lead. I assume they had heard the cheering and popped in to find out the score. However, they don't even glance at the screen. One look in my direction, and they both stride out again.

I learn later that the governor had received a call from Reuters asking him to confirm that I had committed suicide.

Not while we're in the lead against Argentina.

11.00 am

An officer drops in and tells me over coffee that there is disquiet among the officers and staff that sex offenders will in future make up a considerable percentage of our inmates. Officers fear the atmosphere may change from the relaxed state we currently enjoy to one of constant tension, as regular offenders despise paedophiles. It is even possible that one or two of the more violent inhabitants might take it upon themselves to administer their own form of justice.*

---

* Most sex offenders, when housed in an open prison, are given a cover story should anyone ask what they are in for.

The officer goes on to tell me that a murderer at Gartree shared a cell with a prisoner who was allegedly in for burglary. But the lifer discovered from another prisoner, who had been in a previous jail with his cell-mate, that he was in fact a sex offender who had raped his nine-year-old daughter.

At roll-call the following morning, the lifer reported to the main office. His statement was simple and explicit. He had stabbed his cell-mate to death and left him on his bed. The lifer was immediately placed in solitary confinement, charged and later given another life sentence. The judge added that on this occasion, life meant the rest of his life.

6.00 pm

I umpire this evening's cricket match between NSC and a local school. I give the opening batsman from the visiting side out, caught and bowled. When I see the look of surprise on the batsman's face, I immediately feel anxious, because the bowler had taken the catch as he ran in front of me. Have I made a mistake? The batsman is already heading towards the pavilion (a small wooden hut) when Mo (murder, terrorist), who is fielding at silly mid-on, looks at me and says, 'It was a bump-ball, Jeff.' I call the opening batsman back and apologize for my mistake as the rest of the team applaud Mo's sportsmanship.

The visiting team go on to win, thanks to a fine innings from the opening batsman. Funny old world.

It's been a tense day as I wait to discover how much longer I'll have to remain here. My appeal against conviction took Mr Justice Rose two minutes to dismiss, which was no more than my counsel, Nick Purnell QC, had predicted. The appeal against sentence was granted by Mr Justice Brown, so we had all felt more confident that Mr Justice Rose would knock off at least a year, possibly two, allowing me to return home this evening.

At 5.07 pm, Mr Hocking walks slowly into the hospital, looking grim. As senior security officer, he had already set in motion a plan to have me off the premises before the press could arrive. He told me that Alison had rung to say that my sentence had not been cut, even by a day. Although Mr Purnell addressed the judges for over two hours, Mr Justice Rose returned to the court one minute and forty-eight seconds after Nick sat down, and read out a prepared statement that he must have written some days before. Mr Justice Rose could at least have had the courtesy to tell Mr Purnell not to bother, as he'd already made up his mind and wasn't interested in any new evidence.

So much for British justice.

The press are curious to know why Mary didn't appear in court to hear my appeal. She was being interviewed for the chairmanship of Addenbrooke's Hospital at 1 pm, and the date had been fixed for some weeks.

I had told her that under no circumstances was she to request a change of dates, as this was clearly the most important interview of her life. Addenbrooke's, attached umbilically to Cambridge University, is one of the country's leading teaching hospitals. It has a budget of some £250 million per year, and nearly 1,000 doctors and 2,500 nurses. Mary has been vice-chairman for the past two years, and on the board for eight, and although she is up against a formidable shortlist I still feel she's in with a good chance.

We spent over an hour on the phone (until I ran out of phonecards) considering the likely questions that might come up. I want Mary to get this chairmanship job more than I want to be released from jail; otherwise I would spend the rest of my life feeling that I was the reason she failed.

DAY 371   WEDNESDAY 24 JULY 2002

I call Mary to confirm that she will be coming to pick me up on Saturday and take me out on my first town visit, a precursor to home leave. I don't get a chance to ask any questions because everything is overshadowed by the news that she has been appointed chairman of Addenbrooke's.

I'm so delighted that I can't remember why I called.

There has never been a suicide at NSC, despite the fact that there were seventy-three suicides in British jails last year.

Today an inmate made two attempts to take his life. First he tried to cut his wrist, and after being rushed to the Pilgrim Hospital and patched up, he attempted to hang himself. He failed.

He's a young man who recently lost his mother, and last week his girlfriend sent him a 'Dear John' letter. I later learned that during his trial he took 106 paracetamol tablets and although they pumped his body out, he has irreversibly damaged his liver. His crime, by the way, was shoplifting, for which he received six months, and will serve three at most.

However, one good thing came out of it. The Listeners, who have been requesting a room for counselling for some time, were allocated one this morning.

DAY 374   SATURDAY 27 JULY 2002

7.00 am

They have turned off the central heating today, which is all you need to know about the way North Sea Camp is run.

10.00 am

My first day out of jail for a year.

Mary picks me up and, as the press are waiting at the gatehouse, we avoid Boston. We end up in a field of cows, eating a picnic. Heaven, even if the press do get the inevitable picture.*

Over a lunch of turkey and ham salad, followed by Cheddar cheese helped down with a Diet Coke, Mary and I discuss her new responsibilities as chairman of Addenbrooke's Hospital.

After a drive around the countryside, Mary takes me back to NSC just after five, as she is flying to Japan tomorrow, to address a conference.

On your first town visit, you're not allowed beyond the environs of Boston (ten miles) and must return to the camp by

---

* They did. It was published in the *Sunday Mirror* the next day. (See overleaf.)

7 pm. Next week, assuming I've broken none of the rules, strayed beyond the ten-mile limit, had a drink or committed a crime (shoplifting the most common), I will be allowed to travel an 'as the crow flies' distance of fifty-five miles, which takes in Cambridge and Grantchester.

On returning to the hospital, I decide to pick up a phonecard and call Mary to thank her for all she's doing. I go to the drawer by my bed to discover that my phonecards are missing. It's a few minutes before I can accept that a fellow inmate has broken into the hospital and stolen all my phonecards (eight, worth £16). Don't forget that I earn £11.70 a week. But when I check the window opposite my bed, I notice that it's not on its usual notch. So now I know how the thief got in.

I'll have to borrow a couple of cards from David, two from Stephen and two from Tony if I'm going to survive the coming week.

NICE DAY OUT

Strolling Archer gets first taste of freedom

PICTURE EXCLUSIVE

DAY 377   TUESDAY 30 JULY 2002

8.00 am

This morning, four of the Highpoint prisoners were put in a van and shipped out to Lincoln (B-cat) accompanied by six officers and a driver. Just before leaving NSC, one of the prisoners attacked an officer. The governor has made it clear that he will no longer accept prisoners from that establishment.

9.00 am

Five HM Prisons Inspectors arrive unannounced at the front gate. Mr Beaumont (the governing governor) is on holiday in Wales, but rushes back to the camp, along with several other staff.

During the next three days I come across all five inspectors, and am impressed by how quickly they identify the good, the bad and the simply indifferent. They single out the kitchen and the hospital – both run by women – for high praise.

However, the governor wasn't around to hear their final report, as he had gone back to Wales.

As I have completed my first town visit without incident, I am now entitled to travel to Cambridge (within a fifty-five-mile radius of NSC). (See below.) Mary is in Japan attending a conference, and Will is working at the Kennedy Center, in Washington DC, so I spend the day with James.

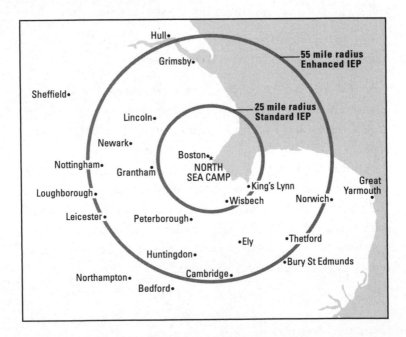

As we drive into Grantchester, I yearn to see the Old Vicarage. I spend the first hour strolling around the slightly overgrown garden – our gardener has been on holiday for a couple of weeks – admiring the flowers, the lake full of koi carp, and the sculptures that adorn the lawn.

James prepares lunch, and after reading the Sunday papers I settle down to slivers of melon with Parma ham, followed by spaghetti bolognaise (my choice) and a Diet Coke. We would normally have a glass of red wine, but not for another year. After a cheese board – I am only interested in the Cheddar – we once again stroll round the garden on a cloudless day, before returning to the house to watch the Commonwealth Games. What a triumph for Manchester.

I leave at 5 o'clock, as I have to report back before 7 pm, when I will be breathalysed and searched. Any sign that I had taken even a mouthful of wine and I would forfeit my job as the hospital orderly, and would not be considered for a CSV job in the future. I would also have to return to a double cell on the north block and be put to work on the farm. Can anyone be that stupid?

Two prisoners were shown to be over the limit on returning this evening. They both lost all their privileges.

DAY 384   TUESDAY 6 AUGUST 2002

All prisoners who have passed their FLED are eligible to work in the outside community as long as they are within twelve months of their parole date (mine is 19 July 2003). A prisoner can then work outside the camp between the hours of 7 am and 7 pm for five days a week, and even have a sixth day of training. Once accepted for the resettlement programme, a prisoner moves into one of the residential blocks located near the gate (single rooms) and is allowed to wear his own clothes at all times. You can also drive your own car to work and have a mobile phone (which cannot be taken out of the car).

The purpose of the resettlement programme is to help prisoners help themselves by earning a living wage (£150–£250 a week). If you are financially independent, these rules do not apply. However, you are still able to work for a voluntary or charitable organization and the prison will pay you £12.50 per week (current salary as a hospital orderly, £11.60 per week).

Governor Berlyn (head of resettlement) has already turned down my application to work for Dr Walling at the Parkside clinic as a trainee nurse. He gives two reasons for his decision: some of the camp staff are patients at the clinic, and Dr Walling, as head of the practice, is technically a member of staff, and therefore not permitted to employ me. However, Mr Berlyn has received a letter from a Mr Moreno at the Theatre Royal Lincoln, who has offered me a job assisting with the theatre's community programme. Mr Berlyn will accompany me to Lincoln next Tuesday for an interviewed. The Theatre Royal Lincoln falls into the category of a charitable organization as it is subsidized by the Lincolnshire County Council.

DAY 386   THURSDAY 8 AUGUST 2002

8.00 am

Some wit has pinned up on the notice board outside the stores, 'If it fits, hand it back.'

It seems that over twenty pads (cells) have been broken into during the past two weeks, and more than two hundred phonecards have been stolen. The old lags tell me that it has to be a crack-head if he was desperate enough to break into the hospital. By the end of the week, the thief has broken into the chapel and the canteen (shop).

Some inmates are claiming they know the culprit.

6.00 pm

A prisoner who recently arrived from Highpoint says he's going to beat me up before he's released. This threat was made during my morning rounds in front of a group of his mates. He must be around thirty and is in for GBH.

I confess to feeling frightened for the first time in months.

DAY 387   FRIDAY 9 AUGUST 2002

8.00 am

This morning the same prisoner turns up at the hospital. I try to look calm. He apologizes for what he said yesterday, claiming that it was a joke and I obviously misunderstood him. 'I would never do anything to harm you Jeff.' I suspect he's worried that his threat may reach the ears of an officer, which would result in his being shipped out to a B-cat. Bullying is considered to be a worse crime than taking drugs. I nod, and he quickly leaves the hospital.

6.00 pm

David (post-office robbery) tells me that the prisoner from High-point who threatened me had a visit from Jim (robbery, antiques only), Mo (terrorist) and Big Al (GBH) in the middle of the night. They explained what would happen to him if Jeff came to any harm, or words to that effect.

I'm touched that three inmates whom I do not know that well feel strongly enough to watch my back.

I gave Big Al out LBW in last week's cricket match, and he hasn't stopped grumbling since.

DAY 391   TUESDAY 13 AUGUST 2002

Mr Berlyn drives me over to Lincoln for an interview with Chris Moreno and Chris Colby, the owner and director of the Theatre Royal Lincoln.

Both men could not have been more welcoming and kind. They make it clear to Mr Berlyn that they need 'volunteers' and would welcome other prisoners to join me. Mr Berlyn seems satisfied that a real job of work exists, and that I could be of some service to the community. He says he will recommend that I start work on Monday.

DAY 393 THURSDAY 15 AUGUST 2002

2.00 pm

A prisoner called Hugh attacks an officer in the north block. She arrives in hospital with a broken cheekbone. Hugh is immediately transferred to Lincoln Prison and will be charged with assault. The officer tells Linda that she will be claiming compensation, and expects to be off work for at least four months.

5.30 pm

'Lucky Ball' arrives at NSC – the man who claimed to have won the lottery and proceeded to spend his non-existent winnings.

7.00 pm

It's my last day as hospital orderly. Stephen (two years, VAT fraud, £160,000) takes my place. I will continue as Saturday orderly so I can keep my daily bath privileges, when Stephen will have the day off.

DAY 396   SUNDAY 18 AUGUST 2002

8.00 am

Jim (gym orderly) drives me to Cambridge so I can spend the day at home with James. Mary is still in Japan. James and I buy four new koi carp from the local garden centre. Freedom is underrated.

5.00 pm

I drive Mary's car back to the camp and leave it in the prison car park. This will be the vehicle I use to get myself to Lincoln and back each day. I decided not to drive my BMW 720 as it would cause all sorts of problems, with the press, the prison staff and the other prisoners. While I'm driving, I feel a little like Toad in his motor on the open road.

DAY 397   MONDAY 19 AUGUST 2002

9.00 am

I began work at the Theatre Royal Lincoln today and enjoy wearing a shirt and tie for the first time in a year. Couldn't find a parking place and arrived a few minutes late. Over a hundred journalists, photographers and cameramen are waiting for me.

The first thing I notice is that my little office has bars on the window.

When I walk in the street during my lunch break, the public are kind and considerate. Find it hard to leave at five, grab a meal and be back by seven.

I reach NSC with three minutes to spare. If I'd failed to make it on time, I would have lost all my privileges on the first day, and probably been put to work on the farm.

DAY 424   SUNDAY 15 SEPTEMBER 2002

I can now leave the prison every Sunday and travel to Grantch-ester to be with Mary and the family for the day.

Today, my fourth Sunday, Mary and I have been invited to lunch with Gillian and Tom Shephard and a few of their friends at their home in Thetford. As Thetford is on the way back to NSC, and within the fifty-five-mile radius of NSC, we decide to take separate cars so I can return to prison after lunch.*

We leave the Old Vicarage at 12.15 pm.†

---

* See map page 414.
† I had no idea how important this lunch would turn out to be on the evening I wrote these words.

DAY 434 WEDNESDAY 25 SEPTEMBER 2002

Five idylic weeks working at the Theatre Royal. *Annie* goes into rehearsal with Su Pollard, Mark Wynter and Louise English. I've been in charge of the children and in particular their accommodation needs, as they go on tour around the country. After the terrible events in Soham, Mr Moreno is adamant that their safety must be paramount. I spend hours organizing where the young girls and their chaperones will stay in each town.

Today, I attend the 2.30 pm dress rehearsal of *Annie* at the Liberal Club and leave the cast after Chris Colby has run through his notes.* I wish them all luck and depart a few minutes before six. I now feel not only part of the team, but that I'm doing a worthwhile job.

I arrive back in Boston at six and go to the Eagles restaurant for what I didn't then know was to be my last steak and kidney pie.

On my arrival back at the camp, Mr Elsen, a senior officer, asks me to accompany him to the governor's office. I am desperately trying to think what I can possibly have done wrong. Mr Beaumont, the governor, and Mr Berlyn, the deputy governor,

---

* When I first entered the Liberal Club, an elderly gentlemen remarked, 'Prison is one thing, Jeff, but the Liberal Club?'

are sitting waiting for me. The governor wastes no time and asks me if, on Sunday 15th, I stopped on the way back to the camp to have lunch with Gillian Shephard MP.

'Yes,' I reply without hesitation, as I don't consider Gillian or any of her other guests to be criminals.

Mr Beaumont tells me that I have breached my licence by leaving my home in Cambridge. This, despite the fact that I remained within the permitted radius of the prison, had been with my wife, hadn't drunk anything stronger than apple juice and returned to NSC well in time.

Without offering me the chance to give an explanation, I am marched to the segregation block, and not even allowed to make a phone call.

The cold, bleak room, five paces by three, has just a thin mattress on the floor against one wall, a steel washbasin and an open lavatory.

DAY 435   THURSDAY 26 SEPTEMBER 2002

5.00 am

I have not slept for one second of the ten hours I have been locked in this cell.

8.00 am

My first visitor is Dr Razzak who assures me that she will inform the governor I should not be moved on medical grounds.*

10.00 am

I have a visit from Mr Forman (chairman of the IMB, the prison's Independent Monitoring Board), who assures me that I will not be moved if my only offence was having lunch with Gillian Shephard.

11.30 am

I am escorted to adjudication. It quickly becomes clear that all decisions are being made in London by Mr Narey, the director-general of the Prison Service. Once I realize this, I accept there is no hope of justice.

---

* I assume that Mr Beaumont was given Dr Razzak's advice. If so, he ignored it.

Mr Beaumont tells me that as a result of this breach of licence, I am being transferred to B-cat Lincoln Prison, despite the fact that I have, until now, had an exemplary record, and have never once been placed on report. He adds that I have embarrassed the Prison Service, following a press story. The paper accused me of drinking champagne at a Tory bash.

'Which paper?' I ask innocently.

'The *Sun*,' says Mr Beaumont, thus revealing which paper Mr Narey reads each morning, and which editorials help him make his decisions.

At North Sea Camp last week, a prisoner who arrived back late and drunk was stripped of all privileges for a month; another, who brought vodka into the camp, was grounded for a month. Only last week, an NSC inmate nicknamed Ginger went on home leave and returned three days late. His excuse was that his girlfriend had held him captive (this provoked a mixture of envy and hilarity among other inmates). His only punishment was confinement to NSC for a short period. Several former inmates have since contacted my wife pointing out that they regularly visited friends and in-laws on their home leave days, as well as taking their children on outings to the park or swimming pool, and it was never once suggested this was against the regulations.

I was given no opportunity to appeal.

I learn later that Dr Walling (the prison's senior doctor) protested about my being put in segregation and moved to Lincoln Prison. Dr Walling told me that he was warned that if he made his feelings public, his days at NSC would be numbered.

3.45 pm

One officer, Mr Masters, is so appalled by the judgement that he comes to the side of the Group 4 van to shake my hand.

30 April 2004

Dear Mr Wragg

INVESTIGATION INTO THE CONDUCT OF MR KEITH BEAUMONT

I understand that you are leading an investigation into the conduct of Mr Keith Beaumont as Governing Governor of HMP North Sea Camp.

As you may be aware, I was in inmate in North Sea Camp from October 2001 until September 2002, when I was summarily transferred to HMP Lincoln by Mr Beaumont.

It is clearly essential that I give evidence to your enquiry about these matters, of which I made contemporaneous records. I can make myself available for this purpose at any time. I can be contacted during the working week at the above number, and over the weekend on 01223 840213.

Yours sincerely

Jeffrey Archer

Jeffrey Archer

cc   Mr Phil Wheatley, Director-General of the Prison Service*

---

* I received a fax from Mr Wragg a week later turning down my request.

On 18 April 2004, Mr Beaumont was suspended from his duties until a full enquiry could investigate his conduct as governor of NSC.

On 30 April 2004, I wrote to Mr Wragg, the chairman of the tribunal, asking to be allowed to give evidence. (See above.)

BACK TO HELL

4.19 pm

The Group 4 sweat box drives through the gates of HMP Lincoln just after 4 pm. Lincoln Prison is less than a mile from the Theatre Royal, but may as well be a thousand miles away.

I am escorted into reception to be met by a Mr Fuller. He seems mystified as to what I am doing here. He checks through my plastic bags and allows me to keep my shaving kit and a pair of trainers. The rest, he assures me, will be returned when I'm transferred to another prison, or released. He fills in several forms, a process that takes over an hour, while I hang around in a dirty smoke-filled corridor, trying to take in what has happened during the past twenty hours. When the last form has been completed, another officer escorts me to a double cell in the notorious A wing.

When I enter the main block, I face the usual jeering and foul language. We come to a halt outside cell fourteen. The massive iron door is unlocked, and then slammed behind me. My new cell-mate looks up from his bed, smiles and introduces himself as Jason. While I unpack what's left of my belongings and make up my bed, Jason tells me that he's in for GBH. He found a man in bed with his wife, and thrashed him to within an inch of his life.

'I wish I'd gone the extra inch,' he adds.

His sentence is four years.

Jason continues to chat as I lie on my hard mattress and stare up at the green ceiling. He tells me that he's trying to get back together with his wife. He will be seeing her for the first time since his conviction (ten weeks ago) at a visit on Saturday. I also learn that Jason served ten years in the airforce, winning three medals in the Gulf, and was the RAF's light heavyweight boxing champion. He left the forces with an exemplary record, which he feels may have helped to get his charge reduced from attempted murder to GBH.

I fall asleep, but only because I haven't slept for thirty-nine hours.

DAY 436   FRIDAY 27 SEPTEMBER 2002

I wake to the words, 'Fuck all screws,' echoing through the air from the floor above.

I haven't eaten for two days, and force down a slice of bread and an out-of-date lemon sorbet.

When they let me out of the cell (forty-five minutes a day), I phone Mary. An inmate from the landing above spits on me, and then bursts out laughing.

Despite the fact that the officers are friendly and sympathetic, I have never been more depressed in my life. I know that if I had a twenty-five-year sentence I would kill myself. There have been three attempted suicides at Lincoln this week. One succeeded – a lad of twenty-two, not yet sentenced.

Jason tells me that he's heard I am to be moved to C wing. He says that it's cleaner and each cell has a television but, and there's always a 'but' in prison, I'll have to work in the kitchen. If that's the case, I'll be stuck on A wing for however long I'm left in here. Jason passes over his newspaper. The *Mirror* gives a fair report of my lunch with Gillian and Tom Shephard; no one suggests I drank any alcohol. *The Times* adds that Martin Narey has said it will not be long before I'm moved. It cheers me up – a little, and then I recall the reality of 'not long' in prison. The press in general consider I've been hard done by, and the *Daily Mail* is in no doubt that the Home Secretary's fingerprints are all over the decision to take revenge on me. I lie on my bed for hour after hour, wondering if I will ever be free.

DAY 437   SATURDAY 28 SEPTEMBER 2002

12 noon

I'm standing in line for lunch wondering if anything will be edible. I spot an apple. I must remember to write to Wendy and congratulate her on the standard of the food at North Sea Camp. A prisoner, three ahead of me in the queue, gruffly asks for some rice. The server slams a ladle-full down on his tin tray.

'Is that all I fuckin' get?' asks the inmate, to which the server replies, 'Move along, you fuckin' muppet.' The prisoner drops his tray on the floor, charges round to the back of the counter and punches the server on the nose. In the ensuing fight, the server crashes his heavy ladle over the other prisoner's head and blood spurts across the food. The rest of the queue form a ring around the two combatants. Prisoners never join in someone else's quarrel, only too aware of the consequences, but it doesn't stop them jeering and cheering, some even taking bets. The fight continues for over a minute before an alarm goes off, bringing officers running from every direction.

By the time the officers arrive, there's blood everywhere. It takes five of them to drag the two men apart. The two combatants are then frogmarched off to segregation.*

---

* One officer pushes the prisoner's head down, while another keeps his legs

DAY 437

5.00 pm

I'm not eating the prison food. Once again, I have to rely on chocolate biscuits and blackcurrant juice. And once again I have a supply problem, which was taken care of at Belmarsh by 'Del Boy'. I quickly discover Lincoln's equivalent, Devon.

Devon is the spur's senior cleaner. He tells me with considerable pride that he is forty-one, has five children by three different women and already has five grandchildren. I tell him my needs. He smiles; the smile of a man who can deliver.

Within the hour, I have a second pillow, a blanket, two bottles of water, a KitKat and a copy of yesterday's *Times*. By the way, like Del Boy, Devon is West Indian. As Devon is on remand, he's allowed far longer out of his cell than a convicted prisoner. He's been charged with attacking a rival drug dealer with a machete (GBH). He cut off the man's right arm, so he's not all that optimistic about the outcome of his forthcoming trial. 'After all,' he says, flashing a smile, 'they've still got his arm, haven't they.' He pauses. 'I only wish it had been his head.' I return to my cell, feeling sick.

6.00 pm

I find it difficult to adjust to being banged up again for twenty-two hours a day, but imagine my surprise when, during association – that forty-five-minute break when you are allowed out of your cell – I bump into Clive. Do you remember Clive? He used to come to the hospital in the evening at North Sea Camp and play backgammon with me, and he nearly always won. Well,

---

bent; this is known as being 'bent up' or 'twisted up'. In the rule book it's described as 'control and restraint'.

he's back on remand, this time charged with money laundering. As we walk around the yard, he tells me what's been happening in his life since we last met.

It seems that after being released from NSC, Clive formed a company that sold mobile phones to the Arabs, who paid for them with cash. He then distributed the cash to different banks right around the globe, while keeping 10 per cent for himself.

'Why's that illegal?' I ask.

'There never were any phones in the first place,' he admits.

Clive seems confident that they won't be able to prove money laundering, but may get him for failure to pay VAT.*

During association, I phone Mary. While she's briefing me on Narey's attempts on radio and television to defend his decision to send me to Lincoln, another fight breaks out. I watch as two more prisoners are dragged away. Mary goes on to tell me that Narey is backtracking as fast as he can, and the Home Office is nowhere to be seen. The commentators seem convinced that I will be transferred back to a D-cat fairly quickly. It can't be too soon, I tell her, this place is full of violent, drug-addicted thugs. I can only admire the way the officers keep the lid on such a boiling cauldron.†

While I roam around association with Jason, he points at three Lithuanians who are standing alone in the far corner.

'They're on remand awaiting trial for murder,' he tells me. 'Even the officers are fearful of them.' Devon joins us, and adds that they are hit men for the Russian mafia and were sent to

---

* I am pleased to learn that David, the friendly schoolmaster at NSC who joined Clive's company on leaving prison, quickly realized what he was up to, and resigned.
† There was a riot the week after I left, and seventeen inmates ended up in hospital.

DAY 437

England to carry out an execution. They have been charged with killing three of their countrymen, chopping them up into little pieces, putting them through a mincer and then feeding them to dogs.

DAY 438   SUNDAY 29 SEPTEMBER 2002

11.00 am

The cell door is opened and an officer escorts me to the chapel: anything to get out of my cell. After all, the chapel is the largest room in the prison. The service is Holy Communion with the added pleasure of singing by choristers from Lincoln Cathedral. They number seventeen, the congregation thirteen.

I sit next to a man who has been on A block for the past ten weeks. He's fifty-three years old, serving a two-year sentence. It's his first offence, and he has no history of drugs or violence.

The Home Secretary can have no idea of the damage he's causing to such people by forcing them to mix in vile conditions with murderers, thugs and drug addicts. Such men should be sent to a D-cat the day they are sentenced.*

12 noon

I go to the library and select three books, the maximum allowed. I spend the next twenty hours in my cell, reading.

---

*I wrote this in *A Prison Diary Volume One – Belmarsh: Hell,* and the Home Office have shown scant interest. There aren't any votes in prisons.

DAY 438

10.00 pm

I end the day with Alfred Hitchcock's *Stories To Be Read With The Doors Locked*. Somewhat ironic.

DAY 439   MONDAY 30 SEPTEMBER 2002

6.00 am

Over the past few days I have been writing furiously, but I have just had my work confiscated by the deputy governor – so much for freedom of speech. He made it clear that his orders to prevent me from sending out any written material came from the Home Office direct. I rewrite my day, and have this copy smuggled out – not too difficult with nearly a hundred prisoners on remand who leave the prison to attend court every day.

8.00 am

After breakfast, I'm confined to my cell and the company of Jason for the next eight hours.

6.00 pm

Mr Marsh, a senior officer, who has a rare gift for keeping things under control, opens the cell door and tells me I have a meeting with the area manager.* I am escorted to a private room, and

---

* An area manager is senior to a governor, and can have as many as fifty prisons under his remit. He reports directly to the deputy director-general.

introduced to Mr Spurr and Ms Stamp. Mr Spurr explains that he has been given the responsibility of investigating my case. As I have received some 600 letters during the past four days (every one of them retained), every one of them expressing outrage at the director-general's judgment, this doesn't come as a great surprise.

Mr Spurr's intelligent questions lead me to believe that he is genuinely interested in putting right an injustice. I tell him and Ms Stamp exactly what happened.

On Friday 27 September, the Prison Service announced that 'further serious allegations' had been made against me. It turned out these related to a lunch I had attended on Wednesday 25 September in Zucchini's Restaurant, Lincoln (which is near the Theatre Royal) with Mr Paul Hocking, then a Senior Security Officer at North Sea Camp, and PC Karen Brooks of the Lincolnshire Constabulary.

I explained to Mr Spurr that the sole purpose of the lunch as far as I was concerned was so that I could describe what I had seen of the drug culture permeating British prisons to PC Brooks, who had by then returned to work with the Lincolnshire Police Drug Squad. After all, I'd had several meetings with Hocking and or Brooks in the past on the subject of drugs. I did not know that prison officers are not supposed to eat meals with prisoners, nor is there any reason I should have known this. Moreover, when a senior officer asks a prisoner to attend a meeting, even in a social context, a wise prisoner does not query the officer's right to do so.

As for SO Hocking, I have been distressed to learn that he was summarily forced to resign from the Prison Service on 27 September under the threat of losing his pension if he did not do so*. PC Karen Brooks was more fortunate in her employers. Her role was

---

* Since Mr Beaumont's suspension, Mr Hocking has addressed the tribunal, and made it clear that he was forced to resign by Beaumont, with the threat of being sacked. But who bullied Mr Beaumont?

investigated comprehensively by Chief Inspector Gossage and Sergeant Kent of the Lincolnshire Police, and she remains with the force. Chief Inspector Gossage and Sergeant Kent interviewed me during their later investigation of the same lunch, and made it very clear that they thought the Prison Service had acted hastily and disproportionately in transferring me to HMP Lincoln.

As Mr Spurr leaves, he assures me that he will complete his report as quickly as possible, although he still has several other people to interview. He repeats that he is interested in seeing justice being done for any prisoner who has been unfairly treated.

It was some time later that the *Daily Mail* reported that the Home Secretary had bullied Mr Narey into the decision to have me moved to HMP Lincoln.

The sequence of events, so far as I am able to establish them, are as follows. The *Sun* newspaper telephoned Martin Narey's office on the evening of Wednesday 25 September and the following day published a highly coloured account of the Gillian Shephard lunch. This provoked the Home Secretary to send an extraordinary fax (see overleaf) to Martin Narey demanding that the latter take 'immediate and decisive disciplinary action' against me. Narey, who had previously stood up against the press's attempts to portray my treatment as privileged, buckled and instructed Mr Beaumont to transfer me forthwith to Lincoln. Narey also went on a number of TV and radio programmes to criticize me in highly personal terms in what the *Independent on Sunday* described as 'an unprecedented attack on an individual prisoner', especially in the light of later pious assertions that the Prison Service is 'unable to discuss individual prisoners in detail with third parties'.

Mr Beaumont found himself in even more difficulty: he had not asked me about the Zucchini lunch, so he could hardly

PRIVATE & CONFIDENTAL

FROM: Home Secretary
Queen Anne's Gate

DATE: 26 September 2002

MARTIN NAREY

Dear Martin

I would be grateful if you would report personally to me on the two incidents you are investigating in relation to Jeffrey Archer.

If either of these incidents are true, I expect you to take immediate and decisive disciplinary action.

I am sick and tired of reading Jeffrey Archer stories about the cushy conditions in which he was placed, the freedom he has been given, the opportunity to do whatever he likes, and the snook that he is cocking at all of us.

Best wishes

DAVID BLUNKETT

make that the basis of an order to transfer me. In the event, the Notice of Transfer which he signed stated simply: 'Following serious allegations reported in the media and confirmed by yourself that on 15 September 2002, you attended a dinner party rather than spend the day on a Community Visit in Cambridge with your wife, it is not appropriate for you to remain at HMP North Sea Camp any longer.'

My licence did *not* restrict me to my home in Grantchester while on release. But, an e-mail was circulated within the Home Office which stated: '*The prison* [HMP North Sea Camp] *had granted JA home leave but his licence conditions stipulated that he should not go anywhere else but home. In light of this, he has breached his licence conditions, and will face adjudication.*' At that time, the copy of my master passbook (a record retained by the prison which records all a prisoner's releases on temporary licence) contained no such stipulation, nor did I ever face adjudication in respect of any breach of such a stipulation.

Mr Spurr later said in a letter he was 'unable to locate' my master passbook when he conducted his investigation into my transfer, a fact which he acknowledged as 'regrettable'. One has to wonder why and how this passbook disappeared. However, Mr Narey told me to stop writing to him on the subject as the matter was closed.

DAY 440　　　TUESDAY 1 OCTOBER 2002

6.00 am

A frequent complaint among prison officers and inmates – with which I have some sympathy – is that paedophiles and sex offenders are treated more leniently, and live in far more palatable surroundings, than the rest of us.

On arriving at Lincoln you are immediately placed on A wing, described quite rightly by the tabloids as a Victorian hellhole. But if you are a convicted sex offender, you go straight to E wing, a modern accommodation block of smart, single cells, each with its own television. E wing also has table tennis and pool tables and a bowling green.

During the past few days, I have been subjected to segregation, transferred to Lincoln, placed in A block with murderers, violent criminals and drug dealers, in a cell any self-respecting rat would desert, offered food I am unable to eat and I have to share my cell with a man who thrashed someone to within an inch of their life. All this for having lunch with the Rt Hon Gillian Shephard in the company of my wife when on my way back to NSC from Grantchester.

Sex offenders can survive in an open prison because the other inmates are on 'trust' and don't want to risk being sent back to a B-cat or have their sentences extended. However, these rules do not apply in a closed prison. An officer recently reported to me the worst case he had come across during his thirty years in the Prison Service. If you are at all squeamish, turn to the next page, because I confess I found this very difficult to write.

The prisoner concerned was charged and convicted of having sex with his five-year-old daughter. During the trial, it was revealed that not only did the defendant rape her, but in order for penetration to take place he had to cut his daughter's vagina with a razor blade.

I know I couldn't have killed the man, but I suspect I would have turned a blind eye while someone else did.

10.34 am

I have a visit from a Portuguese prisoner called Juan. He warns me that some inmates were seen in my cell during association while I was on the phone. It seems that they were hoping to get their hands on some personal memento to sell to the press.

English is Juan's second language, and I have not come across a prisoner with a better command of our native tongue; and I doubt if there is another inmate on A block who has a neater hand – myself included. He is, incidentally, quietly spoken and well mannered. He wrote me a thank you letter for giving him a glass of blackcurrant juice. I must try and find out why he is in prison.

11.17 am

An officer (Mr Brighten) unlocks my door and tells me that he needs a form filled in so that I can work in the kitchen. To begin with, I assume it's a joke, and then become painfully aware that he's serious. Surely the staff can't have missed that I've hardly eaten a thing since the day I arrived, and now they want to put me where the food is prepared? I tell him politely, but firmly, that I have no desire to work in the kitchen.

3.11 pm

I look up at my little window, inches from the ceiling, and think of Oscar Wilde. This must be the nearest I've been to living in conditions described so vividly by the great playwright while he was serving a two-year sentence in Reading jail.

> I never saw a man who looked
> With such a wistful eye
> Upon that little tent of blue
> Which prisoners call the sky.

5.15 pm

Mr Brighten returns to tell me that I will be placed on report if I refuse to work in the kitchen. I agree to work in the kitchen.

DAY 443   FRIDAY 4 OCTOBER 2002

The end of the second longest week in my life.

Jason (GBH) has received a movement order to transfer him to HMP Stocken in Rutland (C-cat) later this morning. He's 'gutted' as he hoped to be sent directly to a D-cat. However, a conviction for violence will have prevented this. By the way, he and his wife did agree to get back together, and she will now visit him every Saturday.

10.00 am

An officer unlocks my cell door and bellows, 'Gym.' Twenty or thirty of us form a line by the barred gate at the far end of the brick-walled, windowless room. A few minutes later we are escorted down long, bleak, echoing corridors, with much unlocking and locking of several heavy gates as we make our slow progress to the gym situated on the other side of the prison.

We are taken to a changing room, where I put on a singlet and shorts. Clive (money laundering) and I enter the spacious gym. We warm up with a game of paddle tennis, and he sees me off in a few minutes. I move on to do a thousand metres on the rowing machine in five minutes, and end up with a little light weight training. When an officer bellows, 'Five more minutes,'

DAY 443

I check my weight. Twelve stone twelve pounds. I've lost six pounds in six days. I join my fellow inmates in the shower room and have my first press-button shower for a year, bringing back more unpleasant memories of Belmarsh.

As we are all escorted back to A block by Mr Lewis, the senior gym officer, we pass E Wing (paedophiles) and not one of the inmates even looks in the direction of the staring faces. Why? Because we are accompanied by an officer. Prisoners are warned that any abuse (shouting, foul language) will be treated as a disciplinary matter, with the loss of daily gym rights as punishment. When you're locked up for twenty-two hours a day, that's incentive enough to remain silent, whatever your thoughts.

5.00 pm

The cell door is unlocked, and my new pad-mate enters carrying the inevitable plastic bag. Jason is replaced by Phil, an amiable, good-looking – despite the scar on his face – twenty-eight-year-old.

He has been put in my cell because he doesn't smoke, which is very rare in jail. Phil talks a great deal, and tells me that he wants to return to work in the kitchen. He certainly seems to know his way round the prison, which turns out to be because he's paid several visits to Lincoln during the past ten years.

He is only too happy to tell me the finer details of his record.

Offence	Age	Length of Sentence	Time Served
ABH	17	18 months	13½ months
armed robbery (post office)	19	4½ years	3 years 2 months
credit card fraud, deception	22	21 months	11 months
driving while disqualified	25	6 months	3 months

driving without a licence	25	4 months	2 months
drink driving	25	community service	80 hours
ABH (car crash, assaulted the other driver)	26	6 months	3 months
common assault (his wife)	27	5 months	10 weeks
Total	28	9½ years	6 years 1 month

Twenty-eight other offences were taken into consideration before the judge passed sentence on Phil this morning.

Phil tells me, 'Never again.' He now has a happy family life – I don't ask how he explains his latest conviction – and a good job to go back to. He can earn £500 a week laying concrete and doesn't need another spell in jail. Phil admits that his problem is a short fuse.

'Strike a match and I explode,' he adds, laughing.

5.40 pm

Mr Brighten unlocks the cell door to inform me that I start work in the kitchen tomorrow at eight o'clock. He slams the door closed before I can comment.

6.00 pm

My cell door is unlocked again and Phil and I, along with three others, are escorted to the hospital. I'm told that I have to take a drugs test before I'm allowed to work in the kitchen. Despite the fact that I don't want to work in the kitchen, Phil tells me that five prisoners apply every day because the work is so popular. Phil and I pass the urine test to show we are drug free, and the duty officer tells us to report to the kitchen by eight. The other three fail.

DAY 443

6.40 pm

During association I phone my agent, Jonathan Lloyd. He goes over the details of tomorrow's announcement of the publication of volume one of these diaries. I congratulate him on how well the secret has been kept. Not one newspaper has picked up that *A Prison Diary by FF8282* will be published tomorrow. This is quite an achievement remembering that at least twenty people must have known at Macmillan and ten or more at the *Daily Mail.*

DAY 444   SATURDAY 5 OCTOBER 2002

5.52 am

This is my tenth day of incarceration at Lincoln.

6.01 am

The publication of *A Prison Diary Volume One – Belmarsh: Hell,* is the lead item on the news. The facts are fairly reported. No one seems to think that the Home Office will try to prevent the publication. However, the director-general is checking to see if I have broken any prison rules. Mr Narey is particularly exercised by the mention of other prisoners' names. I have only referred to prisoners' surnames when they are major characters in the diary, and only then when their permission has been granted.*

A representative of the Prison Officers' Association said on the *Today* programme that as I hid in my room all day, I wouldn't have anything worthwhile to say about prisons. Perhaps it might have been wiser for him to open his mouth after he's read the

---

* Two years and two prison diaries later, and I have not received one letter of complaint from a prisoner or prison officer about the diaries despite receiving some 16,000 letters in the last three years.

book, when he would have discovered how well his colleagues come out of my experience.

7.32 am

My cell door is unlocked so I can be transferred from A to J wing. This is considered a privilege for that select group who work in the kitchen. The cells are a lot cleaner, and also have televisions. My new companion is a grown-up non-smoker called Stephen (age thirty-nine), who is number one in the kitchen.

Stephen is serving a seven-year sentence for smuggling one and a half tons of cannabis into Britain. He is an intelligent man, who runs both the wing and the kitchen with a combination of charm and example.

8.00 am

A group of fourteen prisoners is escorted to the kitchens. Only two of the five who reported for drugs testing yesterday evening are still in the group.

I am put to work in the vegetable room to assist a young twenty-three-year-old called Lee, who is so good at his job – chopping potatoes, slicing onions, grating cheese and mashing swedes – that I become his incompetent assistant. My lack of expertise doesn't seem to worry him.

The officer in charge of the kitchen, Mr Tasker, turns out to be one of the most decent and professional men I have dealt with since being incarcerated. His kitchen is like Singapore airport: you could eat off the floor. He goes to great pains to point out to me that he only has £1.27 per prisoner to deliver three meals a day. In the circumstances, what he and his staff manage to achieve is nothing less than a miracle.

DAY 445   SUNDAY 6 OCTOBER 2002

11.14 am

On this, my eleventh day, I have a second visit from Mr Spurr and his colleague Ms Stamp.

They say they wish to tidy up a few minor points. I'm impressed by Mr Spurr's grasp of what's going on at North Sea Camp, and once again he gives the impression of being concerned.

He leaves promising that he will be able to tell me the outcome of his enquiry on Friday.

DAY 450   FRIDAY 11 OCTOBER 2002

7.30 am

A particularly officious, ill-mannered officer unlocks my cell door and thrusts some papers at me. He tells me with considerable pleasure that I will be on a charge at 4 o'clock this afternoon.

I read the papers several times. I don't have a lot more to do. It seems that by publishing *A Prison Diary* I have broken prison Rule 51 Para 23, in 'naming staff such that they could be identified', contrary to SO 5 Para 34 (9) (d).

8.10 am

On leaving my cell to go to work in the kitchen, I am surprised to find Mr Spurr and Ms Stamp awaiting me. I am escorted into a side room. Mr Spurr tells me that he has completed his enquiry, and I will be transferred to Hollesley Bay (D-cat) some time next week. Do you recall Governor Lewis's words, 'Whatever you do, don't end up in Hollesley Bay . . .'?

10.30 am

I take a break from peeling the spuds, not that I can pretend to have done that many. I notice that Mr Tasker is sitting in his office reading the *Daily Mail*. He beckons me in, and tells me to close the door.

'I've just been reading about your time at Belmarsh,' he says, jabbing a finger at the centre pages, 'and I see you're suggesting that seventy per cent of prisoners are on drugs and as many as thirty per cent could be on heroin.' He looks up, gives me a pained expression and then adds, 'You're wrong.'

I don't comment, expecting him to dismiss my claims, and remind me of the official statistics always parroted by the Home Office whenever the question of drugs is raised.

'Which would you say is the most popular job in the prison?' Mr Tasker asks, folding his newspaper.

'The kitchen, without question,' I reply, 'and for all the obvious reasons.'

'You're right,' he says. 'Every day, at least five inmates apply to work in the kitchen.' He pauses, sips his coffee and adds, 'Did you take a drugs test yesterday?'

'Yes,' I reply, 'along with four others.'

'And how many of you were invited to work in the kitchen?'

'Just Phil and me,' I reply.

'Correct, but what you don't know is that I'm entitled to have twenty-one prisoners working in the kitchen, but currently employ only seventeen.' He takes another sip of his coffee. 'I have never managed to fill all the vacancies during the last ten years, despite the fact that we never have fewer than seven hundred inmates.' Mr Tasker rises from his seat. 'Now I'm no mathematician,' he says, 'but I think you'll find that seventeen out of seven hundred does not come to thirty per cent.'

DAY 450

3.00 pm

The same officious, ill-mannered lout who unlocked my cell door this morning returns to pick me up from the kitchen and escort me to segregation. This time I am only left there for about forty minutes before being hauled up in front of Mr Peacock, the governing governor. Mr Peacock sits at the top of the table with the deputy governor on his right and my wing officer on his left. The thug stands behind me in case I might try to escape. The governor reads out the charge and asks if I wish to plead guilty or not guilty.

'I'm not sure,' I reply. 'I'm not clear what offence I've committed.'

I am then shown the prison rules in full. I express some surprise, saying that I handed over every page of *Belmarsh: Hell* to the prison censor, and he kindly posted them on to my secretary, and at no time did he suggest I was committing any offence. The governor looks suitably embarrassed when I ask him to write down every word I have said. He does so.

Mr Peacock points out that every inmate has access to a copy of the prison rules in the library. 'Yes, but anyone who reads my diary,' – he has a copy of *Belmarsh* on the table in front of him – 'would know that I wasn't allowed to visit the library, or have access to education while at Belmarsh.' I direct him to the passage on the relevant page. At least he has the grace to smile, adding that ignorance of the law is no excuse.

Mr Peacock then calls for my wing officer to make his report. 'Archer FF8282, works in the kitchen and is a polite, well-mannered prisoner, with no history of drugs or violence.' The governor also writes these words down, before clearing his throat and pronouncing sentence.

'Loss of all privileges for fourteen days, and of canteen during the same period,' the governor pauses, 'to be suspended for six months.'

I rise, thank him and leave. I have a feeling he'll be only too happy to see the back of me. But more important, the decision has been made not to remove my D-cat status, thus proving that they had no reason to send me here in the first place.

It was to be another six days before my transfer to Hollesley Bay in Suffolk, and even that simple exercise they managed to botch.

DAY 457   FRIDAY 18 OCTOBER 2002

6.00 am

I rise and pack my belongings into an HMP plastic bag as I
prepare for my next move, not unlike one does when leaving a
no-star motel at the end of a rainy holiday. While I'm gather-
ing my possessions together, I chat to my pad-mate, Stephen
(marijuana, seven years), who tells me that he's been granted his
D-cat status, and hopes it will not be long before they transfer
him to North Sea Camp.

7.00 am

The cell doors on our wing are unlocked to allow Stephen and
his crew to be escorted to the kitchens and begin the day's work.
I try inadequately to thank him for his kindness and help during
the past ten days, while wishing him luck for a speedy transfer.

8.07 am

The cell door is thrown open for the last time, to reveal a young
officer standing in the doorway. Without a word, he escorts me
to reception. It's a protracted journey, as I have to drag along

two large, heavy plastic bags, and however many times I stop, the officer makes no attempt to help me.

When we finally reach reception, I'm placed in the inevitable waiting room. From time to time, I'm called to the counter by Mr Fuller so that I can sign forms and check through the contents of another six plastic bags that have been kept under lock and key. These are filled with gifts – mainly books – sent in by the public during the past three weeks. I sort out those that can be donated to the library (including nine Bibles) and still end up with four full bags, which will have to travel with me to Suffolk.

It's another thirty minutes before the final form is completed and I am cleared to depart for my next destination. Meanwhile, back to the waiting room.

10.19 am

Two young officers from Group 4 appear in the corridor. They are to accompany me and two other inmates from this hell-hole – not that the devils' keepers have been unkind. In fact, with one loutish exception, they have been supportive and friendly.

The Group 4 officers help me with my endless plastic bags, before I am locked into a tiny cubicle in another sweat box. I sit cramped up in silence awaiting a 'movement order'.

11.49 am

The electric gates swing slowly open, and the van eases out onto the main road. I stare from my darkened window to see several photographers snapping away. All they'll get is a blacked-out window.

I remain hunched up in my little box, despite the fact that as a D-cat prisoner I am entitled to have my wife drive me to

Hollesley Bay in the family car. But once again, the Home Office has put a stop to that.

For the next five hours, I am cooped up with two stale sandwiches and a bottle of water as we trundle through four counties on the endless journey to somewhere on the Suffolk coast.

3.19 pm

The van finally arrives at Hollesley Bay, and comes to a halt outside a squat brick building. The three of us step outside, to be escorted into reception. More form filling and more bag checking – decisions to be made about what we can and cannot possess.

While my plastic bags are being checked, the duty officer inadvertently gives it all away with an innocent remark. 'It's the first time I've checked anyone in from Lincoln.' And worse, the other two prisoners who came with me have only two weeks and three weeks respectively to serve before they complete their sentences; this despite the fact that their homes are in north Yorkshire. They have been uprooted because the Home Office is prepared to mess around with their lives just to make sure I couldn't travel by car.

When all the red tape is completed, I am accompanied to the north block by another officer, who dumps me in a single room.

Once again I begin to unpack. Once again, I will have to find my feet. Once again, I will be put through induction. Once again, I will have to suffer the endless jibes and sullen stares, never lowering my guard. Once again, I will have to find a job.

Once again . . .

EPILOGUE

For the past fourteen months, I have been writing two thousand words a day, nearly a million in all, which has resulted in three published diaries.

Although Hollesley Bay turned out to be quite different from North Sea Camp, it was not dissimilar enough to warrant a fourth diary. However, there is one significant difference worthy of mention. Hollesley Bay is an open prison, not a resettlement establishment. It was clearly selected to ensure that I couldn't work outside. After I had completed my induction, the director of Genesis, a Mencap project in Ipswich, offered me a job. His request was rejected by Mr Jones, the prison governor, despite there being three other inmates working at Genesis at that time. I appealed to the Prison Ombudsman about this blatant discrimination, but he said he didn't have the authority to reverse the governor's decision.

I reluctantly settled for the position of library orderly, with a remit from Mr Jones to 'get more prisoners reading'. Thirty-two books were taken out in my first week as library orderly, one hundred and ninety one in my last, eight months later.

However, as the library was only open to prisoners between 12.30 and 1.30, and 6 and 7 pm, I was left with countless hours to occupy myself. It doesn't take that long to replace on the shelves the twenty or thirty books returned each day. I could have occupied those lifeless hours writing a fourth diary, but as I have explained, I felt it would have achieved little.

During those first few months of incarceration at Hollesley Bay, I edited *A Prison Diary Volume Two – Wayland: Purgatory*, and had it smuggled out on a weekly basis by a prisoner who was working in Ipswich. But even that demanding exercise did not fully occupy my time.

My next venture was to write nine short stories based on tales that I had picked up from all four prisons. This collection will be published in 2005 under the title *Cat of Nine Tales*. Unfortunately, even this endeavour, with its several rewrites, only occupied me through to Christmas, leaving me another six months to kill before I was due to be released.

It was the death of an old friend that spurred me into action, and once again gave my life some purpose . . .

A few months before my trial began, I had lunch at Mosimann's with Chris Brasher and a mutual friend, John Bryant. The purpose of the lunch, and Chris always had a purpose, was first to persuade me that I should run in the London marathon and attempt to break the world record for the amount raised for charity by an individual in this event (£1,166,212) and second, that I should write my first screenplay.

While the marathon was postponed by events, I suddenly found myself with time on my hands to write a screenplay. Chris Brasher also knew the subject he wanted me to tackle, and proceeded to tell me the story of George Mallory, an Englishman who in 1924, climbed to within 800 feet of the summit of Everest, dressed in a three-piece tweed suit, with a coiled rope over one shoulder, a fifty-five-pound pack on his back, and carrying an ice axe in one hand and a rolled umbrella in the other.

At 12.50 pm on 17 July 1924 (Ascension Day), he and his young companion Sandy Irvine were enveloped in clouds and never seen again.

Was Mallory the first man to conquer Everest?

It was the untimely death of Chris Brasher that bought the memory of that lunch flooding back.

I resolved to put into action his second suggestion.

DAY 725

MONDAY 21 JULY 2003

5.09 am

I had a good night's sleep and rose early to take a shower. I pack my bags, so that no time will be wasted once the tannoy calls me across to reception.

I am touched by how many prisoners come to my room this morning, to shake me by the hand and wish me luck. However, it is not true, as one tabloid suggested, that I was given a guard of honour as I left the prison.

7.00 am

My last prison breakfast – cornflakes and milk. I can't help looking at my watch every few minutes.

8.09 am

I am called to reception where – no surprise – there is a new bundle of forms to be signed before I can be released.

At last, my release papers are completed by Mr Swivenbank, and he doesn't try to hide a grin as he hands over my regulation £40. I place the notes in the charity box on the counter, shake hands with both officers and depart, with the seventh draft of a screenplay, tucked under my arm, and in my pocket a CD of a song that was performed by The Seven Deadly Sins at my farewell party last night. (See overleaf.)

Will is sitting in my car parked outside the back door, waiting for me. He drives us slowly through the phalanx of journalists who litter both sides of the road. Just as we accelerate away and I think we've escaped them, we spot a Sky TV news helicopter hovering above us, as well as three motorbikes with cameramen glued to the back seats, and another five cars behind them, in close pursuit. Will never once exceeded the speed limit on the journey home to Cambridge.

On arrival back at the Old Vicarage, Mary dashes out to greet me, and I make a short press statement:

Press Release: Embargoed until midnight, Sunday 20 July 2003

Statement by Jeffrey Archer

I want to thank my wife Mary and my sons, William and James, for their unwavering and unstinting support during this unhappy period in my life.

I should also like to thank the many friends who took the trouble to visit me in prison, as well as countless members of the public who sent letters, cards and gifts.

I shall not be giving any interviews for the foreseeable future.

However, I have accepted an invitation to address the Howard League for Penal Reform's conference at New College Oxford in September, and several requests to do charity auctions in the run up to Christmas.

* * *

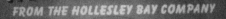

JEFFREY

(to the tune of 'Daniel' by Elton John)

Jeffrey is leaving today down the lane
I can see the paparazzi, flashing away in vain;
Oh, and I can see Jeffrey waving goodbye;
God, it looks like Jeffrey might have a teardrop in his eye.

Oh, ooh, Jeffrey our brother, bet you're glad to be free;
Now you can tell the world what you think of Narey.
You did time well, it's now your time to tell;
Jeffrey, you're a star, go on, son, give 'em hell.

I have not given an interview to the press, or appeared on radio or television, since.

During the last year, I have addressed a dozen or so organizations since speaking to the Howard League, including the Disraelian Society, Trinity College Oxford, the Thirty Club, the Hawks club and the Criminal Law Solicitors' Association.

I have also conducted twenty charity auctions, raising just over a million pounds, and run the Flora London marathon (5 hrs 26 mins) where I was overtaken by a camel, a phone box, a cake and a girl walking.

Most of my spare time has been taken up with carrying out research for my next novel – and continuing to work on the screenplay of *Mallory: Walking Off the Map*.